HYPOCHONDRIA
WOEFUL IMAGININGS

SUSAN BAUR

UNIVERSITY OF CALIFORNIA PRESS
BERKELEY · LOS ANGELES · LONDON

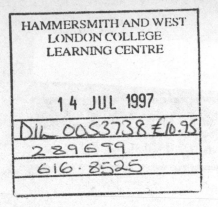
University of California Press
Berkeley and Los Angeles, California

University of California Press, Ltd.
London, England
Copyright © 1988 by The Regents of the University of California

Library of Congress Cataloging-in-Publication Data

Baur, Susan
  Woeful imaginings.

  Bibliography: p.
  Includes index.
  1. Hypochondria.   I. Title.
RC552.H8B38   1988   616.85′25   87-19144
ISBN 0-520-06107-1
ISBN 0-520-06751-7 (ppb)

Printed in the United States of America

2   3   4   5   6   7   8   9

■

For Louisa, Judi, and
my father, Jack Baur

289699

√Contents

Acknowledgments ix

Introduction 1

1   Being a Hypochondriac 10

2   "A Disease So Grievous, So Common" 21

3   The Social Significance of Being Ill 40

4   Pathways toward Childhood Hypochondria 49

5   Hypochondria in the Family 72

6   Hypochondriacs and Their Doctors 93

7   Hypochondria among the Elderly 113

8   Hypochondria and Our Cultural Values 134

9   Hypochondria in Other Cultures 160

10   Occupational Hypochondria 170

11   Getting Better 185

Appendix 211

Notes 213

Selected Bibliography 237

Index 249

Acknowledgments

WHAT PLEASURE TO acknowledge publicly the help of friends who have added to or commented on the manuscript. There are medical doctors, including Robert Reece, Tom Sbarra, E. Langdon Burwell, David Babin, and Virginia Biddle; and there are therapists, Milton Mazer, Bill Hallstein, Art Baur, and Judi Horgan. Doris Haight typed the first draft, Jeannie Smith the second, and Judy Ashmore tracked down references. My thanks also to anonymous contributors, both the hypochondriacs who described their struggles to me, and my family, who cheered the long project on.

Better I were distract;
So should my thoughts be severed from my
  griefs,
And woes, by wrong imaginations, lose
The knowledge of themselves.
                              —Shakespeare

I promise all Hypochondriacal People (the
meanest of which I have generally found Men
of tolerable Sense), that . . . what they shall
find in plain English, will be sufficient to give
them a greater Insight into the Nature of
their Distemper that can be furnished with
anywhere else; and . . . that many upon the
reading of this Treatise will be able to
penetrate into some first Causes of their
Affliction that were hid from them before.
        —Bernard de Mandeville
        *A Treatise of the Hypochondriack
        and Hysterick Passions*, 1711

INTRODUCTION

Hypochondria is a preoccupation with health
or disease, physical or mental, whose
intensity disrupts normal living habits and is
disproportionate to any medical problems that
may actually exist. A hypochondriac's concern
responds only temporarily, if at all, to
reassurance.

■

THERE ARE IN ORDINARY lives rare but disagreeable moments of panic when thoughts of tumor or heart disease flash
uninvited into the mind. These thoughts are sometimes triggered
by a recurrent headache, a racing heart, or a siege of breath-
lessness, and for an instant it seems that these signs are symptoms of serious disease. For most people such brief jolts are all
they experience of hypochondria, and a preoccupation with illness
never expands to dominate their lives. For millions of others,
however, the puzzling tendency to convert all kinds of problems
into physical illness operates on a more continual basis. Why do
we translate so many of our problems into bodily complaints? Is
it really an advantage to fear cancer rather than rejection or some
other emotional hazard? Is the chronic back pain of the frustrated
autoworker a useful form of rebellion against an unjust social situation?

1

But perhaps these are the wrong questions to ask. Could the delusion of disease be the result of the brain's chemistry gone awry? The hundreds of questions raised by hypochondria lead through some of the most fascinating areas of medicine, psychology, history, sociology, and philosophy. We could learn a great deal about ourselves if we could explain hypochondria.

Hypochondria is one of the oldest and commonest expressions of malaise. Springing from the great root stocks of anxiety and depression, it has passed in and out of public favor and medical fashion for the past two thousand years and has continued to express more gradations of disease than almost any other disorder. For centuries hypochondria attracted the attention of great doctors and philosophers who, believing the disorder to stem from a mixture of physiological imbalance and social frustration, tried every drug and therapeutic regime at their command to control this common misery.

During the nineteenth century hypochondria came to be associated with emotional rather than physical problems and, once identified as a mental disease, quickly acquired pejorative connotations. Not only did the disorder lose its status as a yardstick by which other miseries were measured, but it was broken down into a dozen different pieces and parceled out among the psychoses and neuroses. Hypochondria became merely a symptom of deeper troubles.

In the middle of the present century an effort was made to overcome the confusion that this dismemberment of hypochondria produced by ignoring the disorder altogether. Almost no research was undertaken, no papers written, and the term itself dropped from national and international registers of recognized disorders. But hypochondria continued to exist, as any candid observer could see, and the disorder gradually made its way back into medical consciousness. Now interest in this most ancient and absorbing disorder is reviving, especially among doctors who specialize in problems of aging, social critics who believe our lifestyle is conducive to mental distress, and neurologists who believe biochemical imbalances cause many cases of hypochondria.

To paraphrase Sir William Osler's famous observation on syphilis, know hypochondria and you come round, more or less the worse for wear, to most of the critical observations and fundamental disagreements concerning the nature of functional (nonorganic) complaints.

What can people who are studying hypochondria tell us about this elusive mimic of physical disease which makes life so unhappy for millions and which so frequently confounds and embarrasses doctors and therapists? And what can writers, painters, and poets—the articulate sufferers—add to their theories?

Up to this point I have spoken of hypochondria as if it were a specific disorder, a "clinical entity," the way unipolar depression or the anxiety states are thought to be. To use the word this way implies that hypochondria is characterized by symptoms that almost always occur together and that do not overlap, except marginally, with the symptoms of other disorders such as disease phobia or cardiac neurosis. In addition, elevating hypochondria to the status of a specific disorder suggests that hypochondria responds to treatment in characteristic ways and that sooner or later it resolves itself according to one of several patterns.

Unfortunately none of this is true. Hypochondria seems to be a symptom of (that is, a response to) so many different kinds of troubles that the disorder assumes dozens of different forms. Taken together the hypochondrias are so common, in fact, that some doctors believe that they are among the most common symptoms of emotional distress.[1] Is this because among certain groups hypochondria is a more socially acceptable expression of distress than divorce, child abuse, alcoholism, and the like? Is it biologically or psychologically more efficient than other defenses?

Although the questions hypochondria raises radiate in all directions, it is possible to place some limits on the subject by saying what hypochondria is not. Hypochondria is not malingering in which a person intentionally pretends to be sick, and it is not psychosomatic illness in which psychological stress triggers, exacerbates, or maintains a physical problem such as peptic ulcer

without necessarily involving the patient in a life-style that re-
volves around disease. A person with an ulcer might become hypochondriacal and a hypochondriac might get an ulcer, but the
two disorders do not necessarily go together.

Using these distinctions, the users and abusers of bodily
complaints examined here are persons who unwittingly center
their lives on health or disease and yet who function well enough
to live in normal society. Those who are overtly anxious or depressed might want to give up their preoccupations. Others appear moderately content with the multiple restrictions that control their lives and regulate the lives of those around them. In
either case, hypochondriacs are using a concern for their health
as a way of coping with stress.

Although lip service is paid to the belief that hypochondria
is caused by the interaction of psychological, biological, and sociological factors, almost everyone who studies or treats the disorder acts as if one of the three influences were vastly more important than the other two. Psychodynamic therapists, to pick
one group within psychology for example, generally feel that a
person is the product of early childhood experiences more than
anything else. Consequently, their explanations of hypochondria
center on the conflicts and confusions that can beset a young child
when his needs run counter to the rules of society or the desires
of his parents. A common psychodynamic explanation suggests
that hypochondria is one of several maladaptive patterns of behavior that can start when a young child has difficulty separating
himself from an overprotective mother. Rather than gradually
developing the sense of being an individual living among other
individuals, such a child maintains a fundamental confusion concerning the boundaries of his thoughts and even physical feelings.
Some psychologists say this child has failed to develop a sufficiently strong sense of self; others, that he is enmeshed in a mutually dependent relationship with his mother. In either case the
child feels he cannot survive on his own. He must have the protection of a powerful parentlike figure, yet this protection always
seems dangerously unreliable. Many such children apparently feel

that to obtain the love they need, they must relinquish their independence and do whatever their protectors wish.

Being sick is one way of agreeing to be helpless. In fact, hypochondria is almost the perfect solution to this common predicament, for in being ill—either as a child, wife, husband, employee, or in-law—the vulnerable person simultaneously obtains the protection and attention he craves, excuses his excessive dependence, binds his protector to him (who could leave someone who is seriously ill?), causes the protector a good deal of trouble which punishes him or her for being so annoyingly indispensable, and also punishes the hypochondriac for having hostile feelings toward his protector and himself. A hypochondriac thus tries to manage the confusion concerning his dependence, hostility, and guilt by confining these problems to one corner of his life—his body—and at the same time denies the primary result of this confusion, which is a pervasive lack of independence and self-esteem. He substitutes illness, a blameless form of failure, for his sense of general worthlessness. Put another way, he desperately maintains his belief that he would be strong, independent, and lovable if only he were not sick.

Biochemical explanations of hypochondria replace the constructs of dependence and self-esteem with considerations of the biochemical state of the central nervous system both as acquired genetically and as affected by life's varied experiences. Research on the specific chemical problems that seem to accompany some forms of depression and anxiety dates only from the 1950s, but already there are indications that panicky or phobic hypochondriacs may be having trouble shutting off or quieting some of the regulatory systems in their brains. In other words, there may be a physiological basis for the centuries-old observation that hypochondriacs tend to be sensitive, high-strung individuals in "noisy bodies."

The sociological explanation of hypochondria shifts the focus from the individual to the society that may be stressing him beyond endurance. If people try to adjust to a society that is so unsupportive that it makes it almost impossible for the poor, the very old, and certain other groups to attain physical security, self-respect, love, and other essentials, then, sociologists argue, these deprived persons will not have the resources to maintain mental health any more than malnourished persons can maintain physical health. Such groups will be predisposed to many kinds of mental disorders. If, in addition, they live in a society that singles out mental illness as the ultimate sign of weakness but sanctions back pains and headaches as "normal" problems, then disenfranchised persons will be more likely to suffer from hypochondria than from any undisguised form of mental distress.

Where can we go to find an integrated description of these hypochondriacs? Who has gathered all the reasons for this old and inadequate form of rebellion? Which pressures and people work to maintain hypochondria and which labor against it? What is likely to become of a hypochondriac?

To the extent that answers are available, they must be pieced together from information provided by physicians who treat, therapists who analyze, neurologists who test, sociologists who generalize, and philosophers who contemplate hypochondriacs. Each has part of the explanation. A comprehensive understanding of hypochondria must come from such a broad and unfortunately unwieldy range of observations, for the disorder seems fundamentally indicative of a problem in living.

Most important to any explanation are the feelings of the hypochondriacs themselves, for the objective of any study of human behavior is, in my opinion, to reconcile the private experience of the individual with the scientific theories that claim to explain his behavior. So to anchor theory in reality it is essential to listen to hypochondriacs as they confide in their friends or private journals. We must follow those who, like Alfred Lord Tennyson, thought "more about his bowels and nerves than about the Laureate wreath he was born to inherit,"[2] and prayed,

> Be near me when my light is low,
> When the blood creeps and the nerves prick

And tingle; and the heart is sick.
And all the wheels of Being slow.[3]

And we must proceed with others who have recorded their attempts to outwit disease by writing complicated diets or by corresponding at length with their doctors. Wrestling with their fears with desperation or a wonderful wit and cunning, some remain hypochondriacs all their lives. Others leave their preoccupations behind and, as Freud is supposed to have said of hysteria, exchange neurotic misery for common unhappiness.

For many of my chapters, as I move through what might be called the life cycle of a hypochondriac, I have chosen two or three well-known persons to serve as examples. James Boswell, the distinguished biographer of Samuel Johnson, introduces the disorder as he sets off "with a kind of gloom upon my mind" to spend a winter in Holland completing his studies in law. I have chosen Boswell not only because his journals and letters express so earnest a mixture of depression, humor, poignancy, and self-pity but also because the eighteenth century was a time when hypochondria was considered a major problem and was understood to be an amalgam of social, emotional, and physical complaints—a view close to my own.

In subsequent chapters on the modern hypochondriac's life-style, the poet Sara Teasdale, with her chronic retreats to convalescent homes and her growing terror of stroke, demonstrates hypochondria used to deal with problems that seem too threatening to be faced directly. Charles Darwin is another whose lifelong vomiting and insomnia developed in step with his inability to reconcile his ideas and desires with what he believed society demanded of a good person. Immanuel Kant, Robert Burns, Molière's "Argan," Smollett's "Matt Bramble"—these and other hypochondriacs are included to round out the picture of how hypochondriacs live, how they use and are used by, love and are loved by family, friends, and doctors.

Because hypochondria has a lot to do with the management

of relationships and the management of blame, I have tried to find out how the persons dealing closely with hypochondriacs feel and behave. Does the wife of a worrier really want her husband to get well? Or is she unconsciously afraid of the changes his recovery would initiate? And what happens when a chronic complainer whose life-style is rooted in semi-invalidism confronts a doctor whose self-esteem depends on curing patients?

Other disabilities—personally useful and socially sanctioned—could be used to explore the relationship between the marginally out-of-step individual and his society. Alcoholism, dependence on drugs, or obsessive eating—each with parallels to hypochondria—are some of these. Yet the study of hypochondria has a philosophical advantage. Although a preoccupation with disease is a poor road map for getting through life, as a way of living it cannot help but address our most fundamental concerns.

"For the present," wrote Miguel de Unamuno, "let us remain keenly suspecting that the longing not to die, the hunger for personal immortality, the effort . . . to persist indefinitely in our own being . . . that this is the affective basis of all knowledge and the personal inward starting-point of all human philosophy."[4]

There is a more purely practical reason for examining this variety of human limitation as well: the profound effect that hypochondria has on the cost and operation of national health insurance programs. Britons, Swedes, Indians, and others who have put such programs into practice have learned that "free" doctoring exaggerates the differences between persons who act as if they are invulnerable to disease and those who seek constant reassurance. When the second type—among whom are hypochondriacs—number in the hundreds of thousands, the health insurance system is quickly besieged. The common discovery has been that the desire for medical care (and whatever else that stands for) is boundless and can be controlled only by imposing economic limitations.[5] These limitations restrict the number of doctors, hospitals, and other resources a country provides so that the initial promise of medical care that is inexpensive and accessible becomes a scramble for limited services. Under these conditions hypochondria becomes a financial burden for the taxpayer and a logistical problem for both the doctors and the health plan's other users.

Ubiquitous and annoying, hypochondria has been called the ultimate test of health care plans, yet the more poignant challenge is the one the hypochondriac presents to himself. "Asleep or awake he is haunted alike by the spectres of his anxiety," wrote Plutarch almost two thousand years ago. "Awake, he makes no use of his reason; and asleep, he enjoys no respite from his alarms. . . . Nowhere can he find an escape from his imaginary terrors."[6]

Any malady that can be so frightening and invasive brings to many of its sufferers an intense desire to get better or at least to exchange continuous doubt and preoccupation for more concrete and manageable misfortunes. For some this leads to a lifelong search for the physical disease that they believe lies at the root of their present unhappiness. But for some the misery relentlessly pushes them toward a confrontation with the real fears and conflicts that underlie their affliction, be these psychological, social, or biochemical. In short, hypochondria presents many sufferers—whether they want it or not, whether they use it or not—with an almost intolerable opportunity to move toward a more honest way of living.

"*Sperate miseri; cavete felices,*" wrote the melancholic Robert Burton in 1611. "Take hope, you wretched ones; beware, you who are happy."[7]

1

BEING A HYPOCHONDRIAC

This afternoon, by taking too much physic, I
felt myself very ill. I was weak. I shivered,
and I had flashes of heat. I began to be
apprehensive that I was taking a nervous
fever. . . . I was quite sunk. I looked with a
degree of horror upon death.

—James Boswell's
London Journal 1763

■

IN AUGUST 1763 THE generally vivacious but now distressingly
subdued young Scot, James Boswell, glided slowly into the
Dutch city of Utrecht on a canal boat. A week earlier he had set
off from London "with a kind of gloom upon my mind" to study
law at the famous University of Utrecht. Now, a month before
his classes began, he arrived—a complete stranger. Boswell and
his baggage were taken to a hotel that stood near the city's cathedral. Its bell tower looked back upon a cloister, and from there
a somber row of saints and gargoyles gazed impassively at the
university buildings next door.

"I was shown up to a high bedroom with old furniture,"
wrote Boswell to one of his friends the next day. "At every hour
the bells of the great tower played a dreary psalm tune. A deep
melancholy seized upon me. I groaned with the idea of living all

winter in so shocking a place. . . . I was worse and worse the
next day. All the horrid ideas you can imagine, recurred upon
me. . . . I sunk quite into despair. I thought that at length the
time was come that I should grow mad. . . . I went out to the
streets, and even in public could not refrain from groaning and
weeping bitterly."[1]

Boswell was plunging into what he later called his most
severe hypochondria. Thoughts of disease, madness, failure, rid-
icule, and death "in all the various ways in which it has been
observed" trampled through his mind and he was powerless to
repulse them. On that Sunday morning in August he tried touring
the historic city on foot but saw nothing. He searched for someone
to talk to but found only an unsympathetic clerk at the English-
speaking Calvinist church. Boswell walked faster. His thoughts
kept pace, and soon the flushed and perspiring young man was
running frantically down the narrow cobbled alleys, across public
squares, and along quiet canals, sobbing without restraint.

Boswell dreaded spending another night in Utrecht; the
cathedral bells reminded him of frightening Calvinist sermons he
had heard as a child, and he knew from personal experience that
"night is universally the season of terror." But as evening fell he
forced himself into his chamber, determined to leave Utrecht the
next day and to spend the hours until dawn writing to his friends.
At noon the following day he reboarded a canal boat and, at approximately three miles per hour, "fled" to Rotterdam. There he
sought shelter in the home of a recent and somewhat surprised
acquaintance.

Thoroughly demoralized, Boswell was not easy to comfort.
A lot depended on his winter sojourn in Holland, for although his
career as a lawyer was already assured, the ten-month stay in
Utrecht was half of an important bargain he had struck with his
stern and generally uncompromising father. The two had agreed
that if the younger Boswell studied civil law and learned French,
his father would give him a grand tour of Europe. The twentythree-year-old Boswell saw this extensive holiday as a major step
toward the reputation he desired as a worldly gentleman and a

"Great Man," so he was prepared to study hard. Besides, in earnestly applying himself he had hopes of changing from a rakish, somewhat rebellious youth inclined to plumpness and other expressions of self-indulgence into a man of inner strength, outward calm, and regular habit. Yet after thirty-six hours alone in Utrecht, he had repacked his bags and written his friends begging them to meet him, write him, pardon him, and, above all, *help him.*

"The pain which this affair will give my worthy father shocks me in the most severe degree," he wrote William Johnson Temple. "O Temple! all my resolutions of attaining a consistent character are blown to the winds. All my hopes of being a man of respect are gone."[2]

Boswell was in a state of profound irresolution. Should he retreat to London or return to Utrecht? Should he seek a physician or try to hide his distress? Could he fight his fears and "think them down," or was he preordained to suffer?

His moods fluctuated wildly. "Let not this dreadful affair affect you too much. There is no real harm done," he added at the end of a letter to Temple, fearing he had painted too grim a picture of his wretchedness. Then, at the very end, he tacked on, "O dear! I am very ill."[3]

Boswell had long known that the streak of hypochondriac passion ran through his family, and that streak, he believed, consisted of a physical disorder combined with a morbidly overwrought imagination. He knew it had not passed him by. "My grandfather had it in a very strong degree," he would frequently say to explain his own black moods, and he described his mother as having been "an extremely delicate girl, very hypochondriac."[4] His younger brother John struggled with insanity all his adult life.

As a child Boswell was timid. He was afraid of ghosts and especially of being left alone in the dark. By the age of twelve he had contracted a "nervous ailment" that required treatment at a spa. His first real attack of hypochondria occurred when he was about seventeen, and throughout his life "the black foe" periodically attacked him, though not always with equal force or frequency.

When Boswell was in London preparing for his forthcoming trip to Holland by soaking up all "the delicate felicity" the city had to offer, he met the famous literary figure and fellow sufferer, Samuel Johnson. Boswell was immediately attracted to the gruffly eccentric, honest, and articulate Johnson and went out of his way to meet him several times. Almost on the eve of his departure for Utrecht, Boswell got up the courage to confess his torments. He told the much older Johnson of his long periods of lassitude when nothing seemed worth doing or striving for and his terror of illness. At times, he explained, he feared a nervous fever or an "almost madness" and at other times he became morbidly preoccupied with venereal disease or other purely physical disorders. He had, for example, contracted gonorrhea that winter and for weeks afterward was afraid that it would recur and eventually kill him.

"Upon my coming home, I felt myself not so well," he had written in his journal in February. "I dreaded the worst and went to bed. . . . I lay in direful apprehension that my testicle . . . was again swelled. I dreamt that Douglas [a surgeon] stood by me and said, 'This is a damned difficult case.' I got up today still in terror."[5]

To Boswell's relief, Johnson understood this kind of suffering and said that he himself "had been greatly distressed with it."

> He advised me to have constant occupation of mind, to take a great deal of exercise, and to live moderately; especially to shun drinking at night. . . . It gave me great relief to talk of my disorder with Mr. Johnson; and when I discovered that he himself was subject to it, I felt that strange satisfaction which human nature feels at the idea of participating distress with others; and the greater person our fellow sufferer is, so much the more good does it do us.[6]

Johnson's intellectual and moral support was a great help

to Boswell, and the famous author of the *Dictionary* and of so many fine essays even made the day-long trip to Harwich with his new young friend when it was time for Boswell to take the packet boat to Holland.

But when Boswell actually found himself in Holland, among persons who spoke languages he had not yet learned, Johnson's powerful friendship was too far away to comfort him. As he toured through the flat Dutch countryside, Boswell compulsively examined his problem from a dozen different angles, explained it a dozen different ways, and constructed as many unmanageable solutions. In spite of these spasms of convoluted reasoning, he gradually came around to a fairly obvious conclusion: idleness and solitude were no good for him. If he could keep immensely busy, he might survive Utrecht.

In early autumn, therefore, when classes got under way, Boswell set up housekeeping near Cathedral Square. Each morning he arose about 6:30 A.M. and, arming himself against loneliness, wrote out an intricate memorandum. Each began with an evaluation of his previous day's work (or, rather, behavior), then listed objectives for the day at hand. "Read Latin 7 to 8, write French from 8 to 9," begins a typical timetable. "Breakfast from 9 to 10, Latin again from 10 to 11; 11 to 12 get shaved and dressed, 12 to 1 Trotz's lecture, 1 to 3 walk and dine, 3 to 4 French Master . . ."[7] and so on until 10 P.M., at which time he began working on his private journal, writing to friends and doing whatever light reading his remaining strength allowed. The evaluations that proceeded from these relentless schedules gradually changed in tone as the term wore on. Anxious nagging gave way to expressions of cautious approval and finally of astonished delight.

"You was a little irregular yesterday," he wrote of himself in his characteristic style, "but it was but for one day." "You did charmingly yesterday." "You read an immensity of Greek. . . . It was a dismal day and you eat too much wild duck, so was a little gloomy. However, you said not a word of it, nor have you said a word of it near these three months."[8]

But if Boswell hoped that his hypochondria was not a real recurring malady—and he sometimes did—he was dismally reminded of his susceptibility when he returned to Utrecht after the Christmas holidays. He had kept himself in check for three months and was tired of the routine. Moreover it was winter and the weather was dreary beyond all description. More and more of his memoranda were critical.

"You was sad and gloomy." "Yesterday you was lethargic and still hippish [a slang expression for hypochondriacal]. . . . Force activity and drive off this gloom."[9]

Boswell teetered on the verge of another collapse until early March, when he was pushed over the edge by the death of his illegitimate son, an infant he had never seen but was supporting. At first Boswell became lethargic and found it difficult to keep his mind on Latin and law. His thoughts fastened instead "upon all the evils that can happen to man," and in his dreams he again suffered "death in all the various ways in which it has been observed."[10] "How direful the thought of death is when one lies awake in the middle of the night,"[11] he wrote plaintively.

"Nobody but a sincere friend can listen to my complaints when opprest with melancholy," he confided to Temple, explaining further that the very thought of company now made him irritable and peevish. Cheerfulness had "the effect of an insult though unintentional."[12] He wanted friends who, if not hypochondriacs themselves, at least dreaded what he suffered. "It was old-womanish of you to complain so," he would scold himself when, by repeated miscalculations, he revealed his hypochondria to some cheerful, uncomprehending person. Nevertheless throughout March and April Boswell felt driven to demand solace and advice from almost everyone he encountered.

Five days after a particularly horrible night when "you awaked in great disorder, thinking you was dying and exclaiming, 'There's no more of it! Tis all over!' Horrid idea!"[13] Boswell overcame his squeamishness and summoned a physician to bleed him. He hoped that this would rid him of some of the poisons that he believed rose to his head nightly and caused such ghastly nightmares. Besides, having tried "all the modes of cure" except medicine, it was time, he felt, to ask for professional help.

The bloodletting did not ease his apprehensions, however, and a month later Boswell visited the famous doctor, Jerome David Gaubius, who told him that although he had no choice but to tolerate his hypochondria for the present, he would outgrow it by the age of thirty. This cheered Boswell considerably (although the prognosis proved inaccurate), and faced with the delightful prospect of leaving Utrecht in June and gradually outgrowing his hypochondria, Boswell regained his spirits. Toward the end of his stay he wrote out a brave and "INVIOLABLE PLAN— to be read over frequently."

> You believed that you had a real distemper [were mad]. On your first coming to Utrecht, you yielded to that idea. You endured severe torment. You was pitiful and wretched. You was in danger of utter ruin. This severe shock has proved of the highest advantage. Our friend Temple showed you that idleness was your sole disease. . . .
> Remember that idleness renders you quite unhappy. That then your imagination broods over dreary ideas of its own forming, and you become contemptible and wretched.[14]
> Bravely, naively, he added, "Let this be no more."

On a fine day in June Boswell swung into a coach and four and went clattering out of Utrecht. For the duration of his grand tour he was rarely troubled with a dreary or lumpish thought. It was one of "the clear seasons of his existence." Some ten years later, however, long after he was to have outgrown his hypochondria according to Dr. Gaubius, Boswell sank back into familiar apprehensions.

"It vexed me to find a return of that distemper of mind which formerly afflicted me so much. . . . But when the mind has been hurt by hypochondria, it is not soon quite easy again."[15]

Boswell was afflicted with hypochondria on and off for the rest of his life, though never so severely as in Utrecht. He became fairly adept at reading or writing the malady out of his system, and between 1777 and 1783 (as a man in his late thirties and early forties) he passed along his experience and advice in a long series of essays called "The Hypochondriack." Seventy installments appeared anonymously in the *London Magazine*. He was writing, he said, not for the young and gay or for "the solid tranquil species of men," or again for "those whose minds are concentrated by the necessity of providing support for their lives." Rather, he said, "I write to people like myself . . . , who are arrived at the age of serious thinking; to beings whose existence is compounded of reasons and sentiments; who can judge rationally, yet feel keenly; who have an incessant wish for happiness, but find it difficult to have that wish gratified."[16]

"I snatch *gratifications*," he had said of his own life, "but have no *comfort*."[17]

Two centuries after Boswell struggled with fears of illness in Utrecht, the loneliness of solitary travel is still triggering bouts of hypochondria among the susceptible. The anxiety and misery seem scarcely to have changed, but the focus of concern is cancer or heart disease rather than "nervous fevers," and the stresses that impinge upon the sufferer have changed also. It may be well to look briefly at a modern hypochondriac's troubles, to transcribe Boswell's descriptions into a more modern idiom.

When Kate was eighteen and a student at Connecticut College for Women, she took the money she had saved since childhood and went to Europe. Having flown to England, she crossed the channel as Boswell had at Harwich. It was her intention to visit the Dutch university towns of Leiden, Nijmegen, and Utrecht before proceeding south into France, where she had been offered a job as a live-in baby-sitter. It was the first time Kate had been away from home without family or friends. She was traveling alone and loving it.

For a week Kate toured the Dutch countryside, walking everywhere, looking at everything, and except for the strain of trying to speak Dutch or French and the loneliness of eating dinner by herself each evening, she was pleased with her vacation. In June she traveled to a small town in the north of France and there, four blocks from a cobbled square with a broken fountain and an American tank, she took up residence with a family of ten. She was given a low-ceilinged room in the attic under the eaves. A single small window looked down through the branches of an old chestnut tree onto a gravel courtyard below.

Kate congratulated herself on being part of "the real France." She spoke only French, ate only French food, and began dressing like local girls in sandals and dirndl skirts. She fit right in. Yet several weeks after her arrival she began to daydream more than usual—not about home but about falling in love. She was surprised when these fantasies turned into a terrible feeling of loneliness. Getting ready for bed one night, she began sobbing without reason. The next morning her throat felt slightly constricted, and because it tightened further during the day she assumed she had caught cold. That night she tied a T-shirt around her neck to keep warm. It was a useless gesture. She had a horrible nightmare of being lost in an enormous rotting carcass. It was a dream that had often terrified her as a child. By the end of the week the thought possessed her that she had cancer of the throat and was dying.

Like her throat, which now tightened so severely that her breath sometimes rasped, the whole world constricted around her. The chestnut tree that had extended gently moving branches toward her window now froze in place and became a rigid, incomprehensible pattern of brown and green. The children she watched all day became unreal too, and she quickly became short-tempered with them. Letters from her parents were meaningless and so were her mechanical replies. In fact the entire outside world was switched off, shut out, and Kate retreated into intense introspection.

Like Boswell, Kate picked and pried at her problem endlessly and in two contradictory ways. On the one hand, if her throat were really closing, she should rush home to her family and family doctor. She considered this option every time she felt her neck, but she never acted on it. On the other hand, if her illness were really an admission of failure and a sign that she was too immature to be on her own, she should confront that issue. This she never did either. Boswell had been horrified at the thought of admitting his weakness to his worthy father, and Kate was unable to admit even to herself that her resources were not sufficient for the task at hand.

As the summer wore on the civil war in Kate's head intensified, and she became increasingly involved with her symptoms. She monitored them continuously, compared them to the sensations of the day before, and tried to force them into some meaningful pattern. She also began gaining weight at an alarming rate. Although at mealtimes she ate no more than two helpings of anything, she began to sneak food from the pantry when the children were napping and the cook was in town. Gingerbread and candies did not make her throat feel better, and getting too fat for her clothes did not make Kate feel better, but she seemed driven to eat by the same pressures that forced her to feel her neck and mull over her symptoms.

Several weeks later, on the allotted day of her return and not a moment earlier, Kate boarded a plane in Paris and flew home. Late that summer night her father drove her along the Connecticut River to the house where she had always lived. Her mother ran out the door to greet her, and as Kate smelled the familiar lavender cologne and felt her mother's embrace, her throat began to close instead of open. There was no protective circle to reenter, she realized with disheartening certainty. Even in her mother's arms she was still alone with her secret disease and alone to puzzle over the loss of innocence and security that accompanied her fearful acknowledgment of death.

As the American philosopher William James had written of his own crisis,

> after this the universe was changed for me altogether. I awoke morning after morning with a horrible dread at the pit of my stomach, and with a sense of the insecurity of life that I never

knew before. . . . I remember wondering how other people could live, how I myself had ever lived, so unconscious of that pit of insecurity beneath the surface of life.[18]

For Kate, for Boswell, for William James, the sudden awareness of vulnerability, accompanied by dismal imaginings and an intense fear, was an experience that reverberated throughout their lives.

"When the mind has been hurt by hypochondria, it is not soon quite easy again," Boswell had written. This has not changed for centuries.

2

"A DISEASE
SO GRIEVOUS, SO COMMON"

I am very sensible that a surprising Diversity
of Symptoms renders the Knowledge of this
Distemper vastly difficult to be attain'd to.
—Richard Browne
Medicina Musica

■

THAT "TEDIOUS AND long protracted Disease, whose Symptoms are so violent and numerous that it is no easy Task either to enumerate or account for them," [1] has had a remarkably constant clinical picture for the past two thousand years. Few disorders have had so continual or so long a history as hypochondria. Although the disorder has been given a dozen auxiliary names and ten times that number of explanations, the "bad and peevish disease" has been a recognizable entity for at least two millennia. The earliest written descriptions of hypochondriacs who were much troubled with indigestion, vertigo, insomnia, and bad dreams were immediately recognizable to sixth-century Byzantine physicians, to seventeenth-century chroniclers of disease, and even to us.

As far as anyone knows, the word *hypochondrium* first appeared among the Hippocratic aphorisms relating to fevers:

"If jaundice arise in a fever on the seventh, eleventh, or fourteenth day, it is good," Hippocrates is supposed to have said some four hundred years before Christ, "unless the right hypochondrium be hard, in which case it is bad."[2] Used this way, *hypochondrium* is an anatomical term referring to a specific place in the body, namely *hypo* (under) and *chondros* (the cartilage of the ribs). Thus the right hypochondrium includes most of the liver and gall bladder and the left hypochondrium, the spleen. The stomach and the rest of the epigastric apparatus sit between them. It was not uncommon to hear of someone wounded in one or both of his hypochondria (plural), and even as late as the 1700s it was reported that Deacon Sam'll Field of Massachusetts fought with the Indians and was shot clear through his right hypochondrium.[3]

Although the word *hypochondria* persisted for centuries as an anatomical term, during the second century A.D. it took on its second and more popular meaning. At that time the influential physician Galen of Pergamon linked the term to a broad range of digestive disorders. Hypochondria's other attributes—preoccupation with disease, inexplicable periods of anxiety, nightmares, and the rest—were gradually added over the next four hundred years, after which the clinical picture, or "presenting symptoms," as doctors would say, changed very little. In contrast, the explanations for hypochondria remained pretty much as Galen had formulated them for about fifteen centuries and then changed with increasing frequency, as did medicine in general.

Throughout most of its history hypochondria was linked to melancholia, which, being one of the four directions a personality could tend toward, was a common temperamental type. In fact, during Hippocrates' time the problems we now call mental illnesses were loosely ranged in two categories: mania for agitated disturbances and melancholia for tranquil, depressive forms. The latter were understood to be caused by an excess of black bile, and hence the name was derived from *melas* or *melanos*, meaning black, plus *chole*, gall or bile. When Galen coined terms such as *morbus hypochondriacus* in the first century A.D., he was attempting to differentiate among a vast collection of melancholic complaints.

During the Middle Ages interest in hypochondria waned, as it did generally in many aspects of corporeal existence. As attention was focused on salvation and eternal life more than on the flesh, a fascinating kind of spiritual hypochondria flourished briefly. This religious hypochondria was called *pusillanimata*, or scrupulosity. The condition was characterized by morbid doubt as to the adequacy of one's devotion and a terrible fear not of disease and death but of eternal damnation.

During the Renaissance, when Aristotelian and Platonic ideas were revived and the belief grew that only the melancholic were capable of inspiration and other forms of creative madness, the physical variety of hypochondria reappeared as part of the new stance. Among Italian artists of the 1500s, for example, there was a gradual movement away from an earlier image of the competent craftsman toward one of the eccentric and slightly mad artist.

Federico Barocci of Urbino, a popular painter of emotional religious works, amazed his friends by being able to paint at all. He was constantly sick. He painted one hour in the morning and one hour in the evening. "All the rest of the day he spent in pain from stomach cramps, caused by continuous vomiting which overcame him as soon as he had eaten. At night he hardly slept, and even during that short time he was tormented by frightful dreams."[4] Barocci was sick for fifty-two years, and although it is by no means certain that he was a hypochondriac, he did fulfill the role of the fragile and exquisitely sensitive artist until he died in his eighties.

The fashion for being moody, extremely sensitive, and somewhat ailing (as opposed to vulgarly and insensitively healthy) swept north from Italy and soon found expression in poems and plays as well as in the habits of superior persons. As part of this worldly image, hypochondria was on the rise. In fact when the melancholic bachelor Robert Burton published his famous book, *The Anatomy of Melancholy*, in 1621, there were so

many people either suffering or desiring to suffer from love melancholy, religious melancholy, hypochondriacal melancholy, and
all the other forms he described that the book went through an
amazing eight editions by the close of the century.

Burton, who lived the greater part of his life at Christ
Church College, Oxford, reading classics, medicine, mathematics,
astrology, and divinity, drew together the observations that had
been made on melancholia, including hypochondria, since antiq-
uity. He did not himself propose any new causes or suggest more
effective cures, yet his empathy for the emotional suffering of
melancholics was such that Samuel Johnson maintained, "there is
great spirit and great power in what he says," and Boswell ha-
bitually listed *The Anatomy* as the first line of defense against
recurrent hypochondria. "*Experto crede Roberto!*" "Believe the
experienced Robert!" "I was not a little offended with this malady," Burton tells his readers at the start, and since melancholy
is "a common infirmity of body and soul and such a one that hath
as much need of spiritual as a corporeal cure, I could not find a
fitter task to busy myself about."[5] After lengthy preliminaries,
Burton endeavors to describe the overwhelming variety of symptoms attendant upon Melancholia. For hypochondriacal melancholy alone his list goes on for pages. The commonest complaints,
he says, are physical, such as "sharp belchings, fulsome crudities,
heat in the bowels, wind and grumbling in the guts . . ., cold
sweat . . ., ears ringing, vertigo and giddiness."[6] But some symptoms are emotional, such as the periodic fear and sorrow that
beset all melancholics and the fear of disease so characteristic of
hypochondriacs. "Some are afraid that they shall have every fearful disease they see others have, hear of, or read and dare not
therefore hear or read of any such subject."[7]

The cures Burton cites cover the entire spectrum of known
therapies, from diet and exercise to the resolution of intimate
problems and the selection of a good doctor wary of purges. Some
sufferers are helped by the logic and good counsel of friends, he
continues, but others, frankly deluded, must sometimes be
tricked out of their preoccupations.

If they say they have swallowed frogs or a snake, by all means grant it and tell them you can easily cure it—'tis an ordinary thing . . . A woman . . . swallowed a serpent, as she thought; [her physician] gave her a vomit and conveyed a serpent such as she conceived into the basin; upon the sight of it she was amended. The pleasantest dotage that I ever read was of a gentleman at Senes in Italy who was afraid to piss lest all the town should be drowned; the physician caused the bells to be rung backward and told him the town was on fire, whereupon he made water and was immediately cured.[8]

Burton's treatise with its tone of genuine concern was immensely successful, for it spoke to a widespread concern for personal health. His book inspired similar compendiums and even plays, masques, and poems.

Medical treatises on hypochondria were also appearing with increasing frequency, and because of the growing interest in anatomy the names of these tracts were changing from *Discourse on the Hypochondria Melancholy* by John Hawkins (1633), for example, to treatises on the parts of the body that seemed affected. The spleen was usually thought to be the offending organ in men and the uterus in women. Hence men were splenetic and women hysterical (from the Greek word for uterus, *hystera*). Other organs, including the brain, were believed to be secondarily affected, and in the eighteenth century both hysteria and hypochondria were reclassified as weaknesses of the nervous system. As such, symptoms could occur throughout the body. And they did.

Thomas Sydenham, who began the reunification of the two disorders late in the 1600s, calling them similar as two eggs, stated that the complaints were extremely common. Not only did studious, sedentary men suffer hypochondriacal complaints but "as to females . . . , there is rarely one who is wholly free from them—and females, be it remembered, form one half of the adults of the world."[9]

And something else was happening to hypochondria besides its proliferation among the upper and middle classes. It was filtering into the working class as well. This was confusing, for it cast suspicion on the venerable assumption that hypochondria was the mark of a superior person and that it was caused by a rich diet, boredom, and a marvelous sensitivity.

It is difficult to determine exactly what pressures allow a disease to infiltrate—or be adopted by—a new population. In the case of the occurrence of hysteria and hypochondria among the lower classes, some of the reasons are to be found in industrialization and urbanization. These movements brought thousands of laborers into the cities, where many lived in poverty cut off from the support of family and community. As Andrew Duncan, a physician practicing in the Edinburgh Royal Infirmary, noted concerning one of his hypochondriacs, "he is a poor indigent man without house or family and to him the accommodations of an hospital are luxurious."[10] Whatever the reasons, more and more poor were requesting treatments at the "voluntary" or, as we would say, charity hospitals, and one of the illnesses they presented was hypochondria. Duncan himself treated some of these cases, and although the records he kept at the infirmary have been lost, his comments are preserved in the notebooks of medical students who took down his lectures verbatim in shorthand.

A typical case of the new lower-class hypochondria was forty-six-year-old James Smythe, who arrived at the infirmary in February 1795 complaining of a fear of syphilis and occasional numbness in his arms. Dr. Duncan could find no sign of illness. After several examinations he concluded that the syphilis, supposedly contracted seven months before, was imaginary but the hypochondria was real. As was customary, Smythe was kept on the ward with the physically ill patients and was given simple food, no tea or coffee, watered wine, laxatives, and tonics such as iron filings to rebuild his lax nerves.

"After 10 days of medicines he began to get tired of them as is generally the case," Dr. Duncan told his students. Eventually Smythe refused to take his purgatives and this gave Duncan the right to discharge the patient.

I was therefore not displeased to have this opportunity of dismissing him for irregularity. An hospital is a bad place for hypochondriacs. They have too much time to brood over their complaints and their companions are affected with real diseases so that they suppose themselves affected with all the complaints they hear of. The best remedy is certainly . . . [the] exertion of mind and body. I think he will be better by returning to his former occupation than by any remedies we could have given him during his stay in the house.[11]

Whether or not "an hospital" was the proper place for hypochondriacs they came, and faced with this new clientele, doctors were forced to expand their understanding of what caused the disorder. Simultaneously hypochondria was divorced from its aristocratic implications.

"The HYSTERIC and HYPOCHONDRIAC DISORDERS, once peculiar to the chambers of the great are now to be found in our kitchens and workshops," wrote the American physician Benjamin Rush with obvious pride in 1774.[12] And back in England James Boswell took that unfashionable belief a step farther by publicly contending that "hypochondria, like the fever or gout, or any other disease, is incident to all sorts of men, from the wisest to the most foolish."[13]

By the end of the eighteenth century, then, hypochondria and its dozen namesakes were among the commonest of disorders and were believed to afflict every kind of person. George Cheyne, a popular physician and author of *The English Malady* (1733), claimed that roughly one-third of his countrymen suffered from hypochondria and hysteria. (Cheyne apparently included anxiety, depression, and the mental distress attendant upon syphilis, gout, scurvy, and consumption all under the term "English Malady.")

And yet for all their commonness, there continued to be something elusive about these diseases. Although understood to have a physical, inheritable basis and to affect the "animal spirits" that supposedly passed through the hollow tubules of the nerves, there was no essential cluster of symptoms that characterized hypochondria and hysteria the way there was for other diseases. As the century wore on, however, the disorders developed a trademark of another sort, a kind of moral signature. Both hypochondria and hysteria were increasingly said to reflect a weakness of moral fiber. There was, after all, something self-pitying and at times self-serving about the hypochondriac's continual troubles.

In 1822 the French clinician Jean-Pierre Falret published a two-part treatise, *De l'Hypochondrie et du suicide*, which went a step beyond the commonsensical notion that hypochondria involved a moral weakness and declared that it was *primarily* a mental disorder.

> In this work, I especially wish to show that the public's opinion of [this type of] madness is better found than that of most doctors. The expressions crazy-headed and brainless . . . point quite directly to the source of the trouble.[14]

No more spleen or uterus for Falret. "Moral and intellectual causes are, without contradiction, the most usual causes of hypochondria.[15]

The idea that hypochondria was primarily a mental disease gradually gained acceptance and in so doing exerted a profound effect upon the history of the disorder. Reclassification as a mental problem not only determined who would study and treat hypochondria but also, to a significant degree, who would suffer from it. Toward the end of the nineteenth century hypochondria turned a corner, historically speaking, and nearly dropped out of sight.

This brings us to the present, but with a question to answer. How did common hypochondriacal complaints, once estimated to have affected one-third of England's population, and even today considered one of the most common symptoms of mental distress, fall into their current position of disregard? The answer lies largely with hypochondria's reclassification as a mental illness.

In the last quarter of the nineteenth century, as Sigmund Freud began his studies in Vienna and the famous Parisian neurologist Jean-Martin Charcot observed the hysterical women on the wards of Salpetrière, the nervous disorder known interchangeably as hypochondria and hysteria began to split in two. It did not simply return to its former arrangement wherein hysteria was a female complaint and hypochondria solely for men. Now either sex could have either complaint, but hysteria became a pure example of mental illness—the epitome of neurosis, in fact—whereas hypochondria floundered between mental confusion and physical illness. Freud himself reinforced the ambiguity of hypochondria's status by calling it an "actual neurosis"—that is, a neurosis with a physical basis. He believed that there were actual changes in a hypochondriac's organs that arose "without any of the complicated mental mechanisms we have been learning about . . . [and were] the direct somatic consequences of sexual disturbances."[16] Furthermore, Freud stated that unlike hysteria's symbolic gestures or those of psychosomatic disorders— asthmatic wheezing, for example, was the repressed cry of the child whose mother had withdrawn her love—the symptoms of hypochondria contained no hidden explanations of past problems and were therefore of no use in psychoanalysis. Being unanalyzable, hypochondria was of little interest to psychoanalysts, and being resistant to medical treatment, it was not a disorder that medical doctors wanted to treat either, as we shall see.[17]

These developments left hypochondria in a peculiar position, for just as psychoanalysts were rejecting the disorder as unprofitable (insufficiently neurotic, if you will), the splenetic man in the street and the medical doctor were also rejecting hypochondria, but for the opposite reason: it was too "mental." If the mind were more to blame than the body in producing symptoms, this strongly suggested that the hypochondriac was some kind of crank. This evaluation neither appealed to invalids with mysterious aliments, nor to physicians. Once the germ theory took hold, the goal of the latter was to treat specific infectious diseases. Doctors wanted to believe that each germ led to a single disease and could best be treated with one particular drug. No more wasting time on the old compound mixed maladies such as hypochondria.

A long period in the history of hypochondria was over. For hundreds of years, millions had agreed to call their troubles hypochondriacal because this seemed an apt and acceptable label for a distemper that was understood to be a mixture of physical and emotional problems. The complaint seemed largely inherited, which, like the physical symptoms themselves, took the blame off the sufferers. They couldn't help it. In addition, the disorder evoked sympathy from doctors who had little to offer any of their patients beyond reassurance. Today the culturally acceptable maladies that come closest to hypochondria's former status are called psychogenic or stress-related. These have risen in popularity as hypochondria has declined.

The time has come to set historical considerations aside and look at the most ordinary kinds of twentieth-century hypochondria. With "hypochondriac" referring to any person who is so preoccupied with the possibility (or actuality) of being ill that a concern for health overshadows daily thoughts and activities far beyond reason, it becomes obvious that the disorder covers a wide range of behavior. There are worriers who are terrified of getting certain diseases and dismal complainers who are unshakably convinced that they already have them. There are thousands of hypochondriacs who masterfully use their headaches and upset stomachs to manipulate others into waiting on them, staying with them despite the others wanting to leave, or compelling others to feel guilty and responsible for the hypochondriacs' suffering. There are probably just as many who quietly and unconsciously manipulate themselves. There are hypochondriacs who are physically well and others who are sick, ones who outgrow their preoccupation in a few months and others who suffer undiagnosable ailments throughout their lives.

There are several ways of categorizing this diverse and unwieldy group, although it is well to realize that modern classifications do not shed a great deal more light on the dynamics of hypochondria than did ancient nosologies. The easiest classification to make is based on the symptoms that hypochondriacs complain of; the most difficult, on the underlying causes of the disorder. Following the easy route first, hypochondriacs can be categorized according to the part of the body with which they are most concerned.

According to Dr. F. E. Kenyon, a British psychiatrist who has spent most of his professional life working with hypochondriacs, the most common location of symptoms is the head and neck region, followed by the abdomen, and then the chest.[18] Complaints from the head and neck include dizziness, hearing the pulse at night, loss of hearing, lump in the throat, throat clearing or cough, and floaters that drift across one's field of vision. These complaints have not changed for centuries. "These 'animals' [floaters] you mention are very distressing," wrote Nobel Laureate Alfred Lord Tennyson to his aunt, "and mine increase weekly; in fact I almost look forward with certainty to being blind some of these days."[19] (Tennyson worried about blindness his entire life but died in his eighties with tolerable sight.)

Among gastrointestinal complaints, indigestion in all its forms is most common, followed by pains and bowel disorders. "You ask me about my sickness," wrote Charles Darwin, who suffered from every imaginable form of dyspepsia. "It rarely comes on till 2 or 3 hours after eating, so that I seldom throw up food, only acid & morbid secretions otherwise I sh'd have been dead, for during more than a month I vomited after every meal & several times most nights."[20]

And finally in the chest the most usual complaints are palpitations, skipped heartbeats, pain on the left side, racing pulse, inability to take a deep breath, involuntary sighing, and a sensation of increased blood pressure.

Of course, listing the most common symptoms in head, chest, and gut by no means exhausts the symptoms about which modern hypochondriacs complain. There are sexual complaints, skin problems, backaches, insomnia, fear of halitosis and body odors, distortions of features and limbs, mental symptoms, and, in at least one case, a profound hypochondriacal fear of becoming a hypochondriac. Many doctors have noticed that the majority of complaints occur on the left side of the body—Kenyon says more than 70 percent—and centuries-old paintings of figures representing hypochondria and melancholia are often shown bent to the left or clutching the left side. This could be a cultural artifact stemming from our association of "left" (from the Latin *sinister*) with evil or undesirable, or, as some suggest, the result of the different ways in which the right and left hemispheres of the brain perceive and process body noise. In some instances the left-side bias could simply be a result of the arrangement of our innards. For example, intestinal gas is more likely to produce discomfort on the left because it has trouble negotiating the splenic flexure, a sharp turn in the large intestine.

A more sophisticated way of classifying hypochondriacs by complaint is to see which symptoms cluster together. Several factor analyses have been made of the thirty-three items related to hypochondria that appear on the best known of the paper-and-pencil inventories, the Minnesota Multiphasic Personality Inventory (MMPI).[21] The dimensions of hypochondria thus indentified include digestive difficulties, bad eyesight, poor bowel function, and so forth.

The idea of grouping hypochondriacs according to symptoms advanced when Dr. I. Pilowsky constructed a questionnaire that probed a hypochondriac's attitudes toward illness rather than specific symptoms.[22] When the principal components were extracted from the answers to these questionnaires, three factors were revealed. Pilowsky called them Bodily Preoccupation (characterized by depressed complaining), Disease Phobia (expressed as anxious worrying), and Conviction of the Presence of Disease with Non-response to Reassurance. Broadly speaking, Pilowsky regarded the first two as reactions to stress and the third as pure or primary hypochondria. (See the appendix for the questions most likely to be affirmed by each of these kinds of hypochondriacs.) Subsequent analyses (for example, that described by Bianchi[23]) have confirmed the sense that some hypochondria is associated with depression and some with anxiety and arousal.

This leads us to consider how hypochondria might be classified according to underlying causes such as the affective (mood) and anxiety disorders. (This concept is more fully discussed in chapter 11). Many clinicians maintain that the great majority of hypochondriacs are suffering from "masked depression"—the old melancholia. The best way to understand and treat such persons, they say, is to overlook the bodily complaints that are really superficial symptoms and focus on the depression itself with its classic signs of sadness, hopelessness, a feeling of loss, disturbed sleep, lack of sexual interest, fatigue, and disinterest in the outside world. Although these symptoms are not apparent in all hypochondriacs by any means, clinicians who link hypochondria to depression maintain that the classic signs will emerge in the course of therapy as the hypochondriac loosens his grip on the health problems he may be using to keep sadness and hopelessness at bay. This certainly seems to be true in many cases of hypochondria, and once the underlying depression is acknowledged and ameliorated, the accompanying complaints of dizziness or racing pulse disappear by themselves. Of course sometimes they don't, and the preoccupation with symptoms drags on like a bad habit or an entirely separate problem.

Hypochondria is increasingly linked to anxiety disorders as well as depression. Therapists who see this connection point out that anxiety sets a person up for imaginary diseases by heightening his sensitivity to pain and by arousing the autonomic (involuntary) nervous system, thus producing more grumbles, thumps, and spurious sensations. Persons who suffer from panic disorder, with that problem's dramatic respiratory and cardiac symptoms, are especially likely to interpret their sensations as serious illness. The acute anxiety associated with hypochondria in these cases may stem in part from "life events," as psychologists like to call "the slings and arrows of outrageous fortune," and may also arise from biochemical imbalance. Thus classified as a metabolic disorder, some hypochondria has been treated with drugs that enhance or block one or more of the brain's neurotransmitters. This approach has been tried only for some fifteen years, but the dramatic improvement produced in some chronic hypochondriacs suggests that there may be a biochemical component to the disease.[24]

Not all psychologists agree that the core disorder underlying most hypochondria is depression or anxiety. Behaviorists who believe that the environment conditions the individual and that neuroses are in fact learned habits of a maladaptive nature maintain that hypochondria, psychosomatic illness, and other physical manifestations of emotional stress are essentially poor habits. They argue that for any of a hundred reasons hypochondriacs have gotten into the habit of responding to emotional stress with uncomfortable bodily sensations rather than confronting the emotional demands directly. In other words, for behaviorists, hypochondria is a learned somatic response to stress and should be treated by unlearning the bad habit and substituting a more appropriate response. Behavior therapy seems to work about as well as other forms of therapy with hypochondriacs, which may suggest that certain aspects of the disorder can profitably be seen as a poor habit. (For a discussion of various therapies, see chapter 11.)

When hypochondria is examined by sociologists or cultural anthropologists, a very different picture emerges, for these persons are more concerned with exogenous factors—namely, the external stresses that impinge on a person from social and cultural conditions. Consequently the core disorders underlying much of the hypochondria that a social worker encounters among the elderly and the poor, for example, are construed as powerlessness and vulnerability. The therapy of choice in these cases is employment, good housing, a sense of community, and other external signs of security and self-esteem. Although the effectiveness of social therapy can rarely be measured, the proponents of community mental health services maintain that empowering the individual can prevent the common retreat into hypochondria.

Finally, there are a few investigators, as mentioned earlier, who maintain that a certain number of hypochondriacs simply cannot be fit into the more tractable categories of dysphoria. There is, they maintain, such a thing as pure hypochondria.

Where does all this disagreement leave a classification of hypochondria based on underlying disorders? Admittedly in confusion, but not hopelessly so. The picture that is beginning to emerge is one in which depression and anxiety head major lists of factors that predispose certain people to hypochondria. Under both depression and anxiety are two important subcategories—internally generated problems that include genetic susceptibility and metabolic disorder, and the not unrelated category of externally caused problems that include family conflict, losses, medical mismanagement, and social inequities.

The latest attempt to categorize hypochondria formally—as much for the benefit of insurance companies as for a greater understanding of the ailment—is the five-axis method used in the third edition of the *Diagnostic and Statistical Manual* (1980) of the American Psychiatric Association.[25] This extensively revised guide gives a definition of each disorder and also provides five separate axes or dimensions along which an individual's dysfunction is rated. For example, the basic definition of hypochondria given in *DSM-III* is "an unrealistic interpretation of physical signs or sensations as abnormal, leading to preoccupation with the fear or belief of having a serious disease."[26] No other mental disorder may be present. (Pilowsky's primary hypochondria would meet these criteria.) According to the diagnoses listed along Axis I, Kate, whose hypochondria was described in the first chapter, would be diagnosed as suffering from either a generalized anxiety disorder or hypochondriasis, the latter being one of the somatization disorders.[27] She might also receive a diagnosis along Axis II, which includes personality disorders such as narcissistic, compulsive, and dependent disorders. Any physical disorder that contributed to the hypochondriasis would be noted on Axis III, and the level of psychosocial stress that she was under from being alone in a foreign country would be rated on Axis IV. Axis V evaluates the individual's highest level of adaptive functioning in the past year. Thus instead of being given the general label "hypochondriac," popular in the middle of this century, Kate might now be described as a generally anxious hypochondriac possibly with a dependent personality disorder and no physical disabilities who, under a fairly high level of stress, had dropped from a "very good" level of functioning to a "fair" or "poor" level. This is an improvement, although, as in Galen's time, in all likelihood Kate would be given a different diagnosis by every therapist she saw and would be diagnosed differently still by medical doctors who do not use the *Diagnostic and Statistical Manual*. As C. V. Ford points out in his book on illness as a way of life, the inability to reliably diagnose hypochondria stems from a poor understanding of the disease and from the importance that the doctor's relationship with the patient plays in determining the diagnosis.[28] Ford might maintain that young Kate would be diagnosed as having an anxiety disorder until she lost her looks, at which time her problems might be redefined as hypochondria.

It has already been said that hypochondria in all its forms is responsible for as much misery, wasted effort, fear, and despair as any form of emotional disorder. The only unhappiness that may be more common is depression. So just how common is hypochondria? Because clinicians cannot agree on the diagnosis, statisticians cannot reliably estimate its prevalence, but they try. Consider this statement in an editorial in the *American Journal of Psychotherapy:*

> Conservatively speaking, patients with primary hypochondriacal symptoms or hypochondriacal overlay superimposed upon minor somatic disorders represent more than 50 percent of all patients seen by physicians, general practitioners, and specialist alike.[29] Others have commented as follows:

> Ninety percent of my ʾ[psychiatric] practice consists of de-
> pressions of various sorts, and at least half have some hypo-
> chondriacal problems.[30]

> A great many, perhaps even the majority of hypochondriacs
> are "in the closet." They almost never go to doctors.[31]

Anecdotal evidence suggesting that hypochondria is the
most common of symptoms is easy to come by, but doctors' reports can be misleading. It may be that because hypochondriacs
generate a lot of emotion every time they walk into the doctor's
office, "physicians *feel* there are more of them around than there
actually are."[32]

Although no one knows how many hypochondriacs there
are, some sense of the pervasiveness of the problem may be
gained by estimates of institutionalized persons. For example, in
a clinic at the Johns Hopkins Medical School it was estimated that
45 percent of a group of 226 unselected patients were hypochondriacs. (This was in the 1930s, when the term was somewhat more
popular.) A large hospital in New Delhi, India, reported that 12.5
percent of its patients were hypochondriacal, and a hospital in
Finland gave an estimate of 29.5 percent.[33]

Considering persons who go to doctors as another group,
it has been variously estimated that in the United States from 4
to 18 percent of all visits made to the doctor are made by the
"worried well," the hypochondriacal, and the emotionally upset.
Potentially higher estimates are available, for if one agrees with
Drs. Barsky and Klerman's assertion in the *Harvard Medical
School Mental Health Letter* that no serious medical disease is
found in 30 to 60 percent of all visits to primary care physicians,[34]
then a sizable portion of these may be persons who have con-
verted emotional problems into physical complaints.

In Britain, where record keeping is more complete under
the National Health Service, estimates of neuroticism and hypochondria among patients range from 6 to 23 percent.[35] Purely

subjective estimates made by physicians run higher, and a 1970 Harris Poll reported that 46 percent of U.S. doctors believed they saw "a great deal of hypochondria and psychosomatic illness."[36] "Physical pains and fears are the two primary diseases which our patients bring to us; and the latter are generally brought to us in the guise of the former."[37]

A third group, which undoubtedly includes a large number of hypochondriacs, is comprised of disease phobics—persons who are excessively afraid of disease. Estimates vary wildly as to how common this is, but a study conducted in Vermont in the 1960s and occupying the middle ground found that 12 percent of the men interviewed and 20 percent of the women admitted to being somewhat afraid of illness. Although only three percent of the population seemed intensely afraid of disease, this was the most common phobia encountered.[38]

The last and largest group in which to look for hypochondriacs is the so-called normal population, and if, as S. Weir Mitchell stated over a hundred years ago, "the elements out of which these disorders arise are deeply human and exist in all of us in varying amount,"[39] it would not be surprising to find that everyone has occasionally suffered at least a mild and temporary form of hypochondria. For some it might be triggered by a pamphlet from the American Cancer Society showing seven danger signals; for others, by the death of a close friend; and for the most resistant, perhaps only by their own near-fatal heart attack. Under any of these circumstances a temporary preoccupation with disease can be a normal and appropriate response.

Results obtained from hundreds of thousands of personality surveys attest to the commonness of mild hypochondria. The MMPI, originally constructed in 1942 to screen military personnel and now used extensively in clinical settings, includes 566 true/false statements. The significant items from this pool are divided into ten or more scales or areas of concern. The hypochondria scale includes thirty-three specific statements concerning symptoms, and if a person scores high on these, it is generally agreed that in two out of three cases he will match the clinically agreed-upon picture of a hypochondriac. On the MMPI the two items most likely to be checked as true by hypochondriacs are these: "I have a great deal of stomach trouble," and "I am troubled by discomfort in the pit of my stomach every few days or oftener."

After administering thousands of these MMPIs, the authors of the inventory concluded that "a sizeable proportion of the so-called normal population overlaps the hypochondriacal group."[40] This and other studies[41] suggest that hypochondria may best be thought of as a problem that is present to varying degrees in different individuals rather than an entity, such as pregnancy, which is either present or absent.

Taking the various estimates together, it seems that the flatulent Romans in Galen's time, the sensitive, suffering artist, the peevish clergyman, and the unanalyzable neurotic are still with us. Hypochondria remains one of the commonest expressions of emotional, social, and, in some cases, biochemical stress.

3

THE SOCIAL SIGNIFICANCE OF BEING ILL

Sociologists view the medical system as a
system of social relationships: "sickness" is a
social role (as opposed to "disease," which is
a *biological state*) and it is the business of the
medical system to control entry into sick
roles and to define the behavior appropriate
to them.

—Barbara and John Ehrenreich
American Health Empire:
Power, Profits and Politics

■

ECAUSE SOME hypochondriacs use illness to try to manage
personal problems, we need to know how being sickly or
being prone to physical suffering is viewed in our society. Unless
we are familiar with the privileges and liabilities that go along
with being ill, and unless we know how these are modified for
the particular kind of disease hypochondriacs think they have and
for their particular positions in society, it will be difficult to understand how being sick could possibly profit anyone (liars ex-
cepted). This chapter, then, is a brief detour into the nature of
"straight" sickness, for like "student," "lawyer," or "head of
household," "ill" is one of the social roles that the hypochondriac
has adopted.

Our social values and traditions influence our understanding of ill health in two ways. First, society colors our definition of illness. In conjunction with whatever scientific insight is available, our customs have a lot to say about what constitutes sickness, what kinds of things or events cause sickness, what can be done to control illness, and which diseases and disorders are to be tolerated (considered unavoidable) and which must be hidden, denied, or fiercely combated. Second, social mores color our understanding of sickness as a role and teach us, in effect, how sick persons ought to act and how others ought to treat them.

Taking the definition of illness first, how "social" is our current definition? Although many interpretations of ill health coexist in our society and it is possible to find a narrow one that claims that only "morbid processes" should be considered, the dominant definitions that are actually used by ordinary people, doctors, courts, and insurance companies are broad statements that define ill health in terms of physical, mental, and social disability. One such definition equates illness with "a failure to respond adaptively to environmental challenges resulting in a disruption of overall equilibrium."[1] It goes on to say that such challenges include not only germs but pollutants, speeding automobiles, social disruptions such as the loss of a job, and psychological difficulties. The World Health Organization says essentially the same thing when it defines as ill anyone not functioning at optimal physical, mental, and social levels.[2] Especially in the United States, where health is closely related to performance, illness is commonly equated with an inability to work or fulfill other obligations.[3]

These broad definitions of sickness are full of social judgments. They—or, rather, we—acknowledge not only that the social milieu in which we live and work affects our health but also that our relationships with other people are influenced by our health. Moreover modern definitions have gradually expanded to include within the realm of ill health problems such as suicide, delinquency, and alcoholism—disruptions that were formerly considered sin, crime, and social maladjustment. These and similar reclassifications occur when something new is learned of the biological processes involved, but frequently they arise from social considerations. At present the general trend is to reclassify more and more kinds of deviant behavior as illness, although movement in the opposite direction sometimes occurs. Homosexuality, until recently included in the directories of emotional pathology, has been removed. But by and large "acts which in the past would have been defined as sin, and controlled by religious sanctions, or crime, and controlled by the legal system, are increasingly defined as illness and controlled through the agency of medical care."[4]

Thus we have a situation in which doctors commonly deal with social problems that have been defined as medical. For example, when a doctor certifies that a person is suffering from an incapacitating backache or is suicidal, he is not usually commenting on a demonstrable biological condition that he could substantiate with a blood test or an X ray. He is making a personal judgment. This is certainly the case when a doctor sets out to treat a hypochondriac, and it is well not to confuse this social interaction with the somewhat different exchange involved in the diagnosis and treatment of a more purely biological disorder such as pneumonia or cataracts.[5]

When we move from definitions of illness in general to considerations of specific ailments, we can again see social values affecting our understanding. Usually the less that is known about a disease, the more society's apprehensions and concerns will be expressed in the lore that surrounds the disease's imagined cause and control. Cancer provides notorious examples. In Victorian times when emotions—especially those associated with sex— were of deep concern, it was believed that sexual promiscuity, including coitus interruptus practiced by married couples, predisposed women to cancer of the reproductive organs.[6] It was also reported by doctors that persons expressing violent emotions such as rage or grief were particularly susceptible.[7] These "causes" then underwent a gradual transformation as concern for the sexual act and its concomitant emotions was replaced by a worry that sexual and emotional repression might be the greater problem. For a time there was a vague but pervasive suspicion that cancer was more prevalent among the sexually fearful and among persons who did *not* express their violent emotions. More than one "cause" of cancer has been reversed because of a shift in what our society views as dangerous or undesirable.

To bind social values and disease still closer, once our customs have influenced our definition of illness in general, and our explanations of specific ailments, we then turn around and use the threat of disease as a form of control—an incentive to make the members of our society act in desirable ways. For example, when the movement for Prohibition was in full swing, doctors advocating temperance genuinely believed that "whiskey . . . was directly responsible for one-half of all madness, one-half of all sudden death, and one-fourth of all adult deaths."[8] If you drank, you courted serious illness, and for many people that seemed a more persuasive argument than any moral consideration. During the same period, and illustrating the same use of disease as a threat, it was widely and inaccurately believed that promiscuity predisposed a person to cholera. The righteous were supposed to have a far better chance of surviving the epidemics that sporadically swept the eastern seaboard in the 1800s.[9]

Today we are concerned with other hazards, such as stress and conflict, and as occurred with drinking during Prohibition, these hazards are beginning to find their way into our language of threats and persuasions. A rich diet and an unappeasable desire to achieve, once marks of success, now threaten the ambitious with heart disease. Repressed feelings may lead to cancer, too much sugar to hyperactivity, a skimpy breakfast to malnutrition, and so on. Many of these aphorisms conflict with one another, but regardless of their logic or validity they are used to buttress moral values and social expedients. In somewhat the same way, many hypochondriacs use their own complaints and regimes—"I always get carsick unless we keep the windows open," for example—to buttress personal values and personal expedients.

Turning to illness as a role adopted by an individual, there are advantages and disadvantages conferred upon a person who is or believes himself to be ill. Once a person is labeled ill (i.e., he considers himself to be sick and those around him agree), our society bestows several kinds of privileges upon him. These are conferred because we assume in most instances that a person is not directly responsible for getting sick and cannot spontaneously get well simply by willing himself better. It's not his fault—he needs help, and therefore he is given quite an assortment of exemptions, services, and special gifts.

Primary among the exemptions is the suspension of his daily work. The sick person is not expected to do heavy physical work or taxing mental tasks. Demanding emotional situations, including lovemaking, and social obligations are also suspended. In addition, the ill are exempted from standard levels of good behavior. They can regress to a certain degree and be fussier and more openly depressed. A sick child can suck his thumb again, demand more cuddling, and wet his bed. Other members of the family will usually take over some of the sick person's routine work and beyond this will often give special gifts of books, cards, flowers, phone calls, "healthy" foods, and, above all, attention and reassurance. Usually this pleasant fuss is a temporary state of affairs, but it can be incorporated without notice into a family's routine. Regardless of the origin of the famous biologist Charles Darwin's symptoms, his family's "whole day was planned out to suit him, to be ready for reading aloud to him, to go his walks with him, and to be constantly at hand to alleviate his daily discomforts."[10] As an Irish poet who met Darwin at a lodge noted, "he has his meals at his own times, sees people or not as he chooses, [and] has invalid's privileges in full, a great help to a studious man."[11]

Accompanying these privileges, however, are liabilities, all of which stem from the belief (or social agreement) that it is better to be well than sick. Therefore all sick persons are supposed to want to get well and must accept the restrictions that, like the exemptions, are understood to promote health. First and foremost, a sick person is expected to seek competent help in over-coming the ailment. This may be advice from a doctor, mother, wife, or an internalized voice of any of these.

Once advice is received the sick person is expected to follow it, but there are several ways in which hypochondriacs routinely break or distort this rule. Some solicit so much advice, and from contradictory sources such as doctors, pharmacists, in-laws, and health food store owners, that they give the impression of seeking attention rather than treatment. This seems especially plausible when the promiscuous solicitation of advice is followed each time by a rejection of the proffered information.

At the other extreme are hypochondriacs who refuse help and fail to ask for any advice. Usually such people are genuinely unaware of acting so illogically. For example, Milton Mazer, former director of the Martha's Vineyard Mental Health Center, had a patient who was sure he was going to die of a heart attack. At unpredictable moments this man's heart would start to pound and his chest tighten. He was convinced each time that the dreaded attack was at hand. When these panics hit him on the golf course, he would routinely mask his fear, invent a minor excuse for slowing down, and insist that his companions go on ahead of him.[12] "I was sure I was going to die on the sixteenth green," this man confided to Mazer. Yet was the insistent dismissal of his friends the characteristic action of a man convinced of imminent heart failure? Probably not. A heart attack victim needs help, not seclusion, but a man afraid of making a fool of himself, either by crying wolf, fainting, or trembling with fear, may prefer to be alone. Similarly, the hypochondriac who lives for years and years in fear of having cancer but never sees a doctor is *acting* like a person who is not at all sure he has a straightforward medical problem, although he is sure that something deeply disconcerting is wrong.

The characteristic ambivalence that many hypochondriacs express about their ailments makes it extremely difficult for them to know how to act—like a sick person? like a well person? And it makes it equally difficult for others to know how to treat them.

Many hypochondriacs seem to have placed themselves outside the boundaries of socially recognized roles.[13]

Returning to the liabilities of those who place themselves squarely in the role of sick persons, once they seek competent advice for their ailment, they are expected to follow it. In so doing they relinquish a measure of independence. In Darwin's case he not only followed his doctors' orders but left the arrangement of great parts of his life to his wife. Eventually Emma Darwin scheduled his daily activities, even to determining the length of his conversations with visitors, the choice of his recreational reading material, and the details of his infrequent vacations.

Along with being more dependent than usual, a sick person accepts the status of a relatively weak and useless member of society, although not generally as demeaning a stance as Darwin's idea of a "wretched, contemptible invalid." Especially in America, where health is identified with activity, mastery, and attractiveness, being sick is not fundamentally a respected condition. In many ways the patient is treated as a child.

To complete the liabilities of the sick role, the ailing are isolated either because they need rest, have a contagious disease, or are simply considered different from the well. Finally, they must pay financially for their illness in lost salary, doctor bills, medicines, and many other items. Being ill a lot is something of a luxury that not all can enjoy in its fullest expression.

On balance, the sick role seems a passable rest stop but a poor way to achieve success or self-respect. Hypochondriacs enjoy the privileges and chafe under the liabilities like anyone else and apparently run afoul of the socially agreed-upon rules for being sick on only one or two points. Primary among these is our belief that every sick person is supposed to want to get well. That desire is eventually supposed to produce results. But for the hypochondriac one disorder or complication replaces another, and although he honestly says that he wants to be rid of his illnesses, they keep coming back. Gradually his family and peers feel an ill-defined resentment; he is not playing by the rules. And indeed he is not.

In addition to the privileges and liabilities already mentioned, there are several hidden advantages that make individuals and the society they live in tolerate quite a lot of sickness. If the real trouble with a person is that he is frustrated and unhappy, it may be less disruptive to have that person get sick than to have him rebelliously engaging in antisocial behavior. (Although it is not clear that frustration must express itself as a sickness *or* aggression, societies such as in the USSR which are dependent on a fully functioning labor force and do not tolerate much sickness do seem to have more overt forms of aggression, such as alcoholism and malingering, to deal with.[14])

"Soul-destroying, meaningless, mechanical, monotonous, moronic work is an insult to human nature which must necessarily and inevitably produce either escapism or aggression."[15] For people who find themselves in these intolerable situations with few alternatives, sickness can be a temporary escape and hypochondria, with its escapism *and* aggression, a more permanent retreat.

For certain individuals, being sick may be a more acceptable way of expressing suffering and conflict than direct confrontation, aggression, or the more overt forms of escapism such as dependence on tranquilizers or alcohol. Getting sick is frequently safer and more dignified than coming right out and saying that something is wrong (even assuming the person knows what is really bothering him). How can a man say he feels weak and scared without wounding his self-esteem and risking loss of respect? How can a woman, convinced she cannot survive on her own, state forcefully that she is dissatisfied with her marriage without courting abandonment? "I'm scared" is too personal; "I'm furious!" too risky; but "I don't feel well" is an acceptable expression of distress.

Any time sickness is used to say "I'm unhappy," the sufferer is engaging in a form of indirect communication, and although the underlying message may be fairly clear, deception is involved. The ability to speak the truth is not something that all feel they can afford, and Thomas Szasz has stated emphatically that *"to be able to be truthful one must be more or less grown up and personally secure, and one must live in a social situation which encourages, or at least permits truthfulness."*[16]

This suggests several additional reasons for using the indirect language of sickness. If a person is immature and has not yet learned to articulate certain problems, he simply does not have the vocabulary to explain what is wrong. The child who says "I have a stomachache" instead of the far more sophisticated "I don't want to go to school today because the other kids call me a baby" is a common example. A very young child often cannot say precisely what is wrong even when he wants to.

Insecurity is a more powerful reason for substituting body language for direct verbal communication, and the less secure a person is, the more he tends to rely on this type of exchange. Indirectness allows him to express a need yet at the same time to guard against a direct rejection of whatever it is he is asking for. He can also say a lot more using indirect language than he dares to directly. The headache or carsickness can convey "I need help," "I'm lonely, be nice to me," or "you make me sick" and "I'm not going anywhere with you!" But the sick person is held responsible only for the "I'm not feeling well" part of the message.

A final reason for saying "I'm sick" instead of "I'm lonely" or whatever the real problem is, is that the listener may not be able to understand the real complaint. "What do you mean, you're bored and lonely? Every mother with small children spends her days the way you do." Hives, colitis, and undiagnosable pains in the night will present the problem more forcefully and will get action when words have failed.

4

PATHWAYS TOWARD
CHILDHOOD HYPOCHONDRIA

I am part of all that I have met.
                    —Alfred Lord Tennyson
                    Ulysses

■

FOR HUNDREDS OF years adult hypochondriacs, musing over the origin of their disorder, have peered into the branches of their family trees to locate the source of their discomfort. "My grandfather had it in a very strong degree," wrote Boswell of his hypochondria. "I'm black-blooded like all the Tennysons," Alfred Lord Tennyson explained.

Then, late in the nineteenth century, when hypochondria had become a nervous disorder and nervous disorders were increasingly regarded as malfunctions of the psyche, the predisposing signs were sought among the early experiences of childhood. At first parental mismanagement simply replaced bad bloodlines as the cause, but as psychoanalytical explanations became increasingly sophisticated, they incorporated more and more aspects of a child's social and cultural upbringing. The resulting explanations of hypochondria—some of which are in use today—acknowledge that there is something in the depth and persistence of the hypochondriac's habit that urges careful consideration of the vivid and peculiarly distorted experiences of childhood.

Hypochondria among the young is not an unusual condition, though the disorder goes by so many names that its prevalence is not always obvious. "Psychosomatic problem patient" often means hypochondria, and "patient with recurrent abdominal pain" can too. (Among children the stomachache seems to be the most common of all unfounded complaints, with headache and chest pain a distant second and third.[1] Saying that a child belongs to "the fat envelope group—that is, has an enormous medical record—is another way of implying that hypochondria may be involved, and "kid crock" is unambiguous.

Although it is not possible to estimate how many children exhibit hypochondriacal tendencies and at what ages, pediatricians seem to agree that several forms of hypochondria are commonly encountered in both boys and girls between the ages of five and fifteen. Children younger than five frequently have such diffuse patterns of anxiety and such unrefined techniques of manipulation that it is hard to see what form their fears and insecurities are taking. At the other end of the age range, some doctors believe that a troubled girl may well continue to have stomachaches or a chronic cough, but a boy is more likely to express his troubles more assertively with multiple injuries or delinquency. The hypochondria that accompanies panic disorders most often strikes between late adolescence and early adulthood.[2]

Beyond these general observations two distinctions may be made. One is between acute short-term bouts of hypochondria that a child may experience, usually in response to a specific event such as the death of a parent or grandparent, and chronic hypochondria, which is a style of living that the child adopts over a much longer period. Acute reactive hypochondria can, of course, develop into the chronic variety.

The second distinction is between children who are themselves hypochondriacs and those whose parents are "vicarious hypochondriacs." In the latter category the parent imagines that his child has a serious illness either because the parent is a hypochondriac and is displacing his symptoms onto the child or because the parent is using a "sick" child as an excuse to ask for personal help. In the Boston City Hospital, for example, a pediatrician noticed that parents sometimes brought healthy children into the emergency room night after night almost demanding that the children be admitted to the hospital for some totally imaginary condition. After a few nights the visits would stop as abruptly as they had begun. Becoming curious, Robert Reece, the pediatrician, managed to discover how these curious situations resolved themselves. In most cases the visits to the emergency room preceded an episode of child abuse. To his credit and the hospital's, "turkey admissions" (or "social admissions," as they are formally called) are now made to protect the child while counseling is arranged for the parent.

Returning to children who are themselves hypochondriacal, there seem to be three or four different ways in which they come to regard themselves as ill. These causes of or routes toward hypochondria range from the fairly straightforward copying of a parent's habit or the misinterpretation of medical information to the far more complex involvement of an entire family. Taking the experiences of children as a guide and moving from the simpler to the more complex, hypochondria can be seen as a habit cultivated because of its advantages, as the unfortunate result of frequent illness or a traumatic operation, as the misinterpretation of medical information (especially when such information is received under stress), and as part of a regulatory mechanism used by an unstable family to keep itself together.

As a habit, hypochondria is easy to pick up. For example, of the ten children born to Charles and Emma Darwin, seven reached adulthood and five were variously classified as hypochondriac, invalid, or depressed.[3] Darwin himself was almost constantly ill from the time of his wife's first pregnancy; therefore all the children grew up in a household run to suit the needs of a sick man.

Emma Darwin "was a perfect nurse," wrote one of her granddaughters. "She was like a rock to lean on, always devoted and unwearied in devising expedients to give relief, and neat-handed and clever in carrying them out."[4] Although the first son, William, and the second surviving daughter, Bessy, did not become hypochondriacal, all the others fastened on ill health as the accepted way of requesting their mother's (and later their wives' or husbands') affectionate solicitude. Henrietta spent her entire life warding off illnesses that apparently never materialized; George operated under the constant strain of "ill health"; Francis was clearly depressed; Leonard retired at age forty because of undiagnosed health problems and lived to the age of ninety-three; and Horace, who was "frail," was called "a dear old man" at thirty-eight. "I have sometimes thought that she [Emma] must have been rather too sorry for her family when they were unwell," concluded the granddaughter. "A little neglect . . . might have done them a world of good."[5]

For other children the emphasis is reversed. The pleasures of being sick are not so well defined, but sickness is presented as the method of choice in dealing with problems. Sylvia's father, for example, used to go to bed at intervals throughout the winter for a week at a time. "If only I had a better job," he would moan from his darkened bedroom.

The winter he was forty-six his brother and sister died, and it seemed to Sylvia that he went to bed for the entire season. When Sylvia herself was depressed she would mope and start to act sick. This got her some extra attention, but only as long as she agreed to a strict limitation of personal freedom. Like her father, she felt she "bought" powerful maternal protection and with it the option of retreating from unpleasant situations, but only at the price of her independence. She continued this uncomfortable agreement with her husband, and the hypochondria copied from her father served a similar face-saving function in her marriage. Her father's weeks of undiagnosed exhaustion explained why he could not get a better job, and the dizzy spells and racing heart helped her believe that only poor physical health prevented her from setting up her own home, moving across the country, and in other ways being a capable, independent woman.

In the years between the two world wars an American psychiatrist named Esther Richards became interested in these kinds of experiences. She made several studies of hypochondriacs, first of adults, whom she questioned closely about their childhood acquaintance with illness, then of young hypochondriacs themselves. She found no distinctive event in the lives of these people that seemed to cause what she called the "invalid reaction," and their personalities did not seem significantly different from those of nonhypochondriacs. But there were some differences. As children almost all the hypochondriacs had the constant example of a chronic complainer in front of them. Usually this was a mother or father who had "the doctor habit" or "the patent medicine dosing habit" (this is the group that market research analysts today call "self-medicators"). In addition, the hypochondriacs Richards studied "were persons who early showed evidence of extreme sensitiveness. . . . They were born with a psycho-biologic outfit that made them peculiarly susceptible to their environment."[6] (This second distinction, which is attracting attention today, echoes the old constitutional basis for hypochondria and suggests that there may be a genetic basis for the problem. See Kellner[7] for a review of genetic factors in functional somatic symptoms.)

Richards's conclusion was that most young hypochondriacs are unusually sensitive children who learn by example to substitute illness for other kinds of difficulties and that this pattern can be reversed if caught soon enough. In the twenty cases of childhood hypochondria she treated, nineteen children unlearned their hypochondriacal habits. In comparison, the cure rate among adults was dramatically worse, and Richards contended that the sickness habit had become too deeply entrenched in their lives to be changed.

Among the investigators who subsequently built on Richards's work was Felix Brown at Maudsley Hospital, London. In the 1930s he studied forty-one hypochondriacs and, like Richards, found their abuse of illness to date from childhood. He too believed there was a "body-sensitive" or "body-conscious" type of person who was physically predisposed to hypochondria, and he too was of the opinion that "the care of a fussy and over-solicitous female relative" was an even more potent source of trouble.[8] "The impression is, in fact, that the . . . hypochondriasis is more contagious than hereditary."[9]

In Brown's view it was less a question of a child's copying the "I am ill" behavior of the parent than it was his responding to the oversolicitous relative who almost required him to be sick and who capitalized on these illnesses to enhance her own sense of control or well-being. Recent studies[10] have confirmed that a sickly childhood may predispose a person to hypochondria, but whether the push comes from the child's constitution, the illnesses themselves, or the treatment received is not known.

Today some psychologists wonder if that familiar stereotype, the oversolicitous mother, can really determine the attitude of her children toward health and disease. To try to answer this question, a study was done in the mid-1960s of 350 mother-and-child pairs. The results surprisingly pointed away from the mother as the dominant influence and toward cultural variables such as the age and sex of the child.

"Mothers respond to their children's health and their own in a similar fashion,"[11] the report acknowledged. In addition, women under stress tend to report a few more illnesses for themselves and for their children. However, when these maternal influences were balanced against the distinctive differences in attitude produced by the age and sex of the child and the level of education of the mother, the more purely personal "maternal influences appear to be less influential than we anticipated."[12] It was found, for instance, that the less education a mother had, the less concern she showed for the detection and prevention of disease. With a more fatalistic attitude—what will happen, will happen—she had little interest in detecting the first signs of a cold or any other disorder.

In regard to age and sex, girls were clearly more afraid of getting hurt than boys and more likely to tell someone when they felt bad. Among both boys and girls reports of symptoms were far more common among fourth graders than eighth graders, the two ages selected for the study. In a follow-up study conducted sixteen years later,[13] none of the mothers' attitudes toward their children's illnesses, as rated in the original study, was associated with problems in early adulthood. Other studies, however, suggest that parents' attitudes toward disease have a lasting effect on their children.[14]

Other investigations further suggest that a predisposition to hypochondria is associated with being a firstborn or only child. These children have more symptoms—as reported by their parents—and receive more medicines than second or later children.[15] Although all young children, as well as the elderly, are expected to complain openly of discomfort in our society, mothers act on the complaints of their children far more often than they act on their own symptoms or on those of a resident grandparent. In other words, a common focus for parental anxiety is a sick child, especially if he or she is the oldest.

Another variable that apparently influences a child's predisposition to hypochondria is ethnic background. (See chapter 9.) To take one of several examples, white Anglo-Saxon Protestants often have the attitude that it is wrong to complain unless something is "really" wrong, an approach that produces a group of people who cannot express psychological distress easily but who can seek the support they need by translating nebulous feelings of loneliness, boredom, and apprehension into "real" physical symptoms.

Taking age, sex, birth order, heritage, and social class together, the investigators concluded that "the overprotective, hypochondriacal mother does not necessarily beget a child with similar (or opposite) traits. . . . The child is probably neither as malleable nor as fragile as current psychological theory sees him."[16]

Regardless of whether children's attitudes toward sickness were primarily determined by their mother or by a broader set of cultural factors, both Richards and Brown could clearly see that once their young patients were sensitized to illness, they hesitantly, then adroitly, began exploiting the sick role to an ever greater and more imaginative extent.

Some of the gratifications that these children associated with being sick, such as receiving more attention or not going to school, were obvious. Other advantages were obscure. Among the latter, the late Michael Balint, a renowned psychiatrist, pointed out that being sick can be a way of justifying a strong interest in certain parts of the body while not admitting that this is the case.

> It is impossible not to notice the high emotional importance of eating in all gastric . . . diseases [and] of the digestive functions in intestinal disorders, particularly in chronic constipation.[17]

Balint also considered some forms of regression, such as thumb-sucking and clinging, direct gratifications and raised the interesting idea that initially, at least, such actions may be part of a person's unconscious attempt to get well. "By regressing to a more primitive level the patient may be seeking an opportunity to make a new start in a new direction, avoiding that blocked by his illness."[18] Of course all the advantages of being ill, Balint emphasized, can only partially compensate for the discomfort, apprehension, and limitation that are also part of every illness.

Whereas some children pick up hypochondria as a habit and cultivate illness for the advantages that go with it, others become hypochondriacal as the result of medical mismanagement. When Esther Richards made her original study of sixty hypo-

chondriacs at a Johns Hopkins clinic, she found medical mismanagement to be the second most prevalent condition that can lead
a child toward hypochondria, the first being the example of the
chronic complainer. By medical mismanagement Richards meant
the handling of an illness or operation in such a way that regardless of its seriousness, the child felt intolerably threatened.
Such children believed themselves to be vulnerable and had no
power to protect themselves.

During the calamitous years of the Second World War,
Anna Freud began working along the same lines, often in collaboration with Dorothy Burlingham. Elaborating on the observations made by her father that the causes of hypochondria are part
of the patient's present rather than past situation, and that a
physical illness or a history of illness often triggered a bout of
hypochondria, Anna Freud wrote a paper entitled "The Role of
Bodily Illness in the Mental Life of Children."[19] In it she analyzed
some of the effects that medical operations quite unexpectedly
produced on children. Her interpretations of what she observed
in the Hampstead Child Therapy Clinic, where she was director,
and in the Residential War Nursery for Homeless Children, which
she organized, were based on her belief that children undergoing
almost any medical procedure feel threatened from both the outside and the inside—that is, from the strange and somewhat
frightening external setting and at the same time from the fantasies and anxieties that the procedure activates. According to
Freud, it is the child's interpretation of the seriousness of the
operation, not the doctor's opinion, that determines the psychological effects the procedure will produce. Only the child feels the
combined threats of a strange setting in addition to the punishment, abandonment, mutilation, castration, or other symbolic
meaning that he or she imagines is the real basis of the operation.

Freud realized that even before a child is taken to the hospital he senses a change in the family's emotional climate. He
probably gets more attention than usual, and this extra consideration from parents, and perhaps extra jealousy from a brother
or sister, can confuse him. Then, with or without an explanation

that he understands—and certainly without one he accepts—he is taken to the hospital and, in Freud's day, left alone. No promise of future joy or explanation of present necessity can reconcile a young child to being left alone in a strange place. The sight of his mother backing out of the hospital room, tears in her eyes, crayons and modeling clay clutched in her arms, is terrifying.

"Why am I being left here?" "Why isn't my mother staying with me?" The questions aren't always asked, but they are deeply felt with unutterable misery. As Anna Freud had already discovered during the London blitz, and as John Bowlby and others further documented in the 1960s and 1970s, separation from the mother was the greatest trauma a young child could suffer. To be abandoned—so often interpreted as a punishment—was more terrifying than being bombed or burned or operated on. Furthermore, young children had no concept of how long they would be left in a hospital. Bowlby found their reactions were the same as though their mothers had died. First came several days, even a week, of tearful protest and an urgent effort to recover the missing mother. This was followed by despair as the child began to grieve.

To add insult to what is already grave injury, Bowlby noted that "a child in a hospital is likely to be confined to a cot and to be subjected to a variety of medical procedures that are always strange, perhaps painful, and certainly frightening."[20] As the actual operation draws near and the child is strapped onto what he may well perceive to be his mother's ironing board or kitchen chopping block, his sense of physical restriction intensifies, and his rage and anxiety may rise to intolerable levels. Many young children abhor the momentary restriction involved in pulling on a T-shirt. How much worse to be bound to a stretcher?

Freud goes on the describe the symbolic meanings of the operation itself which she believes are frequently understood by children to be mutilation, castration, attack by the mother, punishment, seduction, or intercourse. The pain itself, which may come as a terrible surprise if the child's parents have not prepared the child, reactivates an unpredictable array of fantasies and anxieties. Pain, Freud said, is an important event for a child and is remembered for a long time.

In addition to all this, the child frequently feels betrayed by his parents. When scratchy toast and soft-boiled eggs arrive instead of ice cream the morning after a tonsillectomy, and when stitches hurt instead of feeling like "tiny pin pricks," the child feels he has been lied to.

If the operation is to leave no psychological scars, the child's defense mechanisms must be strong enough to handle the mother's leaving, the medical procedures, the pain, restrictions, strange food, dark nights, odd smells, and all the deeply hidden fears that these events stir up. If he is unable to master this formidable array of internal and external threats, his normal functioning will begin to break down. Neurotic outbursts then occur as the child uses primitive measures of defense such as regression to infantile behavior or denial of the whole situation in an attempt to ward off unendurable emotions. The operation, Freud maintained, has become a trauma, a classic case of medical mismanagement. The damage may be expressed as hypochondria or as some other form of anxiety, and it may appear immediately or years later. Medical mismanagement leaves a scar, Freud asserted, "and there is no scar in mental life which can not reopen under specific conditions. If this happens, the whole structure of the personality is shaken to the core."[21]

Until recently tonsillectomies have been one of the most common precipitating factors of hypochondria and anxiety attacks in children. Both Esther Richards, the psychiatrist who studied hypochondriacal children at Johns Hopkins, and Leo Kanner, author of the widely read *Child Psychiatry*, singled out this operation as emotionally hazardous:

> I have seen several children whose anxiety attacks, beginning a few weeks after tonsillectomy under ether, reported sensations "just like having ether. . . ." These children had been

poorly prepared for their operations. In some instances they had
been told by playmates and classmates that occasionally people
did not wake up from the anaesthetic. They thus received the
sudden shock of a major threat to their existence.[22]

In trying to ascertain how medical mismanagement is con-
verted into hypochondria and neurotic anxiety, Anna Freud was
given a clue by the behavior of orphans. Unlike other children,
who, Freud felt, had little interest in their bodies between the
ages of about two and puberty, orphans routinely coddled and
comforted themselves, sometimes even murmuring endearments
to themselves. "There, there, my sweetie, it's all right." Freud
wrote,

> When watching the behavior of such children toward their
> bodies, we are struck with the similarity of their attitudes to
> that of the adult hypochondriac, to which perhaps it provides a
> clue. The child actually deprived of a mother's care, adopts the
> mother's role in health matters, thus playing "mother and child"
> with his own body.[23]

Subsequently Freud found that this hypochondriacal concern for
one's own body could develop in children who were not orphans
but who felt neglected or abandoned. She gave as an example a
six-year-old boy with a tic who was having a hard time sharing
his mother's attention with his father and baby brother.

> His tic was a pathological way of playing mother-and-child
> with his own body: he took over the role of . . . comforting and
> reassuring . . . , while his own body represented himself in the
> role of the frightened and suffering child.[24]

It is not difficult to imagine how this game could start after a traumatic operation, chronic illnesses such as allergies or cerebral palsy, or even after more ordinary events such as the birth of a brother or sister. The irrational illness patterns that may result are often further reinforced as the child hears his parents routinely explain that his hypochondriacal behavior is the result of "a bad experience."

Still another variation on the medical mismanagement theme is the irrational sense of vulnerability that may be impressed upon a child through his observation of another's pain and death. When the nineteenth-century writer Charlotte Brontë was five her mother died, and three years later she and three of her sisters were sent away to the penurious and poorly run Clergy Daughter's School in Cowan Bridge. By February of that first dreary winter Charlotte was watching Maria, the eldest sister, sicken with consumption. Maria was given plasters that blistered her skin, then roughly shaken for not having the strength to get out of bed. As Charlotte watched, her sister grew weaker and weaker. Maria died in May: the second sister died in June. Charlotte returned to school only to find its Calvinist director still delivering lectures in praise of death as a protector from sin.

By the time Charlotte was eighteen she was deeply depressed, and part of her anxiety manifested itself as what she called "that darkest foe of humanity," hypochondria. Looking back at her years in boarding school, she insisted that "assuredly I can never forget the concentrated anguish of certain insufferable moments, and the heavy gloom of many long hours, besides the preternatural horrors which . . . made life a continual waking nightmare."[25]

"A horror of great darkness fell upon me," she wrote in her first and largely autobiographical novel. "I felt my chamber invaded by one I had known formerly, but had thought for ever departed . . ., hypochondria."[26]

Medical Students Disease is a rather different form of hypochondria which is based on the misinterpretation or misuse of medical information. Although simpler in nature and more transitory than the deeply embedded hypochondrias, it causes very real distress among a majority of medical students[27] as well as among persons who avail themselves of medical information or misinformation.

Every summer vacation hundreds of unabashedly exaggerated adventure stories suggest to some fascinated eleven- or twelve-year-olds that their mosquito bites are the pox and their poison ivy, leprosy. For most this holds more excitement than fear. Health films shown in high school strike closer to home, and thousands of imagined cases of venereal disease result.[28] But medical students with access to examples and descriptions of the full range of humankind's nefarious diseases are the ones who routinely, and with great earnestness, mistake tension headaches for brain tumors and general fatigue for the onset of ankylosing spondylitis.

"The . . . disease you labour under is your apprehension of many diseases and a continual fear that you are always inclining or falling into one or other," wrote a compassionate doctor to Robert Boyle, the chemist, physicist, and medical doctor best known for his law on the elasticity of gases. "This distemper is incident to all that begin the study of diseases."[29]

Although this is less commonly known, medical students extend their fearful diagnoses to fellow students, teachers, and even members of the public. A woman seen scratching her ankle more than once or twice is suspected of having primary psoriasis, and a student who faints in class is considered by some of his or her peers to be suffering from ischemic heart disease. According to Paul Atkinson,[30] who spent two years accompanying medical students on their hospital rounds as part of a study of medical education, the tendency to see in minor symptoms evidence of major illness is a perfectly understandable reaction that needs no deep psychologizing to understand. Medical students do their third- and fourth-year learning in a teaching hospital surrounded by seriously ill patients. Atkinson believes that in such a setting students do not ask themselves "Is this patient ill?" but rather "What exactly is wrong with this person?" Given this bias, students may soon regard all symptoms as indicators of disease. This is especially likely to happen when a student is under personal as well as academic stress.[31] In most cases when a medical student becomes distraught enough to consult a doctor or request X rays, he or she can accept the information received and reinterpret the symptoms in a more realistic way. Some investigators suggest that psychiatric assistance would be more to the point.[32]

The popular conception that medical students spend much of their time worrying about disease has recently been challenged. A study comparing medical students with law students[33] found that although the former paid more attention to physical symptoms and briefly exhibited the symptoms they read about, the groups contained an equal number of real worriers. Fewer than 10 percent of each group were judged to be hypochondriacal. This study does not invalidate earlier findings but suggests that Medical Students Disease is a fleeting phenomenon likely to affect only a small portion of students at any one time and that similar concerns (especially the fear of cancer) are prevalent among other students.

In studying this process whereby a person interprets a symptom as either insignificant or dangerous, medical sociologist David Mechanic has stated that most persons react appropriately if they have either experienced the sensation many times before or have been told about it in sufficient detail.[34] Sometimes, however, these same experienced and/or well-informed persons react inappropriately, either ignoring signs of a serious disease or building a minor symptom into a sign of terminal illness. The latter tendency has been the bane of many medical students and other hypochondriacs for centuries.

Before becoming a famous colonial minister, Cotton Mather studied "Physick" at Harvard University (at the age of thirteen) and later admitted that "I was unhappily led away with Fancies, that I was myself troubled with almost every Distemper that I read of in my Studies; which caused me to use medicines upon myself, that I might cure my Imaginary maladies."[35] And almost two hundred years later, as Charles Darwin prepared to embark are only upon the *Beagle*, he was equally distressed with palpitations and pain about the heart.

> Like many a young ignorant man, especially one with a smattering of medical knowledge, [I] was convinced that I had heart disease. I did not consult any doctor, as I fully expected to hear the verdict that I was not fit for the voyage.[36]

Mechanic believes that these hypochondriacal responses frequently arise from "morbid cues" such as the sight of sick people or the reading of case histories that are present just as a person experiences the normal symptoms of stress. He describes a study in which two groups of college students were given adrenalin without being told what it was or what sensations it would produce. As the chemical elicited the usual symptoms of arousal, members of one group were put in the company of euphoric companions who were supposedly other students taking the test. Members of the second group were paired with angry, anxious companions. It was observed that all students underwent a two-step reaction. First, each became physically aroused: heart rate increased, mouth felt dry, and so forth. Then each student defined the meaning of this arousal. In this second step (i.e., during the interpretation of the symptoms) the cues received from each subject's companion were of great importance and largely determined whether the experience was interpreted as a great trip or a frightening disruption.

As Mechanic put it, "the same internal state can be labeled in a variety of ways, resulting in different emotional reactions."[37] Students stressed by new experiences, a heavy course load, and exams, he continued, are frequently in a state of emotional arousal in which they experience a large number of transient symptoms. These "little strugglings of nature," as Boyle's doctor termed them, are considered normal, when considered at all, by most students but are given specific and fearful meaning by medical students or others who are receiving morbid cues. Such cues need not come from medical literature. They are equally powerful if present as the reactivated memory of a past illness, the death of a well-known person, or the presence of a sick relative or friend. All such invitations to fearful misinterpretation are particularly hard to ignore when received by persons already predisposed to hypochondria by parental example, chronic illness, or family dynamics. Medical students may fall squarely within one of these predisposed groups, as their very interest in medicine is often motivated by a conscious or unconscious fear of disease.

The most complex and possibly the most intractable form of hypochondria to be embedded during childhood is the variety that forms an integral part of a family's way of life. One or more children are singled out as "sickly," and whether they are then coddled or, oddly enough, even punished for being sick, their role in the family drama is fixed. Because the very survival of the family seems dependent on each member playing a consistent part, the children labeled "sickly" will receive no real encouragement to exchange their hypochondria for more constructive behavior. Almost from birth such children are funneled into the role of hypochondriacs.

Obviously this family-generated and maintained hypochondria is not completely different from the kind in which the child copies an ailing parent. There may be a difference in degree, however, the "family plan" apparently blanketing a child with more intense and pervasive motivations for being sick. The difference may also lie in the perspective of the observers, meaning that a doctor or psychologist may see a case of hypochondria as being generated largely by the child or may see the ailment as being produced by an entire family working together.

In an anxious or downright neurotic family, the child labeled "sickly" is frequently treated in one of two distinctly different ways. Either he is extravagantly overprotected, with each cold and bruise eliciting great concern, or he is just as remarkably underprotected (as far as illness is concerned), with sore throats and stomachaches brushed aside or even punished. Although the development of hypochondria is easier to follow in children who are overprotected, the two family styles have much in common.

The American poet Sara Teasdale, an unhappy example of the intimate connection that can arise between overprotection and hypochondria, was born in 1884 to parents whose youngest child was already fourteen. According to Sara's excellent biographer, William Drake, she was brought up in St. Louis in a home that reflected "the best taste and manners of the upper and middle class with its pretensions of English aristocratic refinement."[38] Sara's father, a prosperous and well-respected wholesaler, seemed pleased but only marginally affected by her arrival. She remembered him as kindly and mostly absent. Conversely, her mother had emerged from a sickly childhood to become a restless and formidable force in her family's life. In some ways the middle-aged Mrs. Teasdale resented having to resume the tasks of early motherhood, but she buried that "tangle of negative emotions," as Drake sees it, beneath a "public demonstration of lavish concern."[39] In addition to assuaging whatever guilt Mrs. Teasdale might have felt concerning her own resentment, the incredible fuss she made over Sara's health also allowed her to indulge her propensity to manage. It was a trait she was never comfortable admitting but one she strongly and consistently expressed. By labeling Sara "delicate" and truly believing that she was, Mrs. Teasdale transformed what she could not bear to think of as domination and manipulation into the far more acceptable qualities of caring and good management.

Although Sara's father seems peripheral to his daughter's upbringing, he allowed (in fact probably encouraged) his wife to translate their marital conflicts into problems in child rearing. Instead of arguing openly over travel and vacations, for example, which Sara's mother loved and her father disliked, they seemed to agree that the central problem in their lives was Sara's health, not their own disagreements.

To validate their bogus problem, the Teasdales frequently called in physicians to the big old house on Lindell Boulevard, and Sara was put to bed—to save her strength—for every reason imaginable. Sara lived among neat piles of extra blankets and rows of tonics. She was kept indoors and not considered strong enough to attend school until she was nine years old. By then Sara herself was convinced of a profound physical inadequacy. Although she had not yet fastened upon the kinds of weaknesses that would be characteristic for her and was only beginning to realize that being delicate could be worked to her own (as well as to her mother's) advantage, she was thoroughly and irrationally apprehensive.

When Sara was fourteen she was far too old to continue to attend the private school one block from her home and so was sent to a prestigious girl's school in St. Louis proper. It is possible that this step toward greater self-reliance jostled the status quo and that both Sara and her mother felt ambivalent about the change. "If one is asked to do something [grow up] and not to do it [stay home] at the same time," noted the imaginative therapist Jay Haley, "a possible response is to be unable to do it—which means indicating that one's behavior is involuntary. The physiology of the human being seems to cooperate in this situation even to the point of producing symptoms."[40] Not surprisingly, the ride to and from school by streetcar proved too exhausting for Sara, and she returned to the suburbs. The habit of a lifetime was set. Everything outside of poetry—and frequently that too—exhausted Sara and made her sick. A year rarely passed without extended retreats to an inn or convalescent home. The most disabling part of this pattern was the ingrained belief that it was necessary to relinquish her independence in order to receive love. It had been so with her mother, who seemed to give love only on condition that she be in control of a weak, dependent Sara, who in turn assumed that the same trade would have to be made with a husband. The stress that this impossible situation created for a willful intelligent woman gave her illnesses unrestricted scope and function (see chapter 5).

The mechanism of family involvement can be seen still more clearly in a modern case that, like Sara Teasdale's, involved a domineering mother but was different in that the mother focused her children's attention on illness by punishment rather than treatment.

Anita was the eldest of four children in a family that moved, without apparent reason, from a series of homes in the suburbs of Philadelphia to equally well-kept houses on the outskirts of New Haven, Connecticut—and back again. Her father, a consultant for a large company, traveled a fair amount and even when home would sometimes return to his office after dinner. Her mother cared for the children and the house and apparently had neither the confidence nor the ambition to expand her sphere of influence.

Anita's earliest memories of sickness were of her mother heaving a tremendous sigh and repeating, "Oh, Anita, what a terrible inconvenience." There was more to the message than annoyance, however, and although Anita at five and six years old could not understand why being sick was being bad, she was sure that her mother's sighs and her father's admonitions not to upset Mother really meant that she was being naughty. As she grew older and the association between being sick and being bad coalesced, Anita got into the anxious habit of trying to hide her sore throats and stomachaches until they went away or became more than she could bear. She would sometimes go to bed at night with an earache, believing that if she were truly a good girl she could make the hurt go away. If it did not, she felt as guilty as the times when she had dissected a bug or worm with her mother's manicure set, a practice her mother particularly hated.

When she was seven Anita had two unfortunate experiences that abruptly removed illness from the category of simple sin and placed it in the terrifying position of imminent and personal danger. First was the death of a playmate during an operation that was supposed to cure her of a congenital heart defect, and second was the sudden death of a neighborhood boy who had been skating with Anita only the day before.

Anita was badly shaken. Not only was there no protection from a benevolent God or loving parents, as she had been led to believe, but there was no warning either. "I can never be sure this day is not my last," she remembers saying to herself. From then on Anita worried almost continuously both about contracting terrible diseases and about her mother's predictable annoyance, reinforced as it always was by her father's distant approval. The pattern was set: for the next twenty-five or thirty years she tried to hide the sore throats, swollen lymph glands, chest pains, and disabling diarrhea that she frequently imagined were the first signs of cancer or heart disease. During this time she felt trapped between her desire to ask for help and her conviction that such admissions of inherent insufficiency and badness would be met by the old pattern of parental rejection. During times of stress she had become a reluctant hypochondriac.

Anita's distorted ideas of sickness, like those ingrained in her two sisters and, to a lesser extent, in her brother, were fostered primarily by Anita's mother and agreed to by her father. Anita's mother had had a miserable childhood by almost anyone's standards. She had been raised by an alcoholic mother who was also a flagrant and imaginative hypochondriac. She suffered continually from exotic and incurable illnesses until she died in her seventies. Anita's mother also had to contend with a younger, prettier, smarter, and infinitely more fragile sister who was raised in a manner reminiscent of Sara Teasdale. Anita's mother was shut out from the close relationship between mother and favored sister which revolved around their constant illnesses and special regimens. A sick person, she soon learned, had the right to be self-pitying and rejecting.

As a married woman, Anita's mother apparently carried over her unresolved conflict with her sickly sister and overbearing mother onto her own four children, especially the girls. Sickness in her children seemed to reactivate memories of her sister, and in spite of her efforts to be a good mother the old jealousy and dislike reappeared, this time directed at Anita and her sister. Memories of her mother were reactivated too, and because she thought she was treating her children exactly as she wished her mother had treated her when she was a child, she was confounded by their lack of gratitude, obedience, health, and beauty. Their shortcomings suggested that her child-rearing methods were not perfect and, more important, that her control was not complete.

Anita's mother was especially anxious to control her husband in a way that would guard against overt rejection. When he was busier than usual with his work, Anita's mother vividly expressed her anger—but at the "damn telephone" and at his "stupid," inconsiderate clients, never at her husband for being so involved in his work. "How can I handle four children, especially with one of them sick?" and "How can I manage this impossible house?" became an endless refrain which allowed her covertly to criticize her husband for pursuing his career so independently, while skirting the real question that she never dared ask: "Am I important to you at all?" For his part, her husband was content to pretend that the real problems in their lives centered on the children and the house and had nothing to do with him.

Such a brittle and indirect way of expressing but never resolving conflict has been sufficient to keep Anita's parents together for fifty years but has passed along a disagreeable legacy to all four children. It has taken years for Anita to even partially divest sickness of its hidden meanings (see chapter 11).

Having progressed, haltingly, from the relatively simple processes of misinterpretation of medical literature and the copying of an ailing parent to the complicated dynamics of family conflict diffused and rerouted through hypochondria, we can see that for most chronically hypochondriacal children three or four events or mechanisms interact to perpetuate their distress. A child who copies a chronically sick parent who has a distorted view of illness will learn that however the illness game is played, it has certain advantages for the child as well as for the parents. Copying sickness thus gradually becomes cultivating illness for its advantages, at least on some occasions. By this time the child has become unusually sensitive to the emotional connotations of illness and is particularly susceptible to medical mismanagement. Noticing the signs of illness around him more than other children, the child is also more likely to be deeply affected by the death of a peer or to read terrifying and personal meaning into what he sees and hears. Such misinterpretation feeds upon itself, maintaining the morbid sensitivity toward disease, which in turn leads to future misunderstandings. If this unfortunate cycle is part of the way the child's family suppresses and controls aggression, it is probable that his hypochondriacal reactions will become one of the major ways in which he deals with or attempts to control other people. After leaving to start his own family, he is likely to cling to those hypochondriacal methods rather than to risk the unknown dangers of open argument or rebellion. Even with some insight into the problem, a person may be only half cured, and, as Bernard de Mandeville put it nearly three hundred years ago, such a man or woman "lingering under the remainder of her Disease, may have half a dozen children that shall all inherit it."[41]

And so the cycle begins again.

5

H YPOCHONDRIA I N
T HE F AMILY

The individual and his environment are an
interdependent system at all times. Any
attempt to isolate one or the other produces
major artifacts. . . . When we encounter
neurasthenic and hypochondriacal
manifestations in our patients . . ., they tell
us something about what the patient thinks of
himself and of his . . . communal existence.
  —Gerard Chrzanowski
  "Neurasthenia and Hypochondriasis"

∎

S INCE THE 1960S more and more people have approached psychogenic and psychosomatic disorders with the idea that the
family, not the patient, is the basic unit of study. Although their
attention has hardly been riveted on hypochondria, a few family
therapists have tried to discover how hypochondriacs function
within a family setting and, specifically, how they use illness to
regulate their families' transactions. As one might expect, no single mechanism or pattern of interactions predominates. Charles
Darwin's daughter Etty, for whom sickness was champagne, con-
tentedly managed her illnesses, and her husband, Richard, for
decades. Sara Teasdale used far more distressing diseases to keep
her distance from her husband until the couple was painfully di-

vorced. And different by far from either of these households was the morbidly fascinating family life of the de Goncourt brothers—French novelists, art critics, and connoisseurs of hypochondria.

Despite many differences, a few generalizations can be made. Most obvious is the fact that hypochondriacs' symptoms usually mesh with those of their spouses or other important relatives. As Jay Haley has noted, psychogenic symptoms are ways of dealing with another person. They are tactics, and the person they are used on is bound to have tactics of his or her own regardless of whether or not they are called symptoms. "Typically the mate of a spouse with symptoms opposes the symptomatic behavior but also encourages it"[1]—a curious state of affairs that we shall examine shortly.

A less obvious generalization is that hypochondria usually stabilizes a family as well as disrupts it. It is as if the interlocking roles of hypochondriac-indispensable strong person or hypochondriac-devoted but manipulative nurse force most of the family's problems onto a single circular track or, more precisely, into a self-regulating feedback loop. Just as a thermostat and furnace work together to keep changes in the air temperature to a minimum, the hypochondriac's family unit may experience only minor fluctuations in the emotional climate.

In an attempt to substantiate hypochondria's paradoxical ability to stabilize family relations, Norman Kreitman and his colleagues in Britain compared the marriages of twenty-one confirmed hypochondriacs with twenty-one matched patients suffering from depression but having no physical complaints. The doctors concluded that the hypochondriacs had poorer marriages (although what they meant by this was not clear) but further noted that the hypochondriacs had quieter marriages. They showed "less disruption of social, family, and occupational activities."[2]

This stabilizing effect, which works in a disagreeable but nonetheless effective way to ensure the survival of the family, has a parallel in the individual's own emotional economy. G. A. Ladee, a Dutch doctor who wrote one of the first modern books on hypochondria, believes the disorder is capable of safeguarding a person from psychotic disintegration.[3] In his estimation hypochondria is frequently a substitute for deeper conflict. If the latter were to express itself in an undisguised form, it might well overwhelm the sufferer and lead to a breakdown. Thus in the individual as well as in the family, hypochondria might function as a relatively safe way of letting a basic conflict partially express itself.[4]

In addition to hypochondria's stabilizing influence and its tendency to fit with the rest of the family's characteristics, the disorder is also likely to be chosen by persons who have learned to play the oppressor *and* the oppressed but who have had little experience with equal dealings. This suggests that hypochondriacs—Etty Darwin, Sara Teasdale, the de Goncourt brothers, and the rest—by no means resign themselves to being helplessly dependent when they adopt the sick role. A hypochondriac can function as the oppressor in a family quite as easily as the oppressed.

One pattern that hypochondriacal marriages sometimes assume is characterized by the apparently peaceful union of a dominant husband or wife with an agreeably passive spouse. Charles Darwin's daughter Henrietta had that kind of marriage. Aunt Etty, as she was known in the family, was the fourth of ten children raised in a household where it was a distinct and mournful pleasure to be ill.[5]

"I have been told that when Aunt Etty was thirteen the doctor recommended, after she had a 'low fever,' that she should have breakfast in bed for a time," wrote her niece. "*She never got up to breakfast again in all her life.*"[6] Apparently fragile, and undeniably wiry, Etty survived childhood with a minimum of serious illnesses and eventually married Richard Litchfield, "a nice funny little man, whose socks were always coming down . . . [and whose] fuzzy, waggly, whitey-brown beard . . . was quite indistinguishable, both in colour and texture, from the Shetland shawl which Aunt Etty generally made him wear round his neck."[7]

The couple had no children and no lack of domestic help, so Aunt Etty had nothing to occupy her but the management of her house, her husband, and her illnesses—or, rather, her bodily functions.

She would send down the cook to ask her to count the prune-stones left on her plate, as it was very important to know whether she had eaten three or four prunes for luncheon. She would make Janet put a silk handkerchief over her left foot as she lay in bed, because it was that amount colder than her right foot. And when there were colds about she often wore a kind of gas-mask of her own invention. It was an ordinary wire kitchen-strainer, stuffed with antiseptic cotton-wool, and tied on like a snout, with elastic over her ears. In this she would receive visitors and discuss politics in a hollow voice out of her euca-lyptus-scented seclusion, oblivious of the fact that they might be struggling with fits of laughter.[8]

When the affectionate and in no way self-pitying Etty was not taking her own pulse she was likely to start on her husband, for although he had never been sickly in his life, she had decided early in their marriage that he was extremely delicate.

At frequent intervals Janet used to bring poor Uncle Richard bowls of Benger's food—which we called 'Uncle Richard's porridge.' He always seemed surprised when this occurred, and a little saddened; but he set aside his book, pushed his spectacles up onto his forehead, and ate it up like a man. If the window had to be opened to air the room in cold weather, Aunt Etty covered him up entirely with a dust sheet for fear of draughts; and he sat there as patient as a statue, till he could be un-veiled. . . .

I believe that he thought it saved trouble to obey orders; as indeed it probably did. Yet Aunt Etty always managed to com-bine proper Victorian respect for a man and a husband, with this obedience of his over merely material affairs. 'Uncle Richard says' or 'Uncle Richard thinks' were matters of serious importance.[9]

Among the histories of hypochondriacs it is not difficult to find examples of the Aunt Etty-Uncle Richard type of marriage or of complementary ones in which the wife is dominant but the husband is the hypochondriac, the husband dominant and the wife chronically ill, and so forth. Such descriptions as we have of these marriages portray them as stable unions. Each partner seems to have accepted his or her dominant or passive position and is apparently content.

Another variety of peaceful partnership involving hypochondria is one in which the disorder is shared. "We are so fond of one another, because our ailments are the same."[10] One of the most remarkable examples of the hypochondria à deux occurred not within a conventional marriage but in the lifelong union of two brothers, Edmond and Jules de Goncourt. Born in 1822 and 1830, respectively, the two boys lost their father in 1834 (he had constantly been sick with old war wounds) and their mother some fourteen years later. They were thrown together by temperament as well as circumstance and lived in such close association that they shared the same house, the same friends, the same diary, and, for a time, the same mistress. They collaborated on novels and works of art criticism, and even in their private journal no one could tell where the thoughts of one left off and the other began. They also shared the conviction that they were sick. Edmond's complaints centered on his stomach, Jules had a bad liver, and both ministered, prescribed, and even suffered for the other. Although these chronic disabilities caused both men great discomfort, as when an intestinal complaint had Jules writhing "all night long . . . like a cut earthworm,"[11] they cherished their "nervous illnesses" as a major source of artistic creativity.

"Sickness has its place in our talent, and a big place at that," they wrote in their journal. "But this fact, which at present causes displeasure and irritation, will one day be regarded as our great attraction and strength. Sickness makes a man sensitive like a photographic plate."[12]

The displeasure and irritation referred to resulted from criticisms of the de Goncourt's novels, which some reviewers considered repulsively morbid rather than admirably realistic. Their third work of fiction, for example, revolved around a sister of mercy who worked at a hospital. To describe the setting faithfully, the brothers set off early one winter morning to visit the Hôpital de la Charité in Paris.

Tuesday, 18 December

> We got up at seven. It was cold and damp; and although we said nothing about it to each other, we both felt a certain apprehension, a certain fear in our nerves. . . .
>
> The tour of the ward began. We pulled ourselves together and followed M. Velpeau with his students; but our legs were as weak as if we had been drunk, and we were conscious of the knee-caps in our legs and of a kind of chill in the marrow of our shin-bones. . . .
>
> Those pale women's faces, glimpsed on their pillows, almost blueish in colour and transformed by suffering and immobility, have left us with an impression which haunts our souls and fascinates us like something veiled and frightening.[13]

It took several days for the brothers to shake off the effects of their hospital visit for, as Edmond wrote later, these were "the frightened years, the anxious days when a mere scratch or something a little out of order straight away makes us think of death."[14] The novel finally produced was *Soeur Philomène*. It was published in 1861 by the second publisher to read it; the first considered it too gloomy.

By 1865 Jules was suffering from syphilis, yet both brothers clung to the belief that their *real* suffering was the shared anguish that sprung from their total dedication to art. Five years later the younger brother died. "Will death be content with just half of us?" Edmond wrote disconsolately, "or will it take me soon as well?"[15] Gone was "this great thing, unique perhaps in the history of the world, this intellectual companionship . . ., this sharing of our pride, above all, this communion of our hearts to which we have grown as accustomed as to breath itself; a rare and precious happiness."[16]

Whether a couple is composed of a dominant and passive pair, as with the Darwin-Litchfields, or two overtly dependent persons, as with the de Goncourts, the fit between hypochondriac and spouse is rarely so ideal. An underlying struggle is likely to be in progress with both partners angling covertly for control.[17] Such conflicts can assume innumerable guises and disguises, but two of the most common involve wives who feel obligated by their husbands (and by themselves) to be far more submissive than they think they want to be, and husbands who feel obligated by their wives and families (and, of course, by themselves) to be much more responsible than suits their tastes. In this country, where it is believed that hypochondria occurs far more frequently among women (see chapter 8), the first form is familiar. In Britain, where hypochondria is thought to be more common among men, the second is well known.

Taking the ambivalently submissive wife first, what seems to happen when such a woman marries is that she says, in effect, "I need a strong husband to take care of me, and I will trade a large portion of my independence for this necessary protection and direction. But I also need some powerful leverage in this relationship or my husband is likely to leave me." Giving herself these conflicting directions—act helpless but get control—she can neither become totally dependent nor straightforwardly ask for power. In the first case she would abdicate so much control that her husband might treat her like a servant, and in the second, her aggressiveness would anger him and drive him off—or so she believes.

How, then, can such a wife manage to be apparently helpless yet at the same time retain a significant measure of control?
If she has learned to use hypochondria as her stratagem, she will
get sick to indicate her helplessness yet simultaneously use sickness to get her way and to make her spouse feel guilty if he should
ever consider leaving her. Haley offers an example of this process, though with agoraphobia—the fear of going out—rather
than with hypochondria.

A wife became anxious whenever she tried to leave the house
alone. When she attempted to go out, she suffered anxiety feelings and a terrible pain in the eyes. She had suffered this problem for years and her husband was constantly assuring her that
she should go out alone and that it was perfectly safe. However,
he was also fully cooperating in her staying at home by doing
all the shopping, escorting her where she needed to go, and
indicating some uneasiness whenever she started to go out
alone. After several sessions of marriage therapy, the husband
was asked, in the presence of the wife, to do something he might
think was silly. He was asked to tell the wife each day as he
left for work that she was to stay at home that day and not go
out alone. He could say this seriously, or as a joke, or as he
pleased. The husband agreed to follow this procedure. On the
third day that he told her to stay at home the wife went out to
the store alone for the first time in 8 years. However, the next
interview was devoted to the husband's expressions of concern
about what his wife might do if she went out alone, where she
might go, whom she might meet, and would she even get a job
and become so independent that she would leave him. . . .
Although the wife had been behaving like the helpless one,
she was in charge of being the helpless one by insisting on staying at home. When her husband directed her to stay at home,
the question of who was laying down the rules for their relationship was called in question. The wife responded by a sym-
metrical move, leaving the house, which was her only way of
taking charge in this situation. . . . The crucial problem in a
marriage [is]; who is to define what kind of relationship the two
people will have.[18]

Sara Teasdale's marriage is another example. Sara was born too late to have a clear choice—marriage or career—forced upon her. When she arrived at a marriageable age in the 1900s she faced a more subtle dilemma. There was a deceptive flexibility in women's roles by that time, an expectation, as yet unsupported by experience, that a woman could combine a serious career in the arts with a traditional and fulfilling marriage. Although Sara thought a great deal about love and what it would mean when "to my life's high altar came its priest,"[19] her protected and long-protracted childhood insulated her from any actual involvement with a man until she was twenty-eight. Prior to that time she tentatively, and rather prophetically, established an intense friendship with an older woman, Marion Cummings Stanley, who admired Sara's work. Seeing that the young poet needed time away from home to develop a degree of independence, Marion invited her to spend the winter in Tucson, Arizona. Sara accepted but used the visit to bask in what she called "enraptured dependence." Safe with Marion, her chronic stomach complaints, sore throats, and "hurts by the 10,000" placidly receded. "Marion is a perfect dear," Sara wrote a fellow poet, "only she is so easy to manage. It's always a dreadful temptation to make people do your way when you can—but somehow I rather like to feel that I can't do a thing without them, and that I am being managed myself."[20] In the same letter she complained that too many people treated her like a child.

Sara was broadcasting contradictory messages: she was sick and in need of help, but at the same time she was not really weak or dependent. Such ambiguity informed her friend Marion, and later her suitors, that she needed them and was apprehensive lest she lose their affection and admiration. Although she often felt somewhat superior, she was, in fact, ready to please them. Everyone who accepted this curious courtship on Sara's terms found themselves involved in a series of contradictory and only semitruthful exchanges. Some friends became Sara's titular managers or bogus decision makers; others rashly allowed themselves to be cast as healers and doctor-substitutes, positions they inevitably lost. All such friends became accomplices of a sort, for in agreeing to play a role of exaggerated importance in Sara's life, each expressed his or her own need of appearing a little stronger or more important than he or she actually felt. The price of these inexplicit exchanges was a kind of psychological subservience. Neither Sara nor her intimates could afford to say to one another what they really felt.

In the summer of 1912, when Sara was twenty-eight and still single, she traveled through Europe with her friend Jessie Rittenhouse. The poems written during the trip all speak of love, and all point toward the moment when Sara would meet The Man. It finally happened. Returning to New York aboard an ocean liner, she fell in love. Although she let this first flirtation develop only far enough to jolt her into writing a poem expressing revulsion with the physical aspects of love, she almost immediately replaced her shipboard romance with an epistolary affair. When this too failed to develop, she fell in love simultaneously with the wild and impecunious poet Vachel Lindsay and an ardent yet respectable businessman, Ernst Filsinger. Both adored her. Shortly before her thirtieth birthday, Sara decided to marry Ernst. "I do not love him now," she confided in a friend, "but probably I shall in a month!"[21] (She already loved Lindsay but judged correctly that he was too poor and too erratic to take good care of her.)

Ernst Filsinger was a lot like Sara's mother but more polite and adoring. Sara had repeatedly maintained that "my mother, who is a sort of super-woman, nearly drives me mad. . . . She is sixty-seven and has as much strength in her little finger as I have in my whole body." She seemed to Sara "utterly selfish and restless and jealous."[22]

Ernst too was a restless and extremely active person. He worked all days and all hours, took six language lessons a week when his business expanded into Europe and South America, and traveled extensively at a pace that made Sara angry and sick even in anticipation. After a one-week honeymoon Sara was sick with a bad cold and a bladder infection that precluded sexual relations for six months. Moreover, she was dismayed to discover, her own romantic poems notwithstanding, that as Mrs. Filsinger she was still the same person—alone and uncomfortable with sex.

Illness followed illness in the first year of Sara's marriage, and each seemed to enhance Ernst's solicitude and aggressive vitality. He became more protective, better able to manage their household (they always lived in hotels), and, if possible, more energetic. Sara, admitting she felt guilty about being neither a passionate mate nor a sociable companion, and expressing annoyance at Ernst's undiminished ability to carry on without or in spite of her, became increasingly helpless. It was a method of coping with problems she had evolved years before. Sickness not only punished Ernst and herself (by restricting social and sexual activities) but also provided a familiar substitute for the conflicts she sensed might erupt if they confronted their more fundamental disagreements. Sickness also guaranteed extra emotional and financial support from Ernst and created the illusion that the couple had a caring relationship.

In 1915 Sara published her third book of poems, *Rivers to the Sea*, and its enthusiastic reception further exacerbated the conflict she felt between being a gentle, passive woman and a restless, ambitious success. The five or six specialists who saw her in the months following the book's publication could find nothing wrong with her and were unable to suggest effective treatment. Sara went in and out of the hospital, later writing a group of poems called "In a Hospital," then reembraced the treatment of her choice—long retreats at a convalescent home in Connecticut. Ernst was rarely allowed to visit, yet she wrote him almost daily describing, with relief, how much she missed him.

The conflict between wife and poet reached a peak when Sara found she was pregnant. At the height of her popularity— she had recently received the Poetry Society of America's annual award, and two new books were scheduled for publication—she felt she was being asked to set aside fourteen years of work to concentrate what little strength and energy she possessed on motherhood. Could she give up poetry? She was convinced a real woman would say yes. After an agonizing period of doubt, she persuaded herself she was too ill to bear a child and had it aborted.

As far as Sara Teasdale's health was concerned, it is interesting to speculate what a full-term pregnancy might have accomplished. Some hypochondriacal women apparently lose their fears and regain their health during pregnancy and early motherhood. Although this is scantily documented in medical literature,[23] anecdotal accounts are plentiful. According to the latter, pregnancy's most powerful weapon against hypochondria seems to be its ability temporarily to resolve a woman's confusion about dependency. The complicated forces that pull her in two directions at once, toward independence and its concomitant self-promotion and at the same time toward subservience to both her husband's and her own ideas of the good, compliant wife, are sometimes laid to rest. Pregnant, a woman feels she is devoting a large portion of her thoughts and energies to family matters. She is in step with everyone's picture of the "good woman."

In addition, pregnancy seems to make the concern for health legitimate. Since the late 1900s, when pregnancy began to be treated as an illness (albeit a natural one), the proper care advocated for a pregnant woman has been similar to that suggested for hypochondriacs. In articles on the management of hypochondriacs, it is commonly urged that a doctor give hypochondriacal patients regular appointments without regard for symptoms (thus the patient need not fear that getting better will terminate his or her relationship with the doctor). Furthermore, patients are encouraged to care for themselves with good diet, exercise, vitamin supplements, and so forth, and they are involved in the planning of further treatment. The carefully regulated regime advocated for a healthy pregnancy has many similarities and may allow some hypochondriacs guiltlessly to use doctors and other health aids as much as they have always wanted.

Another reason for a remission of hypochondriacal symptoms during pregnancy may be that the hypochondriac's method of operation (i.e., the paradoxical quest for power, privilege, and attention through increased dependency) is expected during pregnancy. A pregnant woman is expected to be demanding, restless, and indecisive. She is expected to send her husband—not herself—for pickles and ice cream at 2:00 A.M. and is actually given minor privileges for being in this relatively childish but manipulative state.

Simpler explanations for a pregnant woman's cheerful outlook—reasons that probably coexist with pregnancy's ability to resolve social conflict—include a new focus for a woman's attention: physiological changes that occasionally seem to stop panic attacks,[24] and the powerful joy and anticipation of having a baby.

But Sara Teasdale did not experiment with pregnancy. "I am alone in spite of love, / In spite of all I take and give."[25] For the next twelve years that remained of her marriage, Sara continued to withdraw from Ernst. She was soon living like an invalid and, following the death of her brother and later a poet she knew, both of a stroke, she became increasingly afraid of high blood pressure and weak blood vessels. Badly bounced in a taxi crossing Manhattan's Central Park, she insisted on being hospitalized for fear a blood clot had formed. She was also convinced that the jolting had caused extensive rheumatism. Poems from this period deal with impending death, and by 1929, when she sought a divorce from Ernst in spite of the despised publicity she knew would accompany it, she was desperately trying to survive by eliminating conflict from her life. Only peace, she felt, could restore her health.

In January 1933 a small blood vessel broke in her hand and Sara, at the age of forty-nine, believed a massive stroke was on its way. After taking an overdose of sleeping pills she climbed into a warm bath. Her nurse discovered her body the following morning.

In one of the poems from "In a Hospital" Sara had written,

> Great Sower when you tread
> My field again
> Scatter the furrows there
> With better grain.[26]

There is no doubt that Sara Teasdale's life was a misery as far as physical health and comfort were concerned. She was sick, terrified of being sick, or convalescent for most of her forty-nine years. Did her profound hypochondria cripple her talents? Or did she manage to convert some of her misery into poems that transcended self-pity and complaint? The answer to both questions is probably yes.

Emerging from childhood with an unshakable conviction of physical inadequacy and a twisted belief that only a dependent woman could expect to receive love, her internal struggles were intensified by a driving desire to be a successful poet. Although she recognized that the resolution of these conflicts was the major business of her life, she never seemed to develop the emotional resources she needed to become self-sufficient. She could partially avoid conflict but seldom could resolve it. At the same time, she managed to pull from her pervasive moods of fear and frustration sad statements that were more than cries of self-pity.

"Even when she was in anguish and panic she was writing those calm poems in *Strange Victory* [her last book]," wrote poet John Hall Wheelock. "She was a sane human being and she had a certain kind of strength that came out in the end."[27]

Sara Teasdale's hypochondria evolved in step with expressions of helplessness, but other adults are pushed toward hypochondria by being forced into a position of responsibility. In the past such a position was often forced on a man by his obligation to support his unmarried sister, orphaned niece or nephew, and elderly parents, or on a woman by her obligation to live with and care for her ailing father or mother. Today the reluctant helper is likely to be a single parent with small children. In any of these

cases a reluctantly responsible person can use hypochondria to
express the unresolvable conflict that arises when the desire to
break away from dependents runs counter to the fear of social
blame or deeper apprehensions.

Matthew Bramble, an irascible old hypochondriac and the
main character in Tobias Smollett's last novel, was beseiged by
unmanageable obligations in the form of his hopelessly romantic
niece, Liddy, his humorless sister, Tabitha, a rowdy assortment
of servants, and an estate that he was attempting to govern *in
absentia*. Each failure to control produced intractable constipation. The novel begins as Bramble and his entourage arrive at
Bath, a popular watering place where many persons "who think
fit to be sick by way of amusement" loved to congregate. In 1770,
when the action of this early epistolary novel took place, it was
widely believed that mineral waters either drunk or bathed in
would ease a great variety of consumptions, indigestions, rheu-
matisms, and hypochondriacal disorders. Bramble, having had
"an hospital these fourteen years within myself, and studied my
case with the most painful attention," was secretly hopeful that
the waters might help him too.[28] But at Bath Liddy flirted, Tabitha complained of stomach flutterings, and Bramble himself was
so appalled at the variety of diseased bodies sharing the baths
with him that he came down with three or four new complications
of his old complaints.
He wrote his doctor and confidant, Dick Lewis,

Hark-ye Lewis, snares are laid for our lives in every thing
we eat or drink; the very air we breathe is loaded with con-
tagion. I say, infection. This place is the rendezvous of the diseased. You won't deny that many diseases are infections; even
the consumption itself is highly infectious. . . . You'll allow, that
nothing receives infection sooner, or retains it longer, than blankets, featherbeds, and mattresses—'Sdeath! How do I know
what miserable objects have been stewing in the bed where I
now lie? I wonder, Dick, you did not put me in mind of sending

for my own mattresses; but, if I had not been an ass, I should not have needed a remembrancer. There is always some plaguy reflection that rises up in judgment against me, and ruffles my spirits; therefore let us change the subject.

I have other reasons for abridging my stay at Bath. You know sister Tabby . . ., well, this amiable maiden has actually commenced a flirting correspondence with an Irish baronet of sixty-five. . . . I believe, [he] has received false intelligence with respect to her fortune. Be that as it may, the connexion is exceedingly ridiculous, and begins already to excite whispers. . . . I don't think her conduct is a proper example for Liddy, who has also attracted the notice of some coxcombs in the rooms. . . . I shall therefore keep a strict eye over her aunt and her, and even shift the scene if I find the matter grow more serious. You perceive what an agreeable task it must be, to a man of my kidney, to have care of such souls as these—But hold, you shall not have another peevish word, till the next occasion, from yours,

Bath, April 28   MATT BRAMBLE[29]

And so, as many guardians and managers have discovered, Bramble found that "every thing that discomposes my mind produces a correspondent disorder in my body."

In some respects men like Matt Bramble had counterparts in the women who fell ill with undiagnosed maladies while nursing their sick parents. A century ago, when Freud was studying hysteria, he frequently encountered this phenomenon, and although he called it hysteria and saw in it more evidence of intrapsychic conflict than of social tension, the maladies of the captive sick-nurse can also produce hypochondria and may be seen as a conflict between social values and personal goals. For example, Freud's famous patient Anna O. found it impossible to reconcile her personal desire to leave home and start a family with her equally strong wish to fulfill her social obligation and stay with her father.

"Notice how similar this is to the dilemma in which many

contemporary [women] find themselves," wrote Thomas Szasz in
The Myth of Mental Illness,

> not, however, in relation to their fathers, but in relation to their
> small children. Today, married women are generally expected
> to take care of their children; they are not supposed to delegate
> this task to others. . . .
>   In both situations, the *obligatory* nature of the care required
> stimulates a feeling of helplessness in the person from whom
> the help is sought. If a person cannot, in good conscience, refuse
> to provide help . . ., then truly he becomes the captive of the
> help-seeker."[30]

Among the expressions of dissatisfaction available to persons in this situation are depression, hypochondria, alcoholism,
and desertion. Hypochondria seems situated between the ex-
tremes of the possible responses—that is, somewhere between
pure depression, with its sense of giving up, and rebelliousness,
with its implications of fighting or acting out. Both weak and
covertly powerful, the hypochondriac can simultaneously give up
and fight *and yet in meaningful terms does neither.* Such a person
may avoid the disdain that is sometimes felt for the depressed
and the rebellious, but in so doing hypochondriacs can too easily
immobilize themselves within their own conflict. As the exasperated Matt Bramble wrote, admittedly referring to his bowels and
only inadvertently to his behavior, "I have told you over and over
how hard I am to move."

C. V. Ford might say that Matt Bramble had succumbed
to the Humpty Dumpty Syndrome.[31] This refers to a situation in
which a person who for years has been wonderfully responsible
for needy family members (a good egg) falls ill himself and never
fully recovers. Typically, says Ford, when such a designated
helper has an accident or gets sick, he falls apart. Then all the
good doctors, not to mention physical therapists and counselors,
can't put him back together again.

In marriages involving hypochondria, be they peaceful or anxious, there is nothing to prevent both partners from adopting the disorder, and cases are known in which the hypochondria alternates between husband and wife. Gerard Chrzanowski describes a woman whose spells of depression and ill health coincided with the times her husband felt best.[32] When the wife shook off her problems, the husband got sick. This seesaw pattern was gradually interrupted by insights that the wife gained in therapy. At the same time, her husband became increasingly upset. Finally, in what appeared to be a last-ditch effort to retain the marital status quo, which included a denial of psychological problems, the husband abruptly developed an excruciating back pain. His wife suggested a psychiatrist; the husband elected surgery.

"An obvious villain for much obscure difficulty in living had been found" in the man's disc problem, wrote Chrzanowski. No one continued to talk of "mutual suspicions, resentment, power struggles, and humiliations. A [physical] cause had been found that could be reactivated if necessary but which was placed outside of psychological boundaries."[33]

As another family therapist remarked, "spouses will sabotage their partner's attempts to remove the very symptoms that appear to cause so much dissension between them, lest this clear the field for exposure of their own pathology."[34] We saw this in Haley's example of the man who did not want his wife to be able to leave the house alone.

Sometimes the anxious twosome in a hypochondriacal family consists of a mother and her child. Often this relationship is merely a shallow disguise for an argument that is really in progress between wife and husband, but in other cases—especially among single parents—the hypochondria colors and regulates the exchange between parent and child. In some instances the child appears to function as (or to be a substitute for) one of the parent's organs about which he or she is concerned.

In *Child Psychiatry*, Leo Kanner described a case in which a mother transferred her chronic constipation to her daughter, then took the disorder back again when the child learned to go to the bathroom normally.[35] Since birth the daughter had been reared on special diets, suppositories, and enemas and had been given milk of magnesia, mineral oil, Ex-Lax, Petrolagar, cascara, castoria, castor oil, and senna leaves. Judy's bowels had become her mother's organ of hypochondriacal agitation. When Judy was given an opportunity to establish her own routine in fecal elimination without artificial help, she discovered within less than a week that she was not really constipated. But from that week on, Judy's mother became severely constipated after an interruption of six years.[36]

Although most descriptions of hypochondria focus on a single person or, at most, on a husband and wife, a few therapists have tried to analyze the complicated interconnections that exist among all family members, even extending their observations to the in-laws if this seems relevant. A series of these detailed studies was made in the 1940s by a Freudian analyst, Melita Sperling, who treated twenty child-mother pairs suffering from some form of psychosomatic complaint.[37] Each pair shared what Sperling called a "psychosomatic" or "symbiotic" type of relationship based on mutual but ambivalent dependency.

> The mother, in every one of these cases, had an unconscious
> need to keep the child in a helpless and dependent state . . .
> [and] the child reacted to the unconscious need of the mother
> with correspondingly unconscious obedience; it was as though
> the child were given a command to get sick, which meant in
> reality, to stay dependent and helpless.[38]

The unspoken remainder of this exchange was, "if you don't stay sick and dependent, I won't love you." A hypochondriacal or psychosomatic disorder, says Sperling, can be seen to equal an ambivalent attempt on the part of the child to break away from the mother but keep her love. The hypochondriac gets sick, which is his way of agreeing to be dependent, yet at the same time his symptoms drive the mother away, which expresses the hypochondriac's desire to be rid of her. As Haley pointed out years later, symptomatic behavior is punishing. In fact he sometimes encouraged a client to ask the family member with the headache at bedtime or any chronic complaint, "Why are you punishing me?"[39] The question is inevitably met with denial—"The symptom has nothing to do with you"—but it makes it considerably more difficult to indulge the symptom fully.

What seems evident from combining the major insights from the lives of Etty Darwin, Sara Teasdale, Matt Bramble, and the others is that the family hypochondriac is often an ambivalently dependent person who wants to think of himself as responsible and fully adult but who is, in fact, unsure that he can make it on his own or assume full responsibility. Afraid to deal honestly with people for fear weakness will show (or, one could say, unable to deal honestly because of unacknowledged fear or weakness), he or she unconsciously disguises dependence as sickness. Whatever the symptoms, they allow the hypochondriac to seek power covertly by engaging in a dialogue of innuendo and half-truths with persons who accept this inexplicitness for reasons of their own. Hypochondriacs thus establish a series of *mutually dependent relationships*. Their sickness, with or without depression, fear of disease, or psychosomatic complication, both disrupts and stabilizes these relationships. Not only does their illness function as a substitute for deeper, more dangerous conflicts but it also provides a way for hypochondriacs to punish their spouses and themselves (yet avoid personal blame, considering that symptoms, as everyone knows, are involuntary). They also sidestep onerous tasks yet avoid social blame because their actions are neither rebellious nor insane. While all this pushing and pulling is going on, hypochondria can still foster the illusion that the members of a family all share a tender concern for one another.

Seen in the family setting, hypochondria appears very similar to the institutionalization of paralyzing ambiguity. The disorder provides a complicated way of avoiding the dangers—and

benefits—of honest expression, and as long as the family's transactions are regulated by hypochondria, the hypochondriac and
spouse and children are likely to go nowhere and do nothing.

"The drunks stay drunk, the Catholics go to Mass, the
bounders bound. We can't have changes—throws the balance
off."[40]

6

HYPOCHONDRIACS AND THEIR DOCTORS

No disease is more troublesome, either to the
Patient or Physician, than hypochondriac
Disorders; and it often happens, that thro' the
Fault of both, the Cure is either
unnecessarily protracted, or totally
frustrated.

—Robert James
Medical Dictionary

•

HYPOCHONDRIACS frequently hold the distressing belief
that doctors don't understand them and that a subtle mismatching of language and intention is leading to petty annoyances
and even permanent dislikes. They are right.

With candor not generally found in the doctor's office,
C. W. Wahl admits that "the hypochondriac occupies a low position on the scale of 'disease acceptability.' Few doctors like these
patients. We refer to them contemptuously among ourselves as
'crocks' "[1]—and "trolls," "gourds," "turkeys," "cruds," "nomads,"
"doctor-shoppers," "problem patients," "neurotics," "professional
invalids," "malingerers," "hysterical females," and, most recently, "GOMERs" (from Get Out of My Emergency Room).

Such expressions of annoyance have centuries of momentum behind them, and a typical seventeenth-century doctor railed against a demanding patient who was always sending for his own "phisitian," with only a little more respect for the goose that was laying him golden eggs than the nineteenth-century doctor who aimed his complaints at "the Abdominal Woman."[2] "There is notable in the first place a general discontent, 'disgruntlement,' and peevishness, added to which is an intense egotism, which leads the patient to regard herself and her symptoms of the utmost importance," asserted the eloquent Dr. Hutchison in his popular *Lectures on Dyspepsia*. "Her incessant demand for sympathy makes the abdominal woman a veritable vampire, sucking the vitality of all who come near her."[3]

The list of the hypochondriac's failings, like his nicknames, continues. In addition to monopolizing doctors' time and energy, "these patients are . . . ungrateful and often unappreciative of the physician's efforts. . . . They seem prideful and happy, rather than frightened, that they have foiled the best efforts of their physicians."[4]

Hypochondriacs also switch doctors, solicit reassurance only to reject it, and demand complicated regimes with medicines and special diets that they then modify beyond recognition. Their weekly visits are reported to produce in their doctors feelings of despair, hatred, the desire to punish, guilt, and overwhelming fatigue. And of all their sins the hypochondriacs' worst is the elusive suggestion of malice that pervades their artful yet innocent way of demoralizing the doctor. No wonder a physician emerges from "an organ recital" feeling he is "a privy to which all those with loose bowels come running from all directions to relieve themselves."[5]

As doctors themselves have pointed out, their dissatisfaction with hypochondriacs has been widely reciprocated. For example, Bernard de Mandeville, himself a doctor, hypochondriac, and author of *A Treatise of the Hypochondriack and Hysterick Passions* (1711), vigorously criticized the superficial, ineffective, contrary, pompous, hasty, and frequently injurious practices of medical men. "The Arrogance of Physicians in general, and the great Knowledge, which they are obliged to pretend to are deservedly Censur'd and Ridiculed by all Men of Sence," he wrote, to the annoyance of his peers.[6]

Since de Mandeville's time other hypochondriacs have added innumerable refinements to what in Britain is called "doctor-bashing." Wrote Matt Bramble sarcastically to his doctor from the Hot Well in Bath:

> Between friends, I think every man of tolerable parts ought, at my time of day, to be both physician and lawyer, as far as his own constitution and property are concerned. . . . And consequently [I] may be supposed to know something of the matter, although I have not taken regular courses in physiology, *et cetera et cetera*. In short, I have for some time been of opinion (no offence, dear doctor) that the sum of all your medical discoveries amounts to this—the more you study, the less you know.[7]

This same opinion was widely held in the United States in the early 1800s. At that time doctors were sometimes called "the nutcrackers of the angels" and were supposedly used by the heavenly host to pry souls out of the shells that surrounded them.

Continuing the modern hypochondriac's litany of complaints, not only can the doctor's social status and special knowledge be devalued but the doctor himself can be called a hypochondriac. "I am thoroughly irritated by the suggestion that information which is harmless to the doctor himself would, if permitted to invade the 'lay' mind, create problems," wrote an exasperated reader of an editorial suggesting that articles in the magazine *Health* might foster hypochondria. "In my own experience . . . , the most gifted hypochondriacs are those with a medical training."[8]

Still another way to cut doctors down to size is to let a good doctor (which often means a recently acquired one) criticize the bad doctors for you. "So he looks at me and says, 'You mean to tell me that with *this back* you haven't had a myelogram? Who's been treating you?' 'Everyone in the whole damn country,' I said, 'that's who.' "[9]

Although hypochondriacs have generally gotten along better with their doctors in the past than at present, the literature of every age illustrates their battles. Almost all suggest that the central problem is not one of personalities—all doctors are not pompous and all hypochondriacs are not wretched complainers—or solely one of mechanical difficulties involving too little time and too many patients. Rather, the problem centers on the uncomfortable relationship that characteristically exists between the two parties. Doctors might complain of disagreeable personalities, but they usually mean that the *encounters* with hypochondriacs are uncomfortable; and hypochondriacs might proclaim that medicine is worthless but mean, in fact, that they feel misunderstood. What is wrong, then, with the relationship between the two, and why, despite earnest efforts on both sides, is the exchange so frequently unsatisfactory?

Part of the answer stems from the fact that it is no longer as economically or socially advantageous to treat hypochondriacs as it was in the past, and this change can be traced without much difficulty to the advent of the scientific method and germ theory, which remodeled both doctors' training and their daily routine. For most of our history, medicine has been an art, not a science, and its practitioners have used experience and intuition to treat maladies that seemed as numerous and variable as human beings themselves. There was, in fact, such a sense that every disorder was an individualized combination of bad climate, imbalanced temperament, poor diet, and emotional distress that Hippocrates, and many after him, classified each case by the name of the patient rather than by the name of the disease. Each case seemed to have more personal idiosyncrasies than it had generalized symptoms, and physicians, many of whom were retained by wealthy families just as painters or gardeners were, fully expected to deal with personalities as well as with what we would call purely physical problems. Hypochondria was typical of the "compound mixed maladies" that physicians were called upon to treat, and although the disorder was often chronic and unresponsive, at least it had the advantage of assuring many doctors a fairly steady income.

John Moore, in his *Medical Sketches* (1786), estimated that his colleagues received five-sixths of their income from the treatment of

> imaginary complaints, or such as would have disappeared fully as soon as they had been left to themselves. But this ought not to be imputed as a crime to the physician; if an old lady cannot dine with comfort till he has felt her pulse, looked at her tongue, and told her whether her chicken should be roasted or boiled, it is reasonable he should be paid for his trouble.[10]

What seems unusual to us about Moore's example is that the doctor is as content to spend an hour each evening with a fussy old lady as he is to care for acutely ill patients. (Of course in Moore's day he could not help many of the latter anyway.)

Not much more than a century later, with the wide acceptance of germ theory and with the more effective treatments that the theory made possible, doctors' attitudes changed. The exciting idea that diseases were specific entities, each caused by a single kind of germ and each best treated by a single drug, soon led doctors to feel most productive when they were treating specific diseases, not compound mixed maladies.

As the focus on acute illness sharpened, the prestige of certain kinds of doctors rose. The surgeon, the clearest example of the kind of "doer" who daily combats life-threatening injuries and diseases and fixes them, came to epitomize social and economic success. He was followed closely by such specialists as cardiologists and anesthesiologists. Farther down the scale came the internists and general practitioners who, in spite of germ theory, still functioned as hand-holders and morale-boosters as well as curers. At the low end of the scale were, and still are, dermatologists, plastic surgeons, and psychiatrists.

The urge to effect swift and dramatic cures—in other words, to act like a surgeon—may spring from a consideration of economics as much as of prestige. The way in which medical practices are set up in America does not make therapy and other time-consuming treatments very profitable. Doctors who are paid by the visit (the fee-for-service method) do far better financially if they encourage short, single visits rather than long ones with many follow-ups. A second or third visit frequently yields 20 to 30 percent less income than an initial visit. Clearly the tedious treatment of hypochondriacs means a loss of both income and prestige. It also takes time away from more acutely ill patients, and for modern doctors who need more time and not more patients, long-winded visitors are a real problem.

According to Ford,[11] the change that often occurs in a doctor—from being patient and altruistic during the student years to feeling pressured and somewhat cynical at the height of a career—typically occurs during the years of internship and residency. Deprived of sleep, regular meals, and other forms of sustenance, the young doctor becomes particularly annoyed with dependent hypochondriacs who want precisely those hours of attentive caring that the doctor misses so much. In this frame of mind the doctor tolerates the acutely ill, but hypochondriacs become the enemy.

Still another reason for doctors' disinclination to take on a waiting room full of hypochondriacs is that it is a tremendous strain to differentiate between the anxious and sick and the just plain anxious. "Every new complaint presents me with a difficult decision," said E. Langdon Burwell, a local internist. "Is this new complaint just another expression of anxiety? Or is it the first sign of illness? How do I make a diagnosis without administering tests which may be frightening, expensive and unnecessary? And if I don't order tests and the hypochondriac really was sick, then I'm left with a bad taste in my mouth for a long, long time."[12]

Taken together the social, economic, and emotional reasons for not treating hypochondriacs make a persuasive case, and one might reasonably predict that problem patients would be cast aside along with house calls, the seven-day work week, and other unrewarding aspects of doctoring. But doctors have not been able to get rid of hypochondriacs, and this enforced attention to a disorder no longer considered either appropriate or profitable is the source of much friction.

If a doctor is forced to consider a class of problems against his or her will, the relationship with the hypochondriac—the person doing the forcing—will be strained. The simplest solution would be to abolish the relationship. But is this what doctors really want? And will hypochondriacs agree to take their problems elsewhere?

Medical sociologist David Mechanic tried to determine why patients insist on bringing nonmedical problems to their doctors.[13] First, he believes that patients who seek to repress anxiety and deny emotional problems feel far more comfortable with a medical doctor and a discussion of "physical" problems than with a psychotherapist. Second, he feels that as opportunities for close personal contacts diminish and as our population becomes more mobile, further weakening the ties of friendship, problems that in the past were handled among friends and family are now taken to formal, paid helpers such as lawyers and doctors. The more affluent the society, the more quickly this transition occurs. Finally, doctors are victims of their own vastly improved image. Our current idea of "doctor," says Mechanic, is of a smart, capable, interested adviser—an attractive ally in times of trouble.

When attempts have been made to separate doctors from their role as counselors, as was done by the Health Insurance Plan of New York City when it tried to divert nonmedical problems to teams of nurses and social workers, it became apparent that most patients were reluctant to consider their problems as nonmedical and, however labeled, to discuss them with anyone but the doctor. "Thus, regardless of whether physicians wish to deal with emotional problems, it is clear that patients with such difficulties will continue to seek their help even when other channels of help are made available."[14]

This is an awkward situation. Physicians trained to treat

physical problems are forced to consider the vaguer dysfunctions of the psyche, and the social and personal reactions that tend to perpetuate this mismatch show no signs of disappearing.

In his study of doctors, patients, and illness, which was based on weekly seminars held over the course of almost three years, Michael Balint, a Hungarian-born psychiatrist, identified six reasons why most doctors try to restrict their practice to physical diseases.[15] In addition to his medical training, which is devoted almost exclusively to physical illness and which treats social and psychological issues superficially or with contempt,[16] Balint maintains that a doctor desires to keep in step with colleagues and not set up a noticeably different kind of practice. Also, simple physical diagnoses satisfy physicians that they have done their best, and even if the patient suffers or dies, the doctor doesn't feel guilty if he or she has made the correct diagnosis.

But psychological suffering cannot be allowed to run its course the way heart disease can, and with the former the doctor may never feel satisfied that he or she has tried the right treatment or done all that is possible. Psychological suffering also involves the doctor on a personal level. Unlike a physical problem in which the distinction is clear between sick patient and well doctor, psychological problems force the doctor to reveal his or her own attitudes concerning sex, maturity, goals in life, health, happiness—in short, a philosophy of life. There are times when a doctor has no stomach for all this introspection.

Balint further points out that the treatment of physical disorders is a good deal simpler than that involved for psychological ones. What does a general practitioner prescribe when the diagnosis is "neurotic"? Finally, Balint feels that doctors consider physical illnesses more dangerous than emotional complaints and therefore more worthy of their attention.

All these factors help explain why a doctor feels uneasy when presented with emotional complaints rather than physical illnesses, but this is only part of the disagreement that exists between the doctor and a hypochondriac. The nature of the patient is as important as the nature of the disease; predictably, doctor and hypochondriac disagree on what constitutes both a "good" patient and a "good" doctor. "Every doctor has a vague, but almost unshakably firm, idea of *how a patient ought to behave when ill*," Balint maintains. "Although this idea is anything but explicit and concrete, it is immensely powerful, and influences practically every detail of the doctor's work with his patients."[17]

The concept of the good patient has changed over time, but in essence doctors have always expected a patient "to wish his own health," as Seneca put it nearly two thousand years ago. In the *Anatomy of Melancholy*, Burton adds that good patients should not hide their symptoms out of shame or for other reasons unduly postpone consultation. They should follow their doctors' orders and not be miserly when it comes to paying. Good patients must have confidence in their doctors and must not change physicians so often that it can be said of them, "they try many and profit by none."[18]

Modern refinements on this picture of the good patient suggest that patients should share, or at least admire, the values of their doctors. Among psychotherapists it is acknowledged that the patient with the YAVIS syndrome has the best chance of receiving good treatment and of recovering. YAVIS stands for Young, Attractive, Verbal, Intelligent, and Successful. Except that it would spoil the acronym, Appreciative could be added.

Recalling the invectives hurled at hypochondriacs, it is easy to see that crocks and turkeys violate almost every rule of good patienthood. Most significantly, they don't seem to wish their own health. This puts doctors and hypochondriacs on a collision course, the doctor's self-esteem demanding he cure the illness, the patient's emotional equilibrium demanding a chronic disability. Their consistent failure to improve makes it difficult for the doctor to feel effective, just as their lack of consideration and appreciation makes it hard for him to like them and thus feel kind and friendly. Few doctors can tolerate being cast in the dual role of nasty person and impotent healer.

Turning to the patients who worry unduly about their health, what do they want from a doctor? For one thing, they want the reassurance that a physical problem lies at the root of their troubles. In other words, they want the doctor to find something physically wrong with them. As far as a hypochondriac is concerned, a good doctor comes up with something more than negative findings and actually helps the hypochondriac to organize his or her complaints along physical rather than psychological lines. The doctor who finds a suspicion of hypoglycemia or gall bladder trouble is an ally and the finding a source of profound relief—for a while.

Like many patients, hypochondriacs also want a smart, kind, and effective doctor who devotes his full time to caring for the sick, who treats all patients equally whether he happens to like them or not, and who places each patient's welfare above his own immediate desires. Obviously doctors don't fulfill the expectations of our society's good doctor stereotype any more than cowboys fulfill the cowboy image or pilots live up to the pilot image, but the stereotype is what a patient expects and points to the areas where doctors are most likely to be criticized.

In addition to having a doctor who finds real diseases, a hypochondriac also wants a special and often intensely personal relationship with the doctor, as did Alice James, invalid sister of the novelist Henry James and psychologist William James.

"I was charmed at first with the Slavic flavour of our intercourse,"[19] she wrote, referring to her treatment by a Russian doctor who claimed to cure nervous diseases with electric currents and exercise. But as had happened nearly a dozen times before, her initial enthusiasm turned to bitterness. It was not that the doctor's electric currents failed to ameliorate her ill-defined complaints; rather, the promise of respectful intimacy of the doctor-patient relationship lapsed quickly into mutual frustration. From feeling "a wonderful change quite as if I had been transformed" and from describing the doctor as "kind and easy to get on with," she soon quit the cure and referred to the doctor as "a creature with the moral substance of a monkey."[20]

Alice wanted a great deal of attention from her doctors.

She wanted them not only to get to the secret heart of her troubles but also to recognize her as a superior person, a diamond in the rough. This paradoxical request for a powerful person who would simultaneously protect her, like a father would a small child, and respect her, like a husband would a self-sufficient woman, made it impossible for Alice to find a satisfactory doctor. She became furoius when, in one way or another, each intimated that she was responsible for her troubles and for their solution. Like so many dependent individuals (and her upbringing made dependency all but inevitable), she spent her life trying to get someone else to make her happy.

Other hypochondriacs want their doctors simultaneously to be gods and scapegoats, mothers and wives, and so forth. Not surprisingly, the ways in which a problem patient and the doctor maintain any of these intense relationships often resemble hypochondriacs' dealings with their families.

The complex interactions whereby two people fit together so as to bring out the worst in each other is a morbidly fascinating topic. In the article "Taking Care of the Hateful Patient," James Groves identifies half the problem when he describes three groups of patients, each with a different kind of doctor-patient relationship.[21] According to Groves, there are "dependent clingers," who need endless support for innumerable ills, "entitled demanders," who want to believe that their doctors' unfathomable incompetence is a major part of their problem, and "manipulative help-rejectors," who seek an indissoluble marriage with a healer whose efforts they consistently frustrate.

B. K. Singh and colleagues complemented Groves's concept of problem patients with what could be called a taxonomy of problem doctors.[22] So, for example, dependent clingers are *both* resented and encouraged to continue their endless complaining by a doctor who is either overcautious, needs his or her patients to be sick so that the doctor can feel well by comparison, or finds it easier to treat trivial physical symptoms than to address a psychological problem. Similarly, entitled demanders might actually be pushed toward their disagreeable stance by a hostile or punitive doctor who sees malingering in every symptom he or she cannot explain.

A different way of categorizing the doctor-patient relationship is suggested by Drs. Szasz and Hollender, who see doctors and patients playing out the kinds of relationships that exist between parents and their children.[23] In the "activity-passivity" model the physician acts like the parent of an infant or very young child. He or she makes all the decisions. More popular in our culture is the "guidance-cooperation" model,[24] which, while still endowing the doctor with the power of a kindly parent does assume that the patient-as-child has the ability to gratefully follow the doctor's "orders." A relatively new kind of relationship is the "mutual participation" model in which the patient, now treated as an adult, takes responsibility for his own health and uses the doctor as a consultant. It is a partnership. Each model is best suited for certain types of patients, diseases, and situations.

As we have seen with Alice James, some hypochondriacs want the protection associated with the paternalistic guidance-cooperation model and the respect, but not responsibility, that goes with the mutual participation model. Viewed in this way, one of the symptoms (if you will) of hypochondria is a distorted relationship with helpers which often takes the form of excessive but vigorously unacknowledged dependence. If this is so, doctors seeking to "manage" hypochondriacs are in a curious position. For genuine improvement to take place in the dependent patient, a change must also take place in the relationship such that the doctor relinquishes power and management and encourages the hypochondriac to take more responsibility for his or her own care. This would move the relationship toward the guidance-cooperation model that traditional physicians dislike. In sum, it is possible that the only doctors who can help hypochondriacs are those who can actively foster an egalitarian partnership and do not unconsciously want their patients to remain obediently childlike.

This sheds new light on the cycle of hope and disappointment that so commonly runs through the relationships a hypochondriac establishes with doctors. Perhaps the sharp-tongued Alice James and others like her who meet each physician with unrealistic hopes and leave in disillusionment may also be expressing some measure of realistic hope for the tentative beginnings of an egalitarian relationship and disappointment at the condescension or rejection of that request that so often is found instead.

Having established that doctors and hypochondriacs disagree about what constitutes appropriate complaints, appropriate doctor and patient behavior, and an appropriate relationship, it is time to confront a different form of misunderstanding: the faulty communication that results from the double meaning of the word "I." Normally a person uses "I" in two separate and easily distinguishable ways. In the sentence "I am tired," "I" is used subjectively and is equivalent to "my entire person, my being." In the sentence "I am sick," "I" is used objectively and means "my body, the object." If a hypochondriac unconsciously uses the subjective "I" in place of the objective one, he is actually saying to the doctor "I am sick," meaning "I am a damaged person." Unaware of this double entendre, the doctor answers, "no, you aren't sick," meaning "you don't have a damaged body."

According to communications analyst Jay Haley,[25] this misunderstanding is one version of a common power struggle in which each exchange between doctor and hypochondriac is both a trading of information and a comment on who is in control of the relationship. To give a simple example, if a doctor tells his patient to take aspirin, the patient might say "Yes," acknowledging that in this situation the doctor is the boss. He might say, "No, I don't think that's a good idea," asserting that he is the boss and risking some negative response from the doctor. Or he might mix the message and say, "No, aspirin makes me sick to my stomach." In this last instance the patient has assumed the role of boss, but because he is not responsible for how his body responds to aspirin (or for any other symptom, such as headache at bedtime), he can deny that he meant to say anything about the relationship at all. Using his symptoms continually to muddle the distinction between the subjective and objective "I," the patient manages to get his way without taking the responsibility that normally goes along with wanting to be boss. The doctor mutters something under his breath about the tyranny of the weak and wonders how he manages to lose control every time he sees this patient. The patient wonders why the doctor is annoyed.

Although the issues that can precipitate misunderstanding between doctor and patient are more numerous than "your heaven hath stars, Horatio," there seem to be three primary ways in which the pair actually deals with the question of illness. In the first the doctor keeps reassuring the patient that he does not have a damaged body and the patient keeps repeating "but I am a damaged person." In the second the doctor says, "Yes, there is some damage to your body," and the two settle down to deal with a lifelong series of physical illnesses that skirt the central problem. In the third the physician reclassifies his patient's complaints as psychological and proceeds as if he were a therapist. Different types of hypochondriacs—for instance, the anxious worriers and depressed complainers—react differently to these three formats, and doctors respond in various ways as well.

The exchange between doctor and patient that is based on continual reassurance is initiated when a patient unconsciously selects an appropriate illness to substitute for some underlying problem. Such a patient apparently tries on a variety of complaints until finding one that is sufficient—that is, serious enough to express his level of psychic distress and legitimate enough to be accepted as a genuine disability by family, friends, and doctor. During this early stage the patient is likely to bring this proposed illness to a doctor, who may well reject the proposal by saying there is nothing physically wrong. Outwardly reassured but inwardly rebuffed, the patient may offer a second illness, and if this too is rejected, even with the kindest reassurance, the patient is likely to feel frustrated and confused for reasons he cannot identify. As Michael Balint states, "when the doctor confronts these people with his finding that nothing is physically wrong, it is tantamout to a demand to give up the carefully constructed fantasies and to face up to bitter reality and its conflicts."[26]

Reassurance, then, pushes the patient to acknowledge that his illness is not the real problem and that the fear or neediness he still feels must stem from some deeper source—a threatening prospect. "If this insight were as simple as the primitive procedure of reassurance presupposes," Balint continues, "most patients would have arrived at it without outside help."[27]

If a physician committed to the "primitive procedure of reassurance" neither punishes nor avoids his hypochondriacal patients, he has the option of committing himself to decades of successive reassurances. One of the fourteen practitioners who took part in Balint's seminars gave a fine example of this time-consuming routine.

For sixteen years Dr. G had a patient who never ceased complaining. Mr. Z suffered pains in every part of his body, and the number of diagnostic tests—all negative—affixed to his medical record was so enormous that his folders required special storage. Although convinced that no one could do him any good, Mr. Z came to the doctor's office almost every Friday for a bottle of medicine. On each visit to the clinic Mr. Z told his doctor which part of his body hurt and what he thought was wrong with it, but week after week his ideas were rejected. Although the doctor kept insisting that there was nothing physically wrong with Mr. Z, he did acknowledge his patient's discomfort, and for those aches and pains he prescribed scores of different medicines. He even handed Mr. Z his pharmacopoeia upon occasion and let him choose a medicine he thought might help.

Recognizing the doctor as a sympathetic ally, Mr. Z did not become a doctor-shopper switching from clinic to clinic. He remained faithful to his doctor, but he resented being told that there was "nothing wrong" and expressed his resentment by repeatedly telling his doctor that "nothing helped"—in other words, that the doctor was ineffective. Because the doctor accepted this role of well-meaning but impotent physician where Mr. Z was concerned, the two got along with each other for more than sixteen years.

Alice James was also told again and again that there was nothing physically wrong with her, but rather than settling with a single physician and accepting partial symptomatic relief, she switched from doctor to doctor in an increasingly desperate effort to find a personally as well as socially acceptable reason for her feelings of failure and unhappiness. "Ever since I have been ill," she wrote, twenty-four years after her initial bout of nervous troubles, "I have longed and longed for some palpable disease, no matter how conventionally dreadful a label it might have, but I was always driven back to stagger alone under the monstrous mass of subjective sensations, which that sympathetic being 'the medical man' has had no higher inspiration that to assure me I was personally responsible for."[28] Only when she got cancer late in life did she experience "the enormous relief of [this] uncompromising verdict."[29]

If the process of continual reassurance with its proposals and counterproposals becomes tiresome, the patient is likely to look for a new doctor or the doctor will get rid of the patient. Within a group practice, problem patients are frequently given to the physician who has most recently joined the group, and he or she will pass these patients along upon gaining seniority. There are rougher ways of getting rid of problem patients, and doctors consciously or unconsciously punish hypochondriacs by tricking them, overcharging them, making them wait, or subjecting them to disagreeable tests and medicines. Bragged W. C. Alvarez,

> I will never forget how when I was an intern, my chum and I thought we could easily cure a psychotic man who said he had a frog in his stomach. . . . We gave him an emetic, and while he was vomiting, we slipped a frog into the basin. The man was thrilled; he felt so justified, and he was grateful. The only trouble was that he returned the next day to tell us we had been a bit too late—a dozen baby frogs had hatched out and were hopping about in his stomach.[30]

Just as thrilled, justified, and grateful as his patient, Alvarez was using an old trick, and every version of the story has the patient quickly returning with a counterproposal. Of course most hypochondriacs do not get the frog treatment, but the use of placebos is a common form of trickery.

The second kind of exchange that commonly occurs between doctor and hypochondriac is one in which a doctor keeps finding things to fix. Like the reassurance that nothing is wrong, the treatment of suspected or minor disorders is often a shot in the dark. However, the initial response of a hypochondriac to the news that something is physically wrong is often one of relief. "I like knowing that something is *really* wrong," wrote a woman who described herself in *Ms* magazine as a profound hypochondriac of long standing who finally went to a doctor to receive a bona fide diagnosis. "Now that my pain has been defined, I feel . . . that I can control it, that I don't have to be its victim."[31] In light of her long history of pains, swellings, and palpitations, it is tempting to predict that her doctor's finding will not permanently allay her fears and that the next time her problems flare up she will return for a new diagnosis as if it were a stamp of approval on her somewhat fragile "cover." The epitome of this *folie à deux* between a naive or perhaps overzealous doctor and his anxious patient is embodied in the relationship between Argan and his doctor in Molière's "The Imaginary Invalid." "Three and two makes five, and five makes ten, and ten makes twenty," Argan counts to himself at the beginning of the play. "Sixty-three francs four sous six deniers. So this month I've taken one, two, three, four, five, six, seven, eight, nine, ten, eleven, twelve enemas; and last month there were twelve doses of medicine and twenty enemas. I don't wonder that I'm not as well this month as last. I'll tell Monsieur Purgon this, so he'll set this right."[32] For his part, M. Purgon knows he has endless opportunities for repair in his faithful patient Argan and takes pains to remind him that this routine must continue. Only his medicine stands between Argan and slow digestion, bad digestion, and *no* digestion at all. Even a well-meaning physician can inadvertently reinforce hypochondria, and whenever it has been fashionable to split the disorder into a dozen or more types (one French variety being *Arganisme*, for example), doctors have included iatrogenic or physician-generated hypochondria on their lists. A German article on *Hypochondria iatrogenetica* written in 1929 lists eleven forms of doctor-inspired hypochondria. *"Hypochondria hypertonica"* is one, supposedly caused by a doctor who repeatedly takes a patient's blood pressure and notes each change with gravity. *"Hypochondria analytica"* is another, presumably caused by too many blood and urine tests. Other doctors have pointed out that psychotherapeutically augmented hypochondria exists too, although this is not included on the 1929 list, and therapists might lead their patients into discussions of bad mothers and unfulfilled relationships that are as fruitless and irrelevant as the treatment of Argan's dyspepsia. In all these iatrogenic hypochondrias doctors are inadvertently helping patients to keep their emotional problems disguised as physical complaints, and they are encouraging dependence while complaining of it in the same breath. As Singh has pointed out concerning doctor-patient relationships, and as Haley has pointed out concerning communications,[33] the mate or, in this case the doctor, of a person with symptomatic behavior opposes the behavior but also encourages it. In terms of a medical practice, "the strategy that maintains the hypochondriac's status as the child, also maintains the physician's status as the authority."[34]

If, on the other hand, a physician with a certain breadth of vision can reclassify his patient's complaints as psychological, he then has the options of suggesting psychotherapy, or keeping the reclassification to himself, of treating the hypochondriac in his own office. This is the third major form that the doctor-hypochondriac relationship takes. When a family doctor elects to treat a hypochondriac himself, he usually tries to "stabilize and maintain" each patient with a quasi-therapeutic program of regularly scheduled visits, pain relievers, and tranquilizers. Judging from the articles written by general practitioners on the management of hypochondriacs, most of these programs fit the guidance-cooperation model of the doctor-patient relationship. Thus Beverley Mead in "Management of Hypochondriacal Patients" suggests that "the physician may function more comfortably as a benevolent, but authoritative person . . . , a kind but firm parent dealing with an immature, demanding child."[35]

Mead advises doctors to prescribe aspirin and vitamins for their placebo effect and tranquilizers intermittently. Every visit should end with "a brief pep talk," which, he maintains, "has the same value as the pep talk given by a good football coach." He adds that it makes no sense to send a hypochondriac to a psychiatrist because the latter can "do little more than follow the same supportive, directive role described here."

Remembering the problems that Sara Teasdale, Alice James, Anita, and so many other hypochondriacs have had in resolving their conflicting needs for dependency and autonomy, it seems obvious that any form of management that maintains their status as children is likely to prolong their hypochondria. Perhaps these patronizing forms of management release a doctor from the usual effort to cure perfectly and forever and allow him or her to relax and assume a more tolerant attitude. And perhaps for the thousands of chronic hypochondriacs who have settled uncomfortably into this way of life, such limited benevolence may be preferable to hostility. Still, it is not exactly what they need. Paraphrasing Michael Balint, the physician's primary task is to identify the original problem that is too frightening, embarrassing, or hopeless for the patient to voice and for which the functional illness is a substitute. The physician must then try to transform the patient's symptoms (i.e., illness) into a series of personally and socially acceptable problems that come closer and closer to the underlying problem.

So much for the theory of treating hypochondriacs. In practice the theory roughly translates into *not* treating and *not* reassuring the patient until the real problem is identified, and in the meantime *listening* rather than actively guiding.

Is this "your Secret in the Cure of this difficult Distemper?" de Mandeville's hypochondriacal character asks his physician. The eighteenth-century physician answers:

> I have several. I allow myself time to hear and weigh the Complaints of my Patients . . . [and] I take pains to be well acquainted with the manner of living of my Patients . . . , not only to penetrate the Procatartick causes, but likewise the better to consult the Circumstances as well as [the] Idiosyncrasy of every particular Person.[36]

In modern terms, Balint feels that collaboration rather than guidance is the only way a doctor can discover a patient's real problems. If the underlying problems are touched on in the course of several "long interviews," the doctor will then need to provide emotional support for his or her patient while the two work together to remove accumulated layers of protective self-deception. This takes time. Balint wrote,

> It is pointless to force the patient prematurely to recognize and then renounce [his use of illness]. His need of love, concern, sympathy, and, above all, to be taken seriously must be accepted and to some extent gratified in the treatment before he can be expected to experiment with methods other than his illness of obtaining the affection and care for which he is craving.[37]

From the patient's point of view, Balint's prescription means that rather than struggling to be either the perfectly compliant patient or the totally independent person who never needs a doctor, the hypochondriac's better road toward recovery lies in actively working with a doctor to uncover the problems that underlie the present dis-ease. It is comforting to believe that in an atmosphere of mutual respect the struggle can be with these problems and not with the doctor.

7

HYPOCHONDRIA AMONG THE ELDERLY

Have mercy upon me, O God, have mercy
Upon me: years and infirmities oppress
me, terrour and anxiety beset me.
> —Samuel Johnson
> 1777

■

WITHIN OUR LARGE and largely unexamined collection of myths about the elderly there exist the contradictory beliefs that the old find a measure of serenity (at last) and that they also spend their golden years carping, complaining, and bemoaning. Poor health, in all its nasty and fascinating detail, is supposedly their central concern.

The first of these two images suggests that emotional disorders, including hypochondria, are on the wane and that by the time people reach sixty or seventy they have made peace with themselves and those around them and have less need of manipulation, self-punishment, and the other disagreeable rewards of hypochondria. The second image, that of the aged as chronic complainers, implies that hypochondria is a common disorder among the elderly.

It is extremely difficult to measure the serenity or discontent of the elderly, but if sociological studies are even marginally accurate, they reveal that health is of primary interest to most of the approximately 25.5 million Americans over age sixty-five, and illness is an overriding concern.[1] Retirement community brochures to the contrary notwithstanding, most old people apparently worry more about their health, take more vitamins and tranquilizers, and spend more time talking about disease than do the young or middle-aged.

"One cannot work in the field of geriatrics without becoming aware of the large number of patients labelled hypochondriacs," states a representative paper entitled "Hypochondriasis and the Elderly."[2] And according to another, "hypochondria is probably the next most frequent functional psychiatric disorder in the later years, behind depressive and paranoid reactions. It is substantially more frequent among older women than men and it seems to increase in frequency with advancing age."[3]

For convenience, complaints of ill health among the elderly may be divided into three categories. Most common are complaints centering on the discomforts and restrictions of physical decline, or, in hospital jargon, "the dwindles." Second are physical complaints that mask social problems—primarily a drop in real income, increasing isolation, and the loss of status. Getting sick frequently seems to be the only way some elderly individuals can get sympathy and support from their relatives, neighbors, and doctors. Third are physical complaints that mask psychosocial problems, and, as with younger persons, this is where most hypochondria among the elderly is found. (There is a curious variation within this category in which anxious middle-aged children project their own hypochondriacal concerns onto their elderly parents. "Father must not go out for fear of bronchitis, he must not smoke because it is bad for his heart, he must not play bridge in the evening because it interferes with his sleep, and so forth.")[4]

With complaints of ill health being used to express dissatisfaction with physical, social, and emotional conditions and with the elderly being particularly vulnerable in each of these areas, it is no wonder that a flood of physical complaints pours from the aged. Most refer to actual infirmities, but certainly a portion can be attributed to hypochondria. It is probably safe to assume that there is an increase in the incidence of this disorder with advancing age, not only because illness is such an effective way of getting care but also because illness is considered a more legitimate expression of frustration for old people than wife-beating, delinquency, and even alcoholism. Especially for men, age narrows the selection of acceptable revenges and defenses.

The important questions to answer, therefore, are these: "How is hypochondria generated among the elderly?"—that is, what triggers new cases? And "under what conditions are the chronic cases left over from youth and middle-age maintained?" For answers we must look at the three kinds of stress—biological, social, and psychological—that all but a tiny minority of the elderly are subjected to and see if these pressures push the aged toward the emotional paralysis of hypochondria.

One man who escaped none of the stresses of old age, who was eccentrically hypochondriacal, and who has done us the service of recording his lifelong battle against this and other infirmities is James Boswell's friend and mentor, Samuel Johnson. Essayist, moralist, literary critic, and author of a famous dictionary, Johnson is still remembered because he was one of the most intensely honest and articulate men ever to fix his attention on the strange adventure of human life and because his own adventure became the subject of the most famous biography in literature, Boswell's *The Life of Samuel Johnson*.

Johnson's mother was forty when her first child, Sam, was born in 1709. Finding that she could not nurse the child adequately, she sent him to a foster mother for several months, where he contracted scrofula, a form of tuberculosis, which severely affected his sight and hearing. His condition required an operation that was performed without anesthesia. (Compared to this experience the examples of medical mismanagement studied by Anna Freud seem mild.) As a young boy Johnson also had smallpox and the usual respiratory and intestinal infections. Many of these conditions returned in exaggerated forms as Johnson entered late middle age. Nor did he escape the normal changes of aging. His thick, unruly hair grew thin and white, his skin wrinkled, some teeth rotted, his spine bent, and his height decreased. Gradually his muscular strength diminished and he was slower to react. His sleep became increasingly disturbed, and his vision and hearing, poor to begin with, deteriorated still further. His heart and kidneys grew less efficient, and he had circulation problems that in many persons lead to brain damage or what is loosely termed senility.

But as Johnson clearly understood, it was disease—the bronchitis he suffered every winter, the eye inflammations, the emphysema and dropsy—that pushed a man toward hypochondriacal self-indulgence and depression more vigorously than the social or emotional insults of aging. "It is so *very* difficult," said he, "for a sick man not to be a scoundrel."[5]

And the elderly are frequently sick. In the United States eight of ten noninstitutionalized persons over age sixty-five have one or more chronic diseases such as arthritis, bronchitis, diabetes, or heart disease.[6] If lesser disabilities such as partial deafness, foot defects, and anemia are included, then virtually all old people fall into the chronically ill category. Certain doctors in Scotland found an average of five to eleven disorders in each of their elderly patients.[7]

All this illness makes the physician's job of distinguishing between organic disease and hypochondria much more difficult. With elderly patients a doctor must expect each complaint to indicate a physical problem, and even if the symptoms are in fact generated by emotional troubles, the doctor will almost surely find some chronic disability that can be blamed.

In addition to complicating the doctor's task, chronic disease can precipitate neurotic reactions. In a study entitled "Sex Differences in the Neurotic Reaction of the Aged," K. Bergmann identified twenty-nine predisposing factors. Among the more important were physical disabilities. In fact being ill and being female were the two factors most closely associated with neurosis.[8] Among elderly men, having a heart attack was especially likely to trigger a combination of depression and hypochondria. Many doctors consider this common postcardiac preoccupation with pulse, diet, and breathing a natural and appropriate reaction, but only if it is transitory (about a year), associated solely with the heart, and does not precipitate withdrawal from other people. Unfortunately, the preoccupation can continue for the rest of the person's life. Similar forms of hypochondria are common among diabetics and arthritics and are probably generated by the same feelings of overpowering vulnerability that can trigger hypochondria among children who are chronically ill.

A man whose excellent health deteriorated into hypochondria after severe bouts of malaria and pneumonia was the Russian novelist and philosopher Leo Tolstoy. In his seventies he fell ill and upon his almost miraculous recovery became extremely preoccupied with his health. "Hour after hour, from morning till night, he thinks of nothing but his body and how to look after it," wrote his wife.[9]

Unlike Tolstoy, Samuel Johnson waged a stubborn battle against self-preoccupations, including the physical concern for his body that was naturally prompted by his bronchitis, dropsy, and arthritis. One of the cruelest aspects of these diseases was that they robbed him of a way of coping with despair. Ever since his first emotional crisis, Johnson had tried to walk off his anxieties. As a young man he had walked from his home in Lichfield to Birmingham and back, a round-trip of about thirty miles, and later in life he roamed for hours around London, swam, rode, and even ran with an awkward and lumbering gait. But in his sixties Johnson's lungs seemed encumbered, as he put it. His breath failed him and it became increasingly uncomfortable to walk. "How much happiness is gained," he had written, then corrected himself, "how much misery escaped, by frequent and violent agitation of the body."[10]

Aging, then, with its physical restrictions and gathering disabilities makes every old person more vulnerable to preoccupations with the body. Not only does the physical discomfort of the disease focus a person's attention on his body but being infirm puts him in a relatively less powerful position vis-à-vis spouse, children, nurses, or peers, which in itself can be distressing. Finally, physical disabilities often deprive an old person of the walking, gardening, swimming, or puttering that consoled him in earlier years.

The second broad category of stresses that impinge upon all but a few of the elderly is social. Money is the most important within this category, mainly because its presence or absence substantially ameliorates or exacerbates the other stresses, such as loss of status as a result of retirement (or children leaving home), loneliness after the deaths of relatives and friends, isolation that arises from moving, and so on.

Sociologists tend to view the aged as an underprivileged minority group in our society, meaning that the elderly do not have the same power or responsibility that younger adults have and do not take part in many of the activities enjoyed by other adults. Work, serious schooling, .and sex (supposedly) are examples.

This lack of social power has not always been characteristic of advanced age. Western cultures have generally considered old age one of the less desirable periods of life but one of considerable responsibility. This was true until the end of the eighteenth century. Whether ancient Greece, medieval Europe, or colonial America is chosen to illustrate the point, it can be seen that among landowners the greatest social power traditionally resided in the eldest male. Even if the patriarch's sons were in their forties and fifties, management of the land and therefore much of the direction of daily life was overseen by the aged father. This often created resentment among the young, and for centuries the grasping old man, hanging on to his domain, was the butt of satire—a form of criticism rarely wasted on the weak.

In *Gulliver's Travels* (1726), Jonathan Swift introduces Gulliver to a repulsive race of immortal Struldbrugs. These perpetually senile old wrecks "were not only opinionative, peevish,

covetous, morose, vain, talkative, but incapable of friendship and
dead to all natural affection."

> In talking they forgot the common appelation of things, and
> the names of persons, even of those who are their nearest
> friends and relations. For the same reason they can never
> amuse themselves with reading, because their memory will not
> serve to carry them from the beginning of a sentence to the
> end.[11]

The reluctant veneration of the elderly did not outlive
Swift by more than half a century. Broadly speaking, the authority of age ended in the same wave of social revolutions that
swept personal freedom to a position of ultimate value and began
to weaken the authority of church, monarch, ruling class, the
white race, and the patriarch. The relationship between young
and old changed profoundly as the result of the new emphasis on
liberty and equality, and these changes were later reinforced by
industrialization, new policies of retirement, and government support of the indigent and the elderly. Today the social power of
senior citizens is vastly diminished, and few people over sixty-
five would maintain that the golden years have enhanced their
status. In fact, the opposite is closer to the truth. Gerontophobia,
the fear of aging, is reflected in our slang, fashions, books, mov-
ies, and lies about age. (Men, not women, between thirty-nine
and fifty are the most likely to round their age off to a lower
number, according to the Census Bureau.) As gerontologist and
popular writer Alex Comfort put it, we view our aged as "un-
intelligent, unemployable, crazy and asexual."[12]

For many elderly men a loss of social standing occurs upon
retirement. The most obvious component of this loss is usually
financial, and it is now the rule, rather than the exception, for
persons over sixty-five to grow poorer year by year.[13] It is a
person's self-esteem, however, including his or her public status,
that often is severely buffeted. Some retirees feel cheated by the

ease with which their business glides on without them, and many find it difficult to discover a substitute activity toward which he or she will feel the same genuine interest and commitment.[14]

"In old age we should wish still to have passions strong enough to prevent us turning in upon our selves," wrote Simone de Beauvoir in *The Coming of Age*.[15] "One would like some fresh unexpected turn," confided the French novelist André Gide, "and one does not know what to invent."[16] It is common to trifle with imitation work and mediocre talents.

One of the remarkably common options available to retired parents and businessmen and women is to redirect their attention toward their own bodies. Among older women this infrequently leads to a conviction that they, and their homes, are infested. Typically they arrive at the doctor's office with complaints of itching and pricking that they believe are caused by mites, lice, nits, or insects. "Their complaints are expressed in a lively, natural, credible way," writes George Ladee, a doctor specializing in hypochondria.[17]

> They describe how they are suffering, and they feel precisely how the vermin move. They are constantly taking counter-measures. . . . They disinfect clothes, bedding, and their dwellings and chase the malefactors with skin-scrapers, dust-combs, and vacuum cleaners. A visit to the doctor is often postponed for quite a while because they feel embarrassed and when neither the general practitioner nor the dermatologist can find any dermatological complaints, they often bring the alleged evidence along in a box.

(The boxes usually contain dust and dandruff.) Psychiatrists rarely see these patients, Ladee reports, but almost every dermatologist has treated at least one case, and exterminators are familiar with dozens. Sometimes these delusions of infestation are classed as circumscribed or monosymptomatic hypochondria,[18] which doctors often feel is only superficially related to common hypochondria. The problem may be more closely akin to the non-schizophrenic delusional states and is reported to respond to the antipsychotic drug pimozide.[19]

The male counterpart of the woman who fills her days fighting dirt and vermin is the "man in advanced middle life, generally retired from business, who makes his health his hobby, and who collects symptoms as others collect stamps or old china. Retired Army men seem to be particularly subject to the complaint."[20]

The epitome of the person who replaces former occupations with concern for disease is the narrator in Jerome K. Jerome's *Three Men in a Boat*, a story the author insists is hopelessly and incurably true.[21]

> I remember going to the British Museum one day to read up the treatment for some slight ailment of which I had a touch—hay fever, I fancy it was. I got down the book, and read all I came to read; and then, in an unthinking moment, I idly turned the leaves, and began to indolently study diseases, generally. I forget which was the first distemper I plunged into—some fearful, devastating scourge, I know—and, before I had glanced half down the list of 'premonitory symptoms,' it was borne in upon me that I had fairly got it.
>
> I sat for a while frozen with horror; and then in the listlessness of despair, I again turned over the pages. I came to typhoid fever—read the symptoms—discovered that I had typhoid fever, must have had it for months without knowing it—wondered what else I had got; turned up St. Vitus's Dance—found, as I expected, that I had that too—began to get interested in my case, and determined to sift it to the bottom, and so started alphabetically—read up ague, and learnt that I was sickening for it, and that the acute stage would commence in about another fortnight. Bright's disease, I was relieved to find, I had only in a modified form, and, so far as that was concerned, I might live for years. Cholera I had, with severe complications; and diphtheria I seemed to have been born with. I plodded conscientiously through the twenty-six letters, and the only malady I could conclude I had not got was housemaid's knee.

This humorous description of rampant hypochondria is what a user of the third edition of the *Diagnostic and Statistical Manual of Mental Disorders* might call "somatization disorder." In these "there tends to be preoccupation with symptoms rather than fear of having a specific disease or diseases."[22] This distinction seems less than significant if, as some therapists maintain, the disease-collector's anecdotal approach to his illnesses represents a fragile defense against anxiety that can give way in the face of mounting stress.

The belief that retirement is a strain that can drive a person toward maladaptive preoccupations is certainly not held by everyone. At least a handful of sociological studies have found retirement to be a relief—a reward for a life well lived. For example, a long-term study conducted at Cornell University in the 1950s found that the health of men who retired improved (or declined more gradually) compared to the health of men who kept working.[23] The study also concluded that if a person looked forward to retirement and felt financially secure, regardless of income, the transition was likely to be agreeable.

By the time men and women retire and, at least in theory, have more time to cultivate their friendships, their social circle is shrinking. Friends, brothers, sisters move to nursing homes or die. One's husband or wife dies, and for Samuel Johnson, the loss of his wife was the severest trial.

When Johnson was twenty-seven years old he married a woman roughly twice his age, and for eight or ten years the two lived in what can perhaps be described as mutual and grateful devotion. "Tetty," as Johnson called his wife, did not enjoy good health for long, unfortunately, and between her illnesses and the alcohol and opium she took to ease her discomforts, her strength failed by the time she was sixty. Tetty retreated into chronic invalidism. She spent more and more of her time in a small country house away from Johnson and, according to her companion and nurse, used the excuse that she was not well to refuse her husband's sexual advances. She simply wished to be left alone: Johnson wished for affection.

Despite the frustration that these repeatedly unresponsive encounters produced, Johnson visited Tetty each week. When she retired early each evening (having spent most of the day in bed), Johnson would go off to talk with a friend or read until two or three in the morning as was his custom. Upon his return Tetty's nurse let him in and gave him a pan of coals to warm his bed. Once tucked in, Johnson would often ask the nurse to come into his room to sit and talk with him until he could sleep. Years later, the nurse told Boswell that as she sat on the side of Johnson's bed, she occasionally laid her head on his pillow. Johnson yearned to respond, and did so in small ways, although never "beyond the limits of decency." Apparently struggling with himself, Johnson would ask her to leave.

In spite of the limitations of this marriage, which, as can happen, became increasingly apparent as the couple aged, Johnson was heartbroken when Tetty died. A friend found him "in tears and in extreme agitation," and the next day Johnson wrote this same friend asking him to "let me have your company and instruction. Do not live away from me. My distress is great."[24]

Johnson's story is not unfamiliar among the elderly. "The longing for . . . intimacy stays with every human being from infancy throughout life," wrote Freida Fromm-Reichmann, "and there is no human being who is not threatened by its loss. . . . I expect . . . it will be found that real loneliness plays an essential role in the genesis of mental disorder."[25] And the survivor—the husband or wife with the "melancholy privilege of remaining alone in a new world"[26]—is not only deprived of the touch and smell and sound of his partner but, as Simone de Beauvoir points out, "the death of someone we are fond of amounts to a sudden violent break with our past. . . . The death of a friend, of one who was close to us, not only deprives us of a presence but of the whole of that part of our lives [past, present, and future] that was committed to them."[27]

Roughly 50 percent of American women will be widows and a smaller but still significant proportion of men will be widowers. "Remember the time when we . . .," they may start to ask, but there is no one left who does. The moves from home to apartment or from home to a daughter or son's house that the elderly are frequently forced to make are wrenching experiences for the same kinds of reasons.

Seven years after Tetty died, Johnson moved from the house they had shared, and the one in which he had written his great dictionary, to rooms in an inn, a "veritable abode of wretchedness." He hated to admit that this "change which I am now making in *outward* things" was of any significance, but at age fifty, with no family, no home, no serious employment, and no money, Johnson began to turn in upon himself. With all the strength and relentless logic that he had developed in his writing and thinking, he began to examine the workings of his own mind with destructive intensity.

"Happiness," he had said long before, "is not found in self-contemplation; it is perceived only when it is reflected from another."[28] Yet Johnson was withdrawing. He knew better than anyone that his hypochondria, with its mixture of depression, tics, obsessions, and desperate fear of insanity, could not be "faced down" by solitary, internal combat, and yet he was doing just that. He was beginning to commit what he had so accurately described in others as "moral suicide."

Considering loss as predisposition to hypochondria, it is interesting, if a bit risky, to compare the death of an elderly person's husband or wife with the loss of a much younger person's parents or siblings, as happened, for instance, with Charlotte Brontë and the de Goncourt brothers. In some respects the character of the loss is dissimilar, the child fearing for his own safety and asking "Who will take care of me?" or "Will I die like my sister?" and the old person suffering more from a loss of companionship and wondering "Who will eat dinner with me?" and "Who will ever again find me physically lovable?" But both old and young feel particularly vulnerable. They do not see how the emotional support they need will be provided.

There are further, less obvious similarities. Consider the orphans whom Anna Freud observed playing mother-and-child with their own bodies and murmuring "there, there, my sweetie," and the lonely old man whom François Mauriac said "gives himself the pleasure of calling on Mama under his breath."[29] "Towards the evening [my] state of mind changed into a longing for caresses and affection," wrote the seventy-eight-year-old Tolstoy in his journal. "I should have liked to cuddle against some loving, sympathetic bosom as I did as a child, to have wept with emotion and to have been comforted. . . . Mama, pick me up, baby me. . . . All this is mad, but it is all true."[30] Some of these elder orphans, like the young, replace the maternal love they crave with solicitous pampering of their own bodies—a reaction, Anna Freud would say, to overwhelming feelings of abandonment and neglect.

There is still another social pressure conducive to hypochondria that, superficially, is the opposite of neglect: too much doctoring. This was not a problem in Johnson's time, but today health insurance plans have made it possible for a person of modest means to visit dozens of doctors, and the prestige that modern physicians enjoy has made them desirable allies in times of trouble. Although studies on the effect of national health plans on the prevalence of hypochondria contradict one another, it is obvious that a person such as the seventy-year-old woman who, in eighteen years, made 548 visits to 226 physicians (and 42 medical students) and collected 164 diagnoses could not have indulged her hypochondria so expansively without Medicare and Medicaid.[31]

In addition to such health insurance programs, which have made medical care more available, there is the strenuous promotion of drugs, vitamins, and health aids which makes doctoring oneself seem both necessary and appealing. The "health industry" encourages persons of all ages, and especially the elderly, to think about their bodies, diagnose every sign of deterioration, and remedy, remedy, remedy. (Senior citizens make up 11 percent of our population but take 25 percent of all prescription drugs and an even greater percentage of over-the-counter remedies.)[32] All this shoring up, holding in check, cleaning out, and preventing increases a person's "body consciousness," which in turn makes it more likely that he or she will see illness as the appropriate response to the stresses of age.

Taken together the loss of income, status, spouse, friends, and home constitutes an impressive array of social threats to the emotional well-being of the elderly. It seems fitting that gerontologist Louis Kuplan classified hypochondria among the "senile delinquencies," a term coined to invite comparison to juvenile delinquency. Both, he felt, were antisocial behavior motivated by feelings of exclusion. If true—or, rather, *when* true—hypochondria can be seen as ambivalent revenge and should be explained primarily in social rather than psychological terms.[33]

> My anger, because I am old, is considered a sign of madness or senility. Is this not cruel? Are we to be deprived even of righteous anger? Is even irritability to be treated as a "symptom?"[34]

The third kind of stress that the elderly encounter and that sometimes leads to hypochondria is emotional, and here the aged, coming face-to-face with the end of their lives, are in a delicate position. Before considering what the proper business of aging might be and why it can be stressful, it should be emphasized that individuals with different personalities and experiences will handle the last period of their lives very differently. This is true for the physical aspects of aging. One French writer stated, "It is a torment to preserve one's intellectual being intact, imprisoned in a worn-out physical shell," and another proclaimed, "Eighty years old! No eyes left, no ears, no teeth, no legs, no wind! And when all is said and done, how astonishingly well one does without them!"[35]

In a study of the neurotic reactions common among the elderly, Bergmann stated that persons who are insecure, rigid, anxious, or hostile run a greater risk of being overwhelmed by the strains of the golden years than do persons who are confident and content.[36] Many among the former will experience aging as a series of constrictions, whereas the latter often report a sense of increasing emotional freedom.

But regardless of differences in personality, experience, and outlook, many elderly individuals feel a need to reminisce. In this process, be it a conscious effort to remember the past or a far more haphazard impulse to revisit and recall, many elderly give the impression that they are attempting to resolve the discrepancies that still linger between how life has been lived and how they still imagine it should have been lived. The aphorism that comes to mind is "life is what happens while we are making other plans."

This reknitting of the weak and troubled spots—a real revision of the person's "autobiography" in many cases—is generally viewed as a constructive process.[37] It is not without its subtle dangers, however, for as a person rambles through childhood scenes, former love affairs, or experiences as a parent, scenes from the past can burst upon him with heartbreaking clarity. Viewed from the far side of life, the sweetest insights sometimes produce a profound sense of loss, and painful realizations—the newly accepted failures—can bring depression.

Among the reminiscers are those who cannot bear to think that they have failed in any significant way, and some of these will fall back on the excuse that illnesses have been the real reasons behind their disappointments. "And because the question of whether one has been a success or failure is often a critical issue during the later years," wrote Adrian Verwoerdt, director of the Geropsychiatric Training Program at Duke University's Medical Center, "we . . . encounter hypochondriasis with greater frequency during this period."[38]

Samuel Johnson was not anxious to undertake a life review or what his recent biographer, W. Jackson Bate, calls the middle-age reconsideration, and throughout his forties Johnson poured his energies into literary projects. With an inordinate amount of "bustle" he deferred the early stages of his life review until his fifties, when "the pressure toward it became very strong."[39] At this point Johnson could no longer hold off "the fearful experience of his fifties, when, after keeping things at bay by the achievement of his forties, life caught up with him, and—with the revenge of what has accumulated through postponement—exacted a fearful psychological toll."

Less is known about Johnson's breakdown than about the other crises and accomplishments of his life, for near the end of his life he destroyed the journals he had kept between 1761 and 1768. His last entry before this period is an Easter prayer.

My terrours and perplexities have so much increased, that I am under great depression. . . . Almighty and merciful Father look down upon my misery with pity.[40]

As Johnson looked back over his life, he found an unbridgeable distance between what he had accomplished and what he genuinely believed he *could* have accomplished. In spite of his essays, dictionary, and, by 1765, an edition of Shakespeare, he felt that "when I survey my past life, I discover nothing but a barren waste of time with some disorders of the body, and disturbances of mind very near to madness."[41]

This sense of failure was unbearably intensified by Johnson's realization that not enough time remained in his life to embark upon a significant detour, much less a new start. Each decision he had made—and for reasons he scarcely understood—had brought with it so much more than he had bargained for, so much he had not wished for and had not foreseen as being inevitable consequences of the original decision.

Johnson's life review proceeded in spite of him, and for three years he hovered on the edge of madness, examining his mind for the symptoms of breakdown, lapsing into long periods of amnesia, fearing sleep, and being terrified of any letting go. There were few memories of overpowering sweetness for Johnson and many that besieged him with guilt and despair. Throughout his late fifties (and intermittently in his sixties) Johnson was so disturbed that he purchased an essential measure of protection from the excruciating anxiety associated with memories of his early life by numbing himself with hypochondriacal preoccupations. His life review reactivated his earlier disorders in full force. "But let not little men triumph upon knowing that Johnson was an Hyphochondriack."[42]

Returning to questions asked at the beginning of the chapter—"How is hypochondria generated among the elderly?" and "Why are chronic cases maintained or, as with Johnson, reactivated?"—it is evident that answers must be framed in terms of biological, social, and psychological stresses. Physically declining, socially disenfranchised, and feeling that life has been far less important than originally imagined or, as Yeats wrote, "a long preparation for something that never happens," each person turns to the coping mechanisms he has developed throughout his lifetime to keep these threats within manageable bounds. If a person has surrounded himself with friends and talked out his problems, then he will visit, discuss, and philosophize with new urgency. If he has worked off anxiety, then in his sixties and seventies if he can still work, he will cope that way. But if he has tended to withdraw from trouble and become depressed, then depression may well reappear in old age. Similarly, if hypochondria or its complement—an illogical insistence on invulnerability—has been used, then under stress one of these may reappear. If, however, the triple stresses of aging are too great to be handled by old techniques, then new, stronger measures will be tried. Some will be constructive, others not. It would be comforting to state that the former far outnumber the maladaptive responses, but if the busywork that passes for work or art is discounted, there are few new pathways open to the elderly. Even Sigmund Freud felt his life thin out in his late sixties. "Something in the nature of a resonance is lacking," he wrote. "I am no musician, yet here I feel the same difference that there is when one presses on the pedal or when one does not."[43]

If aging is to be more opportunity than threat, improvements must be made in each of the three categories under discussion. Medically, a great deal more attention is being paid to the aged, and since the formal organization of geriatrics in the 1950s, a large number of new drugs and techniques have been developed to ease the discomfort of aging. Supportive social remedies have traditionally been provided by the church, and in many communities churches operate homes for the elderly, deliver meals to shut-ins, and sponsor numerous service groups for both men and women. Unaffiliated "senior centers" are augmenting (and, in some instances, taking over) these functions, and government agencies have, until recently, subsidized a larger and larger proportion of medical care, housing, transportation, legal aid, and so forth. Although this sounds like a lot of help, most services are available only to a minority. In addition, material provisions often make it easier for the children of the elderly to live completely apart from them and thus harder for their parents to obtain the warm personal contact they need. Most important, public services do not address the underlying problem of nonworking persons living in a society oriented so strongly toward production.

The psychiatric help available to the elderly also reflects an ambivalent attitude toward age. Although therapists are still less than fascinated by the obdurate complexities of an elderly hypochondriac, they have definitely progressed beyond the inspirational programs of the 1940s and 1950s under which the depressed and lonely were urged to repeat, out loud, "I must sweep the cobwebs out of my mind."

Recently, as more was learned both about hypochondria and the elderly, a feeling developed among some therapists working in nursing homes and mental institutions that hypochondria—being a fairly effective way of coping with stress—should not be tampered with. They felt it was rare that a better coping mechanism—meaning one in closer touch with reality and producing less fear and depression—was within reach of an old person whose resources of time, strength, and social support were limited.

"Both hypochondriasis and paranoia in the aged have the

dual functions of safeguarding self-esteem and also of manipulating others," wrote T. L. Brink, who found that such patients
maintained higher-than-average levels of social activity and with-
drew selectively only from persons they disliked.[44] Others feel "it
is poor practice and uncharitable to assume that the elderly patient's vague symptoms are merely the inevitable effects of old
age, and thereby to miss treatable diseases and psychopatholo-
gies in the old."[45] Robert Kellner goes on to say that treatment
of hypochondria among the aged does not differ from that used
with younger individuals and that such treatment "can make the
difference between contentment and appalling misery."[46]

Since the 1970s family therapy has joined the old stabilize-
and-maintain approach so widely used by general practitioners to
try to ameliorate the intense discomfort that can surround hypochondria. "It seems logical to view this illness as one in which
there is an inability to convey feelings directly and honestly to
'significant others,' " wrote E. S. Goldstein. "If the physician
could help the patient do this, then somatic complaints would not
be necessary."[47]

Goldstein tried family therapy on nine selected cases and
eight responded well. Before treatment these men and women
found it too uncomfortable to come out and ask for help or to get
angry at their families. Pitiful pains and inconvenient disabilities
conveyed these sentiments for them. Once the neurotic interaction was replaced with more direct communication, physical
problems abated. Goldstein went on to point out that if the grown
children or spouse of the elderly hypochondriac is deriving secondary gains from playing the role of strong, silent helper or not-
so-silent martyr, then "neither may have the motivation or
strength to confront the pathologic aspects of the relationship."[48]

At a special clinic for hypochondriacs at Duke University's
Medical Center, Ewald Busse and his colleagues worked for years
with patients, most of whom were elderly women. Busse evolved
a commonsensical form of treatment that involved agreeing with
the patient that she was sick, offering symptomatic relief with
aspirin, antacids, and the like, encouraging relatives to give the

patient additional support, letting the patient gradually shift the discussion from disease to emotional complaints over the course of his visits to the doctor if he so desired, and suggesting psychotherapy if insight began to develop. Following these steps Busse found that "hypochondriasis in the elderly is often a preventable or reversible syndrome" and that coping with socioeconomic stress is often the key to its cure.[49]

Even after reading such sympathetic suggestions, it is wise to remember that "therapeutic interventions have two faces: one is to heal the sick, the other is to control the wicked."[50] In other words, some part of every therapy designed for the elderly is aimed at calming the querulous and pacifying the hand-wringers so that *our* lives may proceed undisturbed. There is danger in this that the unhappy will adjust too much and thus reconcile themselves to an environment that is, in fact, inadequate.

> Disabilities crowd in on the old; real pain is there, and if we have to be falsely cheerful, it is part of our isolation. . . . "What more is expected of me?" Have we got to pretend out of noblesse oblige that age is nothing, in order to encourage the others?[51]

Johnson was horrified by the possibility that he would be given charity (today's social or therapeutic support) out of pity or to keep him happily quiet, and only after a great deal of thought did he convince himself that the offers of a modest pension and, four years later, of a home within the household of Henry and Hester Thrale were freely given rewards for work he had done or was doing. In conjunction with new opportunities for work (notably his *Lives of the Poets*), his pension and home with the Thrales were important components of the cure Johnson was trying to effect after his abysmal breakdown. At the heart of his effort, however, was his continuing search for the real basis of his discomfort. If he could name it truly, he believed he would gradually achieve "the stability of truth." No placebos, compromises, or superficial reconciliations for Johnson. For him the only freedom from the stresses of age lay in the integration of his inner life with reality. In youth and middle age he had thought to win these insights by storming his own fears and battling his own mind, but by the age of seventy he recognized that diversion—the opposite of preoccupation—was a sounder way of letting the mind ripen as it would. It might almost be said that he began to trust himself.

"It is by *studying little things*," he had told Boswell many years before, "that we attain the great art of having as little misery, and as much happiness as possible." And later he added, we must "*divert* distressing thoughts, and not *combat* with them. . . . To attempt to *think them down* is madness."[52]

Less than two weeks before he died, at the age of seventy-five, Johnson attended to his last business. He burned masses of his personal papers and, after so many years, arranged to have headstones placed over the graves of his parents and younger brother. Some days later, when his doctor visited, Johnson quoted a passage from *Macbeth* and asked, "Canst thou not minister to a mind diseas'd; / Pluck from the memory a rooted sorrow; / Raze out the written troubles of the brain?" And his doctor replied in kind, "Therein the patient / Must minister to himself."

Johnson died on 13 December 1784, and having refused opiates once he knew he would not recover, he was in no danger of meeting "God in a state of idiocy."[53] His friends were deeply saddened, as we are now. "He had given them the most precious of all the gifts one can give another," Bate wrote, "and that is hope. With all the odds against him, he had proved that it was possible to get through this strange adventure of life, and to do it in a way that is a tribute to human nature."[54]

"I will be *conquered*," Johnson said for all the brave among the aged. "I will not capitulate."[55]

8

HYPOCHONDRIA AND OUR
CULTURAL VALUES

The national character may be defined by its
ailments as well as its achievements.
                    —George Beard
                    American Nervousness

The new danger to our well being . . . is in
becoming a nation of healthy hypochondriacs,
living gingerly, worrying ourselves half to
death.
                    —Lewis Thomas
                    The Medusa and the Snail

■

THERE ARE THREE difficult questions to answer in this chapter. First, in what ways does our society foster or discourage hypochondria? Second, do the pressures leading toward hypochondria fall evenly on all segments of our society? Third, what are the common forms that hypochondria takes in America today?

In the past thirty-five to forty years Americans have concerned themselves to an unprecedented degree with their bodies, and there is a modern fascination with both health and illness. Consider our health-care industry. It is the largest industry in the country in terms of employees and third (behind construction and agriculture) in terms of income produced. In 1981, for example, Americans spent $247 billion, or almost 10 percent of the gross national product, on health care.[1] Consider also the increasing popularity of television's health and hospital shows, fitness regimes, do-it-yourself doctoring books, save-your-life diets, and articles—not to mention entire magazines—devoted to the prevention of physical decline. Blood-pressure kits are sold in drug stores, and wary runners can wear a ringlike device that measures and displays their heart rate. As the *Wall Street Journal* reported, "a morbid preoccupation with death is a major component of the national scene."[2]

With all this attention directed toward health, and with most Americans spending not just more but a growing proportion of their money to outmaneuver disease, it seems evident that forces exist in our society that encourage us to focus attention on our bodies. In an attempt to discover what these forces are, let us start at a general level with a quick look at the American life-style itself.

It is an oversimplification, but one with a good deal of truth, to say that most of us are brought up to place greater value on publicly acknowledged symbols of success and achievement than on private satisfaction. This has not always been the case in our society, nor have all our members in all spheres of their lives found themselves substituting the approval of those they admire for the more old-fashioned sense of "being right" that can be experienced by adhering to a commonly held system of morality. Yet some sociologists[3] sense that many Americans today fill the vacuum left by older systems of right and wrong and good and evil with subjective and ultimately arbitrary systems that could be described as "feels right" and "feels wrong" or "works for me" versus "doesn't work for me." Although such phrases are given a thousand different shades of meaning, the underlying message of this pragmatic philosophy is that we increasingly guide our actions by the results they produce. And the results that really count, most psychologists will claim, are the reactions of other people. Not so curiously, this concern for the opinion of others leads directly to a preoccupation with oneself.

Anyone who is extremely sensitive to the signs of approval given and approval withheld spends much time evaluating— looks, actions, acquisitions, and all the rest—for their effect on other people. He wants everything about him—certainly including his face and body—to express his most attractive self, a persona that he perversely insists on calling "the real me." This desire to be liked and admired can lead to body consciousness, as well as other forms of self-absorption, and is commonly expressed by beautifying, slimming, strengthening, and treating various parts of the body.

In part this "transcendental self-attention" persists because it encourages the mass consumption of goods and services on which our country's economic health depends. Advertising consultants know that a preoccupation with the self sells all sorts of things, and the sophisticated studies they undertake to identify markets for vitamins, gym equipment, health food, and so on have identified several ways in which the urge to be seen as a successful man or woman motivates a person to buy.[4]

Other forces that seem to foster the self-perpetuating cycle of self-centeredness and need for approval can be found in the early experiences of childhood. The fit between one's early development and a later concern for the good opinion of others can best be seen in the writings of psychologists who concern themselves with the development of the self. Heinz Kohut and Ernest Wolf, for example, believe that in order to develop a sturdy sense of self, two essential ingredients must be present during early childhood.[5] One is the presence of a parent who, like a mirror, reflects and confirms the child's sense of vigor and ability. The second is a parent who can absorb the child's anxieties within his or her own reservoir of calm—in other words, can be a pillar of strength to the child during crises. It seems to be the case that the genuine affirmation of rowdy little children and the deep peacefulness needed to comfort their barely comprehensible fears are not qualities found in an adult who is still trying tensely to satisfy what is expected of him rather than what his soul almost inaudibly tells him is worthwhile. Consequently, ego psychologists such as Kohut believe that a large number of young children get part but not enough of what is needed for the development of resilient self-sufficient selves.

According to Kohut and Wolf, such persons neither retain the nucleus of childish omnipotence, which is the basis of self-confidence, nor develop the essential ability to soothe and reassure themselves. They are vulnerable to stress and crisis. To compensate, they court the approval of others and establish close but often uncomfortable ties with powerful protectors. Entering adulthood more than ready to respond and to reinforce our gregarious and compulsively self-centered life-style, they seem caricatures of the typical American. Again according to Kohut and Wolf, they frequently suffer from our most typical disorders.

At one extreme, if the parents are psychologically incapable of supplying any mirroring or soothing, the child may become psychotic. Toward the other end of the spectrum, minor deprivations account for the crowds of young Americans who are prone to narcissistic behavior disorders (perversions, delinquencies, and addictions) and narcissistic personality disorders that are sometimes accompanied by hypochondria.

Social psychologists offer a different explanation for the apparent prevalence of Americans who are so dependent on others that they are predisposed to adopt a wide variety of maladaptive strategies to maintain their self-esteem and keep in touch with those whom they need too much. In the late 1970s, E. Jones and S. Berglas[6] introduced the term "self-handicappers" to describe individuals such as alcoholics and the functionally ill who create impediments in their lives or exaggerate problems in order to explain and excuse all manner of poor performance. By drinking or having constant bronchial troubles, for example, the self-handicapper has a ready excuse if he falls short of what he hopes to accomplish at work or home. A failure does not mean that *he* is unworthy or incompetent but merely that he was hung over or sick. When such a person succeeds, his self-esteem is given an added boost as he says in effect, "If my lungs had been clear, I could have turned in a really spectacular performance."

Such a person can't lose, or at least he is not able to see a loss for what it is.

Jones and Berglas speculate that the self-handicapping strategy may have its roots in a family situation in which children are rewarded for doing the right things or having the right answers rather than for simply being intrinsically lovable. If such children come to believe that acceptance is based on good performance, they may strive to become overachievers or, declining to compete for love, may adopt the strategy of an underachieving self-handicapper. It is by no means impossible to adopt both these strategies in different spheres of life.

In a paper entitled "The Self-Serving Function of Hypochondriacal Complaints," T. Smith and his colleagues[7] tested the process of self-handicapping among students who scored high on a hypochondriasis scale and those who scored low. Given a bogus test of "social intelligence," some students were told that their scores would not be affected by such extraneous factors as physical health, others were told nothing, and a third set of groups was told that the test was sensitive to disruption by physical health. After taking the test, subjects filled out two symptom checklists, and, as predicted, the students scoring high on hypochondria checked the greatest number of symptoms when told that such symptoms would affect their performance. Hypochondriacal students in the other groups checked a moderate number of symptoms, and nonhypochondriacal students checked a very small number of symptoms regardless of the instructions they received when taking the bogus test.

A more particular reason than family upbringing for the modern emphasis on health and body consciousness is the steadily increasing amount of publicly disseminated medical information that encourages us to monitor our bodies for signs of disease. Television programs and magazine articles have increasingly focused attention on the dangers of our simplest habits. Drinking coffee may predispose us to cancer of the pancreas, breathing polluted air to emphysema and lung cancer, drinking the water carried in plastic conduits to other cancers, and on and on. "More

and more of us are identified as being members of the population who are 'at risk,' " wrote Paul Atkinson, discussing the relationship between medical expertise and hypochondria. "The notion that we may be 'at risk' also encourages a close scrutiny of the day-to-day changes in our physical state."[8]

Techniques for the early detection of disease further focus our attention on what can go wrong with our bodies, as do campaigns to raise money for the National Cancer Society or the American Heart Association. Atkinson concludes that contemporary medicine is in danger of putting us all at risk of becoming hypochondriacs.

Closely related to the dramatization of medical problems is the medicalization of nonmedical topics that were formerly considered the business of individuals, lawmakers, or members of the clergy. The list of daily activities that can be subsumed under the general heading of "health," and for which the doctor is assumed to be the expert, has been growing with amazing rapidity. Doctors and therapists are becoming our experts on diet, sleep, sex (deviant and normal), pollutants, climate, drugs, stress, marriage, aging, abortion, genetic counseling, insurance risks, selection of military recruits, many kinds of crime, and even the comparative worth of human beings. (Should doctors decide which individuals are worth saving when only a few can have access to special drugs or machines?) In 1964, 28 percent of the persons interviewed in a large study of British households agreed with the statement, "the doctor is a good person to talk to about a personal problem." Only five years later a second study found that 41 percent agreed.[9]

Few individuals become either sufficiently uncomfortable with their growing dependence on experts or sufficiently confident of their own judgment to reject the omniscience of doctors, educators, and lawyers. Not willing to embark upon a life free from the powerful protection of experts, we commonly exchange an unmeasured amount of freedom, with its very real pitfalls, for safety that is always expensive and sometimes demoralizing. Surely this is what a hypochondriac does, but more so. And just

as hypochondriacs fail to satisfy themselves with this trade, sensing that in spite of their partial loss of freedom and magnified reliance they have not purchased safety or love, so those persons with our characteristically incomplete sense of self are never satisfied that they are successful enough in the eyes of their peers or protected enough by their reliance on experts. They need more and better doctoring just as they need more and better television equipment, clothes, and even marriage partners.[10]

One of the results of paying so much attention to health hazards and of speaking of so many of life's concerns in terms of health and disease is that personal health has become a symbol of success in itself and as such is a popular retreat in times of unmanageable confusion. When people living through the upheaval of major transitions—say between the ages of faith, reason, and whatever is to follow—find their private lives awesomely complex, their problems unsolvable, and their future uncertain, they will sometimes retreat into one small corner of life in an effort to simplify the confusion, maintain control, and experience satisfaction in a restricted area. Which corner will be chosen—spiritual redemption, a social reform such as Prohibition, or personal health—depends on what patterns of behavior are fashionable and on the particular pressures felt by the individual.

Today one of the most crowded avenues of retreat leads away from a disheartening world toward an exaggerated concern for personal health. Having no hope of understanding the larger world, much less improving it, many people are busying themselves with personal survival. Whether their strategies are based on the latest technologies and include a $300 physical examination every year or on rejection of technology that may ban all additives and preservatives from the family diet, they are attempting to ensure the narrow goals of health, peace of mind, and longevity. The importance of being tied to the larger world, to the past as well as the future, is often repudiated. Some forms of hypochondria seem caricatures of our cultural discontent, an ethic of self-preservation carried one step beyond the "normal" extreme.

Turning briefly to the forces in our society that counter-balance dependency and discourage hypochondria, anything that gives people a sense of being equal to the demands of life moves them away from preoccupations with survival. In simplest terms, the move toward self-sufficiency can be accomplished either by increasing a person's ability to cope or by reducing the demands that are made upon him or her. Most Americans, with their energetic bias toward action and mastery over life, think in terms of the former, and those persons who are temperamentally suited to embrace active solutions are at an advantage in our society over those who place a higher value on adaptation and acceptance.

Among the active there seems to be a growing desire to be directly involved in the production of essential goods and services. There is more backyard gardening, woodchopping, sewing, building, and even cooperative educating and doctoring than has been seen for decades. The neo-pioneering spirit thus manifested by one segment of the middle class is not likely to change the character of our consumer-oriented nation, but, like some aspects of the fitness fad, it is symbolic of a strong desire to be in some measure independent of the system. Although Lewis Thomas deplores the hordes of scowling middle-aged men and women who trudge through Central Park in their undershorts, many of these persons have left sports in which gamesmanship, image, and the lucky shot are all-important and have turned instead to jogging because they want the heightened sense of physical power and independence that fitness through individual training brings.

Jean-Paul Sartre asserted that playing was valuable for the very reason that it erased an individual's awareness of his relation to the Other. Although cycling, swimming, or running may begin as "the desire to do," to conquer, or even to impress, they are frequently "reduced to a certain desire to be." This "being for yourself alone" is, in Sartre's words, "the absolute freedom which is the very beginning of the person."[11] It certainly can be the antithesis of relying on the opinion and expertise of others.

Turning to our second question—"Do the pressures toward hypochondria fall evenly on all segments of our society?"—we encounter two social characteristics that seem to make hypochondria particularly prevalent among the poor.

There is a saying among sociologists that minorities were discovered in the 1950s, the poor in the 1960s, and women in the 1970s, and indeed the first comprehensive studies of mental health that included the poor were made in the late 1950s and early 1960s. Chief among them were the Stirling County Study of Psychiatric Disorder and Sociocultural Environment conducted in Nova Scotia and August Hollingshead and Frederick Redlich's community study of social class and mental illness in New Haven, Connecticut.[12] Because the poor used to be excluded from the medical system by their inability to pay, and are still underrepresented in any census of hospital or private practice patients, sociological studies of mental disorder based on hospital populations or private patients measure only the prevalence of treatment, not the incidence of disorder. Both the Nova Scotia and New Haven studies circumvented this problem by using field studies—that is, interviews, personality tests, and other measuring devices administered to random samples drawn from all neighborhoods.

The outstanding and undisputable result of these and virtually every other comprehensive study is that there is a powerful positive association between poverty and mental disorder. This is true not only for severe mental illness but also for marginally disruptive disorders such as hypochondria. Wrote Marc Fried in his survey of dozens of studies:

> One observation stands out: the greater frequency of mild mental disorders among higher-status groups found in studies based on psychiatric treatment is contradicted by the higher rates of mild impairments (along with higher rates of severe impairments) among lower social class groups found in studies based on field interviews.[13]

One important question was not answered by the early studies. Do the greater social pressures of poverty cause mental illness? Or do mentally ill people end up in the lower classes? A second generation of studies was undertaken to answer this question, and enough data have now been amassed to paint a grimly fascinating picture of the interaction between low social status and mental distress.

Before tracing the route from the slums to the doctor, police station, or mental health clinic, it will be useful to define what is meant by "social classes." Hollingshead and Redlich used five divisions that have been widely adopted by other sociologists. Members of Class I are rich by anyone's standards. They are community leaders and live in the best part of town. Not far below them in prestige come the members of Class II, who are mostly college-educated professionals. Class III includes the vast majority of white-collar office workers, businesspeople, and skilled manual workers such as plumbers and carpenters. Class IV consists predominantly of semiskilled factory workers. Members of the lowest group, Class V, are unskilled workers. Many members of the last group lack a complete elementary school education and are likely to live in tenements or ghettos.

Using these divisions sociologists have documented what most people already knew: namely, that Class IV and V individuals suffer far more than others from narrow job opportunities, substandard housing, overcrowding, forced relocation, and physical illness. Among these the fear of unemployment and the hardships that accompany a loss of income are apparently the most potent threats to mental and physical equilibrium.

M. Harvey Brenner at the Johns Hopkins School of Hygiene and Public Health has shown that a 1.0 percent rise in unemployment (which, of course, represents a much higher percentage among the Class IV and V work force) results nationwide in a 4.3 percent increase in the number of men admitted for the first time to state mental hospitals (2.3 percent for women), a 4.1 percent increase in suicide, and a 4.0 percent rise in commitments to state prisons.[14] Not unexpectedly, the majority of persons entering state hospitals were the least powerful among the powerless—the aged poor and the young poor.

What was not anticipated by early studies of poverty and mental distress was that there appears to be more vulnerability to stress among lower-class individuals. For example, after the Midtown Study compiled a list of deprivations and disruptions it was found that regardless of the kind of problem that each involved, the higher the number of deprivations, the greater the likelihood of mental disorder. Later studies took this finding a step farther and compared individuals from middle and lower classes, each of whom had experienced the same number of deprivations during a certain period of time. In one of these studies 6 percent of a sample of middle-class women developed mental problems, whereas 30 percent—five times as many—working-class women developed similar disorders.[15] Although this greater vulnerability to stress is not well understood, it may be significant that the working-class woman who developed problems was more likely than her middle-class counterpart to have lost her mother before age eleven, have three or more preteen children to care for, and lack an intimate relationship with husband or steady boyfriend.

Taking these studies together, it seems that the greater deprivations of poverty and the greater vulnerability to these deprivations cause a higher rate of mental illness, rather than illness causing persons to move into the lower class.

A case history from the files of a London hospital traced the strains and illnesses of a lower-middle-class woman identified only as Case 9.[16] "Nine" was one of six children raised by a mother who cared little for her offspring and a father who was affectionate but largely absent. "Nine" was a healthy child and had no history of multiple illness when she left home in her late teens to become a secretary. She married at twenty-two. She began to have back trouble when her second child was born, and by the time her fourth baby arrived she was exhausted. Her family doctor told her to rest. As if to justify such an indulgence, she began having a series of disabilities, each of which made it more difficult to care for her children or be sexually responsive to her husband. First her back stiffened and then her feet swelled up. Finally "neuritis" in her arms made it impossible to pick up anything. She went to a nursing home for two months. Upon her return she caught influenza but could not go to bed because she had to nurse her family as each in turn came down with the flu. Further illnesses among her children and serious financial problems preceded a severe bout of back pain, knee discomfort, and indigestion. After numerous treatments and an exploratory operation, her doctors said they could do no more, so she turned to an osteopath and spent nine months in his rest home. Upon her return she "worked like a nigger," she said, although she "could only crawl up and down the stairs." She prided herself on her stoic attitude and on the incredible amounts of work she could do for a family she described as insensitive and undeserving.

"I'll just go on being exhausted until the family will give me a rest," she said grimly. "I always have had to do things thoroughly, and with this worrying all round—people telling me I owed it to my family to be well—it has added nervous exhaustion to the physical one."

Although the remainder of the case history describes "Nine" in such disagreeable terms that it is tempting to discredit her own evaluation of her predicaments, she may, in fact, have been so physically exhausted by caring for four small children and a mild but helpless husband on grossly insufficient funds that she succumbed more quickly and more completely to a neurotic round of disabilities than would a woman of similar personality but with greater financial resources.

Like so many other persons of the lower middle class, "Nine" was taught to "put up" with life when she was a child. Dependent on her parents and later on boss or husband, she always expected to be acted upon, not to act on her own behalf. Once married and economically pinched, "Nine" was further trapped in a position of enforced dependence. As Thomas Szasz has pointed out, helplessness fosters indirect communication, and the poor are likely to wage covert rebellions against the people who seem to control their lives. The powerless cannot afford the luxury of telling the truth, Szasz wrote, and for them the "slave tactics" of continual fatigue, chronic illness, and imminent breakdown are safer and often more effective expressions of discontent than direct rebellion.[17]

Among the poor, mental distress speaks body language, and often anxiety and mental disorder are expressed as physical illness rather than as psychological strain. Class V individuals "are unable to understand that their troubles are not physical illness. . . . They expect 'pills and needles,' " reported Hollingshead and Redlich.[18]

Psychosomatic symptoms, psychogenic pain, and hypochondria are all extremely common among the lower classes, partly because of a lack of insight (which Hollingshead found was rare in any class) but more because of the greater stigma attached to mental illness and the greater danger of being labeled "nuts." For a poor person the possibility of spending the rest of his life in a state hospital if he is diagnosed as "mental" drives him toward alternative explanations. Even the selection of the kinds of physical complaints used to express emotional distress varies according to class. Among the working class there is greater recourse to the "manly" complaints of wrenched backs, torn ligaments, and pulled muscles as explanations of problems that in fact range from insomnia to impotence. Middle-class men and women seem to prefer heart trouble, nervous indigestion, and arthritis as substitutes for problems that seem too dangerous to face.

Not only do the poor have to contend with more than their share of stress, which is often expressed as physical disease but they also face the additional problem of having their disorders routinely interpreted as either more hopeless or more trivial than the aches and pains of the higher class. In other words, a poor person is far more likely to be turned away from a clinic as a chronic complainer or sent to the state hospital with a diagnosis of schizophrenia than to be called a neurotic and given the gentler therapies that neuroses generally elicit. Even compared to the middle- or upper-class persons in mental hospitals, the poor are far more likely to be treated with drugs and electroshock than with talking therapies. In general the upper classes get analyzed; the poor get directed.

In addition to socioeconomic status as a factor that apparently affects a person's chances of becoming a hypochondriac, other differences such as race, religion, gender, and age—in theory at least—could make some groups more or less prone to hypochondria. In the case of race, minority groups are so commonly poor that of the approximately two dozen studies done on the mental disorders of whites versus blacks, almost all show that the higher rate of mental distress among blacks can best be explained by socioeconomic deprivation.[19] When black families belong to the middle classes, their illness behavior matches the class norm.

The very fact of being in the minority puts a strain on people of all backgrounds, and it was discovered that whites living in predominantly black areas or small enclaves of Italians living outside a city's main Italian section have higher rates of mental disorder.[20]

Racial origins may affect a person's choice of symptoms. The impression among some physicians is that Puerto Ricans in New York City suffer an exceptionally large number of headaches and cold sweats, Portuguese women on Cape Cod complain of being sick and dizzy, and Mexican-American males frequently express emotional distress through sleep disturbances, palpitations, and shortness of breath.[21] In all these cases the individuals prefer to be sick rather than crazy, and yet they are not unaware that they are failing to meet standards set by themselves or their peers. When more than two thousand welfare mothers were interviewed, 71 percent agreed with the statement, "A lot of people getting money from welfare don't deserve it."[22] In other words, these women knew that the dominant culture considers welfare recipients failures. How, then, did these welfare mothers cope with their self-accusations of failure?

They coped in three ways. First, many mothers said their

failure was temporary and that they would certainly be working within a year. (Only 10 percent did so.) Second, they maintained that their young children needed them and therefore they could not leave home to work. Finally, they fell back on poor health. Fully 45 percent of the mothers complained of "nerves," and the longer they stayed on welfare, the more likely it became that they would blame their failure on self-diagnosed illness.

Essentially the same pattern was found among black mothers on welfare. If they described themselves as good wives and mothers, they rarely complained of poor health, but if they saw themselves as failures, about half blamed their inabilities on poor health.[23]

When it comes to ascertaining the effect of gender on hypochondria, there is immediate and vehement disagreement:

> "Hypochondriasis is essentially a male condition."
> "Hypochondriasis is three or four times more prevalent in women than in men."
> "The rigid forms . . . and the paranoidal hypochondria appear to be a male privilege."
> "In my experience most hypochondriacs are women."[24]

Each camp has a plausible explanation. Men are more likely to become hypochondriacs because it is socially more acceptable for them to be physically ill rather than crazy, lazy, or weak and because it is easier for a man to find a spouse who will undertake the nurse or mother role. Conversely, women are more likely to become hypochondriacs because it is socially more acceptable for them to express illness of all kinds and because it is easier for them to find a spouse who will take the part of the strong partner. The more complicated psychological explanations are equally contradictory.

Two faint patterns are discernible in this confusion. One is that doctors who use the broadest definitions of hypochondria almost invariably say that the disorder is more prevalent among women. The second is that British and European doctors, living closer to the old tradition that men are "Hypochondriak" and women "Hysterick," tend to see men as the ones more commonly afflicted.

The official view among American therapists falls somewhere in between. As mentioned before, the third edition of the *Diagnostic and Statistical Manual of Mental Disorders* states that hypochondria is about equally divided between men and women but that "somatization disorder," a less pervasive malady that inherited parts of the old hysteria, is the prerogative of females.

Today it is certainly true that from childhood through old age women in many countries report more illness, physical and mental, than men. Women have a larger number of symptoms for any given disease, utilize all health services more, miss more days of work because of illness, spend more money for medicines, and, as is well known, live longer. Understandably these facts give the impression that women worry more about their health and are more likely to express distress with illnesses. The reasons for their greater use of medical facilities are not really known, however, and their concern for illness cannot be used to bear out the impression it first gives. For example, the current patterns of male and female illness behavior would result if women were weaker than men and more prone to physical and emotional disorders. It would also result if women were as resilient as men but were under greater strain. A third possibility is that women actually suffer about the same amount of illness as men but are more aware of changes in their bodies and more willing to seek help. Finally, for some kinds of disorders—notably hypochondria—women may be *imagined* to have a higher rate than men. Not only is a doctor more likely to label a woman with a chronic headache a "hypochondriac" (a man with the same symptom will be sent to the hospital for tests), but the doctor is also likely to report that such a woman has made greater demands on his time than the male patient, even if the number and length of appointments are about the same for both.

In a study aimed at identifying patients who claim to be sicker than their doctors believe them to be, most of the physicians questioned rated their female patients as having more symptoms and less bona fide illness.[25] They were described as being more helpless and complaining than the doctors' male patients and also of being in greater need of tranquilizers and emotional support. When the physicians' office records were subsequently examined, it was found that the *female patients used the medical services with the same frequency as did the males*.

A similar bias seems to extend to therapists as well. When clinicians were given a list of 122 traits and asked to indicate those that best described either a healthy adult, a healthy, socially competent male, or a healthy, socially competent female,[26] it was hypothesized that the male and female would be described in different terms in accordance with society's stereotypes. This proved to be true regardless of whether a male or female clinician was selecting the traits. Predictably, the healthy female was described as less competitive, less independent, more emotional, more excitable in minor crises, and so on. If most doctors and therapists expect this behavior from their female patients, it is easy to see how they could overestimate the claims women actually make on their time.

The study further hypothesized and confirmed that because the phrase "healthy adult" is interpreted by most people to mean "ideal standard adult," the traits ascribed to the adult would match the male list but not the female list. In other words, our culture values the traits that are presumed to be typically male—action, mastery, independence, and the rest—far more than it values the presumably feminine characteristics of submissiveness, caring, feeling, and loving. One implication that can be drawn from this bias is that the exaggerations and distortions of male behavior will not be called "mental illness" as quickly as will the excesses of female behavior. Excessive independence is not judged to be nearly as bad as excessive dependence, although both can be emotionally crippling.

Up to this point we have been assuming that the differences in male and female patterns of illness are the result of cultural conditioning. Are there also biological differences that push men toward pride and aggression and, in times of stress, toward expression of distress such as delinquency, frantic bodybuilding, or workaholism? And are women led by their bodies' capacity for reproduction toward caring and enduring and sometimes toward passive, internalized expressions of distress such as depression and hypochondria? Some psychologists say yes, although most add quickly that the effects of social pressures are impossible to disentangle from biological dynamics except in books.

In *Sex and Fantasy, Patterns of Male and Female Development,* for example, Robert May[27] argues that the differences between men and women lead to different patterns of emotional distress. The "pathologies of pride and caring," as he calls them, are characterized by an overemphasis on fundamental male or female traits and a denial of the opposite traits that in "normal" people temper them. Thus distressed men become all fight and bluster and overburdened women rely on excessive dependency to get them through life. If all else were equal, such biological differences would cause women to become hypochondriacal far more than men, or at least to develop distinctly passive versus aggressive forms of the disorder. All else is not equal, however, and distress cannot be so neatly portioned out.

In the case of hypochondria, the social pressures—the self-centeredness stemming from a need to please, the fear of mental illness, the remarkable attention focused on illness that makes it such a perfect symbol of distress—tend to obscure, although not negate, the effects of any biologically generated differences. Hypochondria covers such a wide range of distress and is fueled by so many different needs and fears that the disorder is commonly used by male and female, active and passive. At either end of the spectrum of hypochondriacal complaints, however, is a hint of sexually generated differences. Cases of mild hypochondria seem more common among women, but at the other extreme the frankly deluded hypochondriacs whose rigidly defined diseases include angry claims of medical mismanagement are more often reported to be men.[28]

Returning to the question, "Do certain groups in our society run a greater risk of suffering from hypochondria?" the answer is a resounding yes. A poor nonwhite woman living in a predominantly white neighborhood is a prime candidate. Her husband, if she has one, is also likely to express the strain of living from day to day with little control over his job or home life and with little expectation of a better future in terms of physical illness. Although this couple's concern for their health will lack the trappings of superficial insight common among upper-class hypochondriacs who attribute so many of their health problems to a fashionable excess of "stress," the disorders of both will function as an uncomfortable way of maintaining mutually incompatible truths about themselves as long as they lack the material and/or emotional resources to face the underlying conflict.

If the character of what a person fears affects the nature of the shelter he or she constructs, and if in addition the person's fears are shaped and molded by the social climate of the time, then it is reasonable to expect hypochondria, that curious shelter, to have changed its countenance over the centuries. Indeed it has. In the eighteenth and nineteenth centuries, for example, when the growing tension between sexuality and morality stood for many other confusions, *syphilis imaginaria* was a common manifestation of hypochondria. Listed as a subspecies of hypochondria by some doctors, fear of the Pox and of the mercury poisoning associated with its attempted cure afflicted thousands. For men like James Boswell, panic was at least initially based on the real possibility of catching a painful, shameful, and frequently untreatable disease. But for others, such as the Dutch physician Bernard de Mandeville, author of *The Hypochondriack and Hysterik Passions* (1711), no sexual adventures—correctly understood to spread venereal disease—were needed to precipitate uncontrollable fear of infection.

Actually describing his own case, de Mandeville had a hypochondriac who had been faithfully married to a faithful wife for thirty years say:

> It is no longer ago than last Winter, that I could not be persuaded but that I was Pox'd . . . [and] for a considerable time I was all Day long examining my Shins and Forehead and feeling for *Nodes*. . . . The losing of my Nose, my Palate, my Eyes and all the Frightful and shameful Consequences of that Disease possess'd my Fancy for hours together, till the Horror of them ent'ring deeper into my Soul, sometimes struck me with such unspeakable Pangs of Grief, as no Torture, or Death could ever be able to give.[29]

Abruptly the fear of another sexually transmitted disease, AIDS, has lept into the ranks of the hypochondriac's fear. Even more than syphilis in the eighteenth and nineteenth centuries, AIDS is a real and extremely grave problem, but in addition its freight of shame, terror, uncontrollability, and blame make it a perfect focus for hypochondriacs. AIDS centers increasingly receive calls from individuals who had one sexual adventure eight or nine years ago and are now terrified that they have AIDS and have given it to their faithful and probably ambivalently loved and resented spouse.

Returning to the diseases most feared in the past, by the middle of the eighteenth century tuberculosis had become the primary cause of death in industrialized societies and the most dreaded chronic communicable disease. TB in its many forms became the focus of hypochondriacal apprehensions. Only slightly less than syphilis, tuberculosis had its own shameful and mysterious implications. Many tubercular patients looked as if they burned with an inner fire uncomfortably similar to sexual passion. Lying on their beds, limp and spent, their eyes glittered and their lips were startlingly red. Doctors, who did not know what caused tuberculosis or how it spread, sometimes got the impression that the disease mainly struck sensitive young men and women who perhaps already burned with sexual longing and so courted the disease with their disruptive thoughts. Later it was as much the discovery of a cause—the TB bacillus—as of chemical cures that gradually removed tuberculosis from the repertoires of hypochondriacs.

Cancer replaced it. Perceived as the equal of leprosy, syphilis, and TB both in mystery and malignancy, cancer is currently the most dreaded disease. Even among persons who run a far greater risk of dying in car accidents or from heart disease, cancer is listed in every survey as being most feared. Serious and often painful, cancer has a frightfulness that fits the vulnerabilities of the twentieth-century imagination. It resembles one of the unmanageable issues of our time—uncontrollable technological violence. As the war machines of powerful nations grow beyond our power to control them, millions could die for reasons that are so complex and unfathomable as to seem absent. Senseless death from uncontrollable proliferation is epitomized by cancer.

As early as 1937 cancer had become an emotional issue on a national scale. In that year the organization that became the National Institutes of Health was established by passage of the National Cancer Act. By the 1950s nationwide surveys routinely rated cancer as more feared than all other diseases including polio, cerebral palsy, arthritis, heart disease, and TB. Fewer than twenty years later the disease seemed such a threat (although it killed roughly half the number claimed by heart disease) that the budget for cancer research was separated from all other biomedical research within the National Institutes of Health. Between 1971 and 1975 allocations for cancer research rose from 17 to 33 percent of the NIH budget.

As fear of cancer grew, so did the belief that the disease was somehow morally reprehensible, a bad mistake. This was (and to some extent still is) reflected by many cancer "victims" decision to hide the nature of their illness from employers, colleagues, and acquaintances. The largest cancer hospital in this country sends mail to outpatients in plain envelopes with no identifying letterhead, and the 1966 Freedom of Information Act cites "treatment for cancer" as exempt. No other illness—not even venereal disease—was singled out in this way.[30]

If an exaggerated fear of cancer is prevalent among the normal population, "cancerphobia" is even more apparent among hypochondriacs. Doctors who specialize in hypochondria find that many of their patients dare not utter the word "cancer" and refer to it only as "that disease" or "C." They are terrified. Twentythree-year-old Miss K, for example, a case presented by Balint,[31] got her mother to check her tongue every night before she went to bed to see if the redness on one side had spread. She was frantically certain that it would eventually turn into cancer. For years she lived with this fear, sometimes even quitting her job as a secretary to live out what she imagined were her last months on earth and also to have more flexibility in scheduling visits to her doctors and surgeons on whom she felt her life depended.

Unlike Miss K, whose fear of cancer was a conscious one, Mr. L's terror lay beneath the surface and inconspicuously animated an irrational drive for safety. Felix Brown[32] reported that Mr. L, who was a steelworker in his thirties when his troubles began, gradually became convinced that most foods did not agree with him. Although he did not consciously fear any particular disease, he felt that it was desperately important to eliminate everything from his diet that caused him any distress. This he did until almost nothing remained. He wrote in his diary:

> Diet has come down to bread and milk except for an orange and an egg at breakfast. More nervous each day.
> Friday: Severe gas pains in stomach. Ate nothing: drank a quart of cocoa.
> Wednesday: Terrible pains in lower stomach. Had injection from doctor, also nose treated, but did not do anything about stomach.

When Mr. L was finally referred to a therapist, the history

of his starvation diet was gradually unraveled. It began after Mr. L had seen a film on stomach cancer. The patient then remembered that his grandmother had died of cancer of the stomach and that he had believed the disease to be inheritable. Without realizing it, Mr. L had put himself on a self-styled anticancer diet.

It seems likely that our irrational fear of cancer, with its intricate trappings of folklore and superstition, will gradually subside as causes for certain cancers are discovered. Articles that irresponsibly claim to delineate "the cancer personality" (often diametrically opposed to the nineteenth-century idea of the cancer personality) cannot survive the discovery that inhaling asbestos fibers and cigarette smoke, not frigidity and the repression of anger, are the significant factors that predispose a person to lung cancer.

In the coming decades when cancer is better understood, AIDS or even the quality of aging will probably follow it along the syphilis-TB-cancer continuum as the focus for persons who are emotionally involved with health. It is already a mark of success to live to the age of eighty, but only if one is active and attractive until the very end. Increasingly the expensive debilities of aging may be considered personal failure.

Fashions in the milder forms of hypochondria have also changed. In the first half of this century Americans suffered from sluggish livers, which made them bilious, and being bilious they were headachy, dyspeptic, bored, and invariably constipated. They took liver pills to tone up their livers and explosive laxatives to boost their spirits. Although the staggering variety of "natural" laxatives still on the market is proof enough that millions still fret over irregularity, liver pills have all but disappeared. Their function, like their shelf space, has been taken over by aspirin, antacids, vitamins, and sleeping pills, which are consumed in astounding quantities. A British survey found that 80 percent of adults had taken an over-the-counter or prescription drug in the two-week period prior to being interviewed.[33]

Among modern hypochondriacs there is a relatively new variation on the old self-medicating theme, and this is the self-directed prescription of emotional remedies. Some "mental hypochondriacs" will not touch medicines—"poisons, unnatural," they claim—but "medicate" themselves with self-help books on meditation, mind control, bioenergetics, EST, Esalen, Arica, rolfing, massage, and other consciousness-raising techniques. Each of these techniques may be helpful, but each can be misused to foster endless cycles of self-absorption rather than a rigorous examination that may lead to change. One psychiatrist believed that he could distinguish "mental hypochondriacs" from persons seeking to understand themselves by the amount and kind of background reading they had done, their glib use of psychological jargon, and their easy acceptance of self-diagnosed neuroses, compulsions, and obsessions. The naive assumption that one's personality can be changed at will could be added to his list.

In every period there are also hidden forms of mild hypochondria—irrational health worries that affect so many people that *not* to be preoccupied seems bizarre. These usually center on health practices that fit so well with a society's avowed goals that the preoccupations are actually considered desirable. Two such hidden forms of exaggerated concern are what could be called "weight-watchers' hypochondria" and "fitness hypochondria." The first centers on keeping slim. From responses to a questionnaire sent out by *Psychology Today* it was clear that attractiveness matters a great deal to most women and that by attractiveness they primarily mean being slim. A woman who feels she is overweight feels out of control, inferior, and unhappy.[34] More than 20 percent of the entire U.S. population is on a diet at any given time, and even among those who are not, weight is of such concern that many Americans weigh themselves once or even twice daily on the bathroom scale. They do not consider this behavior compulsive or their preoccupation with this aspect of their body image excessive. However, when a person examines the inside of his mouth twice a day with a dental mirror or has her mother check the side of her tongue for redness every evening, this behavior is considered extremely odd. The same goes for drugs. Take diet aids or a handful of vitamins every day and you are doing right by yourself. Take sleeping pills, tranquilizers, and patent medicines and you're a self-medicating hypochondriac. Obviously the examples just given of "good" and "bad" behavior are not exactly parallel, but they are close enough to make the point that a compulsive preoccupation that fits the American image of a successful person is tolerated—even encouraged—if it is economically useful, whereas similar preoccupations that are not socially acceptable will be regarded as queer.

The compulsion to keep fit is a more recent phenomenon than the American love affair with attractiveness. Although doctors were adding the health addict and the "physical prig" to their catalogues of hypochondriacs as early as the 1930s, the lopsided athleticism of the middle-aged did not become a widespread occurrence until the 1970s. It was then that jogging, tennis, cycling, aerobic dancing, bodybuilding, and other fitness programs burst into full flower, bringing with them associated concerns for nutrition and sports medicine.

Comparing the life-style of a compulsive runner with that of a hypochondriac, the similarities are striking. Both are preoccupied with their bodies to a degree that is out of proportion to any dangers they face. (Several books on running state that thirty minutes of running every other day is optimum for cardiovascular fitness, but serious runners routinely run one or more hours daily.) Continuing the comparison, a hypochondriac's concerns disrupt his or her normal life-style. A compulsively dedicated runner eats at odd hours so his stomach will be empty when it's time to run; he leaves concerts during intermission to be in bed by 10:00 P.M.; and he runs to dinner parties, showers and changes on arrival, then eschews meat, salt, sugar, or whatever else he has chosen to ban that month. By almost anyone's standards, including his own, this runner's life-style is peculiar.

Finally, a hypochondriac's anxieties are not likely to respond more than temporarily to reassurance. Neither is the bodybuilding narcissist's. He is never doing enough, never fit enough. He is sure he needs more exercise and different exercises, better food and less caffeine, more sleep and a different attitude. An endless flow of compulsions weave in and out of his life replacing one another like a hypochondriac's diseases and, it must be added, probably replacing the runner's prefitness obsessions with smoking, overeating, drinking, or being hypochondriacal.

Returning to the difficult questions that opened this chapter, it seems clear that the American life-style, with its tendency to substitute the good opinion of others for self-satisfaction and with its emphasis on attractiveness and fitness, fosters a pervasive preoccupation with health and body image, which in turn predisposes people to see their problems in terms of physical disability. Lewis Thomas observed that for millions of Americans illness seems to be "the central human dilemma."[35] In addition to this self-centeredness there is a tendency to retreat from the complexities of an unmanageable world and to project our pessimism as well as our managerial propensities onto our bodies instead.

The pressures leading toward these common myopias do not fall evenly on all segments of society. The poor, minorities, women, and both the young and very old are more likely to retreat from a realistic appraisal of their problems and substitute physical failures in their stead. Finally, for those who unconsciously feel that their problems are too overwhelming to face and who choose to concentrate on disease instead, their preoccupation will probably be with cancer if their conflicts are profound and with irregular sleep, eating, and bowel habits if their worries are relatively superficial. They may even choose to be preoccupied with fitness, and sometimes this means they are feeling strong enough to start sidling up to their problems unawares.

HYPOCHONDRIA IN
OTHER CULTURES

Certain races and nationalities seem to get a
reputation for being hypochondriacs. This is
nearly always the opinion of others.
                              —F. E. Kenyon
                              Hypochondria

∎

EVER SINCE THE disorder called *koro* or *su yang* was described in a textbook of tropical medicine in 1936, doctors studying the cultural variations of mental anguish have delighted in describing this dramatic crisis.[1] Called *koro* among the Malays and *su yang* among the southern Chinese, the disorder is an acute castration anxiety with hypochondriacal overtones. The patient, like everyone else in his society, believes that the proper functioning of the male genitals is essential for life. Suddenly he is seized with the conviction that his penis is shrinking into his abdomen. Fighting off panic, he measures and remeasures but finally succumbs to the delusion that his penis is indeed getting smaller. Because he believes that when it disappears he will die, he frantically resorts to accustomed remedies.

The orthodox way to forestall death is for him to clamp his penis in a wooden case used for holding a jeweler's balance, but if he does not have such a device, he may tie a peg on his shrinking member or at least a red string. (Among the Chinese, red is the color that wards off evil.) If his penis continues to shrink, however, he may simply hold onto it or, better still, have his wife or a friend hold it until the crisis is over. His wife may practice fellatio, but even with such dramatic reassurance the poor man may have to be carried off to the hospital until his anxiety attack is over. A female form of the disorder, in which a woman fears that her breasts, nipples, or genitalia are retracting, has been reported, but it is uncommon.

Within the literature of hypochondria, reports of shrinking penises among the Chinese, bowel disorders among the Germans, liver problems among the French, venereal disease among Africans, and exotic mouth disturbances in India suggest that differences exist in how people express their hypochondriacal concerns. There are probably different amounts of hypochondria too, although these can only be hinted at. The hazards of attempting a cross-cultural study are essentially the same as those that bedevil comparisons among social classes. Visibility must not be confused with actual prevalence, and middle-class Western attitudes toward illness must not be considered either the most common or the most healthy: they are not the standards by which all other behavior is to be judged. The list of variables that confound cross-cultural studies could be greatly expanded, and perhaps all that can be said with confidence is that in cultures where mental distress is considered a terrible handicap, the substitution of physical complaints is very common. For example, a study comparing depression among Chinese and Americans found that the Chinese (living both in China and in the United States) expressed a higher proportion of physical symptoms than American patients. These bodily complaints were never acknowledged by the Chinese to stem from depression even when the symptoms cleared up with antidepressant medication. A. M. Kleinman explains that because a mentally ill person in China may be labeled unfit for marriage, he or she has strong reasons to deny the emotional origin of problems.[2]

Differences in the use of bodily complaints are also notice-
able between Eastern and Western cultures and seem to stem
from a deep philosophical division. "Hebraic life has always had
a very different structure from Graeco-Roman," wrote José Ortega y Gassett. "While in Western man the norm—which is perhaps a bit childish—is to be satisfied and only from time to time
to fall like a child into sudden hopelessness, Eastern man has
always lived in a state of desperation. This is his primary and
normal attitude."[3] Ortega goes on to explain that, whereas
Greeks put their trust in reason and Romans in the State, Hebraic peoples put their trust in an all-powerful god. They assumed—and still assume—that humans are insufficient and incomplete. Therefore the Hebrew feels that he is "absolutely
dependent on another superior being; or, what is the same thing,
that he sees himself essentially as an infant."[4]

Such a strong feeling of dependence—seen earlier among
children, the poor, and other groups—fosters indirect communication rather than direct confrontation. Add to this the East-
erner's somewhat fatalistic tendency to adapt and endure rather
than act (and quite possibly perish), and the stage is set for using
sickness and other forms of weakness to gain leverage with the
powerful while simultaneously claiming the protection due the
meek and fearful.

Examples of a culturally or, one might even say philosophically, predisposed hypochondria abound among peoples of
the Mediterranean and Eastern Europe and can also be found in
certain subcultures in the United States. When a medical questionnaire aimed at identifying hypochondriacs was given to
Greeks, Anglo-Greeks, and Anglo-Saxons, for example, it was
found that the Greeks were the most likely to believe that they
suffered from serious physical disease.[5] This finding concurred
with those of other studies of Mediterranean groups and suggested that in spite of their legendary emphasis on emotion,
Greeks, Italians, and North Africans saw their problems very
much in terms of physical illness. (See Kellner for a brief review
of these studies.)[6]

In another study, this one comparing Oriental versus Occidental immigrants to Israel, it was found that roughly 32 percent of the mentally distressed Jews coming from Iraq, North Africa, and the Middle East had hypochondriacal complaints, whereas only 9 percent of the disturbed Jews emigrating from Europe, the Balkans, and Rumania complained of undiagnosable illness.[7] Studies of immigrants suggest that they hold onto their patterns of somatization for at least several generations.

Several waves of Jewish immigrants have come to the United States. In the 1840s families began arriving from Western Europe, and some forty years later large numbers of Eastern Europeans followed. Many of the more educated families came from communities where scholarship was the cultural ideal and the vocation of the greatest prestige. Earning money had been less important, and families were frequently supported by the joint efforts of father, mother, and elder children. When these families came to America they adopted many new patterns. Economic success supplanted religious study—a strain for many men—and a rather fierce kind of homemaking replaced outside work for women who were quick to see that a nonworking wife was an important symbol of a husband's financial success. Given the stress that these changes produced, many families fell back on their traditional expressions of distress—sickness and disability.

"Don't tease God into striking you dead by walking around saying . . . you feel fine," Maurice Sendak's mother used to say urgently to her son. The well-known illustrator of children's books remembered that "when my father came home with good news my mother would press her forefinger heavily on her lips and point to the ceiling as if to say, 'What are you doing? Are you going to bring the world down on us by saying something good has happened?'"[8]

Mrs. Sendak grew up with the common belief that God, fathers, husbands, and employers were far kinder to the oppressed and powerless than they were to the apparently self-sufficient. She knew that if the meek were rash enough to be happy, the powerful would ask more of them. Like so many others, she rarely had a sense of setting her own pace and instead had felt driven through much of life by the demands of others. It was difficult for such a person to stop for a rest or even slow down without an excuse. This naturally led to resentment, and the powerful ones—the drivers—were secretly or even subconsciously disliked. But this was an acutely uncomfortable line of thought, and one that produced a great deal of guilt. How could a good person resent God's laws or despise the husband or employer she depended on? If the powerful learned of this ingratitude, they would punish it. As long as the weak punished themselves first, however, they would not be bothered.

Hypochondria, with its continual succession of headaches, fatigue, and upsets, was both the self-inflicted misery that protected many weak persons from what they imagined would be a harsher punishment at the hands of the powerful and the excuse necessary to justify a temporary respite from endless work.

Mrs. Sendak was doubtless familiar with the Law of Talion too, the idea that a wrongdoing, even if it never progressed beyond her imagination, could be rectified only by the infliction of a closely similar punishment—an eye for an eye. This concept may underlie some hypochondriacs' selection of exactly the same symptom that afflicts or afflicted a parent, spouse, or other person whom they both love and resent. More than a specific religious law, however, it is the Middle Eastern and Oriental tendency to see human beings as utterly dependent on a powerful being that explains part of their greater-than-average use of medical services.

In a small but carefully controlled study of the relationship between ethnicity and illness behavior, Andrew Twaddle at Brown University found that "Jews were likely to seek early treatment for relatively subtle symptoms as compared with other groups. . . . Jews reported relatively trivial conditions as compared with the Protestants or Italian Catholics."[9]

When the Italian Catholics were then compared with Irish Catholics (this time in Irving Zola's study in Boston), it became clear that the Italians were fairly close to the Jews in giving a freer and broader expression to physical complaints. Whereas the Irish tended to deny disease—"I ignore it, like I do most things"—the Italians dramatized and exaggerated their symptoms and apparently felt better for doing so.[10] When all four groups were compared,

> the Irish and American [Protestant] patients said that they prefer to hide their pain, the Jewish and Italian patients admitted freely that they show their pain and they do it by crying, by complaining about pain, by being more demanding and by stating unequivocally that they cannot tolerate pain.[11]

It is not surprising, then, that many doctors get the impression that hypochondria is more prevalent among Jews and Italians. Regardless of absolute numbers, illness and fear of illness among members of these groups are more openly expressed.

Two other groups have a reputation for presenting many of their emotional problems as physical illness: Navaho Indians and Mexican-Americans. Both are poor, which may have more to do with their insistence on equating ill fortune with ill health than with their cultural background; but be that as it may, Navahos have at least thirty-five long and complicated ceremonials, each aimed at driving out a common disease. And Mexican-Americans, especially migrant workers, consistently present physical complaints in lieu of emotional ones.

In many cultures there exists an altogether different kind of subculture whose mores significantly affect its members' attitudes toward illness. This is the military. On the one hand, being a soldier or sailor is a profession with occupational hazards that may or may not foster hypochondria. On the other hand, to be in the armed forces is to belong to a highly regimented and partially isolated society that, in democratic countries at least, is considerably different from the main culture. During peacetime it is the cultural differences more than the occupational ones that are likely to affect the character and incidence of hypochondria.

For our purposes, the most important difference between the military subculture and the main culture is that in the former the doctor is an agent of the armed forces, not of the patient. As such his task is to assure adequate manpower, and he must act in the best interests of the military. If the doctor is under pressure to fill the ranks, he will tend to divide all the complaints he sees into two categories—"real" ones, which he treats, and unsubstantiated ones, which he labels "lying" or "malingering" and passes on for disciplinary action. He does not interpret complaints as hypochondria or as other neurotic misuses of illness.

The hypochondriacs among the recruits quickly respond to this situation in which they are either ailing or lying by exchanging their haphazard symptoms for officially recognized ones that are difficult to verify. Many apparently make the transition from "feeling feverish" and having tightness in their throats to sharp chest pains and dizzy spells without consciously trying to outwit the military doctor.

Whereas the majority of anxious behavior occurs upon enlistment, before combat, and just prior to retirement, some anxious reactions occur during combat that resemble temporary hypochondria. Soldiers whose buddies have been killed sometimes become immobilized by the fear that what has happened to their chums will happen to them "because we were so much alike." Some psychologists are reluctant to take such soldiers' reasoning at face value, however, and feel that their guilty feelings over being the ones who survived rather than their empathy are triggering the anxiety. A survivor may feel so ashamed at how immensely relieved he is that his friend, and not he, was killed that he punishes himself with emotionally produced pain, often in the same part of the body that was irreparably damaged in his companion.[12] Prior to World War I, many of these reactions were thrown together under the headings of shell shock or battle fatigue, but as psychiatrists were increasingly assigned to recruitment offices, field hospitals, and recovery homes, the recognition of mental distress and its division into somewhat more precise categories proceeded rapidly.

By the middle years of World War II, mental disorders resulted in the rejection of more Selective Service registrants and in more disability discharges than any other defect.[13] From 1940 to 1945 the rate of rejection for mental problems rose alarmingly and, with hindsight, can be attributed in large part to the greater number of psychiatrists joining the screening panels. There was also a booming new business in "goofballs" and "4-F pills." Available over the counter from any druggist, these induced just the right amount of jitteriness to lead to immediate rejection.

The Germans, harder pressed for manpower, were far less likely to excuse a man for being nervous or for imagining that he was ill, but they took advantage of the Allies' concern by dropping thousands of leaflets entitled "Better Ill a Few Weeks than Dead All Your Life." Included were complete instructions for faking major illnesses.[14]

One final type of anxious reaction with hypochondriacal overtones that is fairly common in the military is "the old soldiers' syndrome." Found among career soldiers just about to retire, the disorder is characterized by irritability and depression. Commonly it leads to heavy drinking and sexual indiscretion, but some retirees begin to suffer from a series of undiagnosable ailments. They seem especially afraid of diseases that could leave them impotent. "Our impression has been that many of these men are intensively passive-dependent at core," wrote Captain Harvey Greenberg, a military psychiatrist. "The Army, with its ordered, authoritative structure continues to support the soldier's passive needs down through the years."[15]

As his career draws to a close, however, the old soldier questions his worth in civilian society. Is there a place for him out there? Will he be comfortable? "He may unconsciously wish to maintain the dependency relationship implicit in active duty status."[16]

Many of the same features that characterize the relationship between doctor and patient in the armed forces, and which lead to denial of the very existence of hypochondria, are found in the medical systems of countries where doctors are closely controlled by the state and where it is essential to maintain a fully functioning work force. Taking the USSR as an example, the Russian government issues every doctor a limited number of medical certificates, which, when given to a patient, legally excuses him from work. Often the number of certificates given to doctors caring for workers employed in an important industry is proportionally smaller than for doctors with a rural or less important practice. In the past doctors were severely punished for issuing more than their allotted number of certificates even when compliance with the limit meant forcing sick people to work. Gradually government pressure relaxed, but not before workers had learned to manipulate the new system. They became adept at malingering.

The general rule in the USSR is that a person is ill if he or she has a fever. Therefore Russians quickly learned to put mustard seeds or hot peppers under their arms (where their temperature is taken), which gives them the required fever. They also learned masterfully to stretch a "legitimate" illness a week beyond its normal course and at times resorted to self-mutilation. A folklore has grown up around these subterfuges, and every household has its stories of how this aunt, uncle, or friend numbed his or her bottom with a piece of ice, then injected milk to produce a fever or cleverly fabricated a fake welding burn with a cigarette. The simulation of nervous diseases is essentially ignored because those disorders rarely win a medical certificate.[17]

Caught between government regulations and rebellious workers, Russian doctors admit they are less effective than their Western counterparts. They often do not recognize real illness because malingering is so common that they have come to suspect everyone of exaggerating. They also have trouble comforting or reassuring the seriously ill when their patients so often regard them as pawns of the state.

In the few instances in which hypochondria is acknowledged—and these seem to be slightly on the increase though still closely linked to organic causes—the suggested treatment is sometimes a kind of thought reform. After the emotional arousal of an aggressive interrogation, a confession is elicited from the patient to the effect that, unconsciously at least, he was trying to shirk his duty by being sick. The hypochondriac is then given group support and the assurance that he will feel much better once he has fallen into step with the rest of society.

There are, then, differences in the amount of hypochondria that a nation or a large institution such as the armed forces will allow its members to express. How much hypochondria continues to exist in these societies, where it is expressed as a long series of earnestly presented complaints but diagnosed as malingering, is impossible to measure. Also tantalizingly out of reach are answers to questions that revolve around the effects that overt versus covert coercion might have on the prevalence of hypochondria.

Does the straightforward expression of state or military power encourage some people to "select" malingering *instead of* hypochondria? In other words, does a command such as "you will work or you will be jailed" actually predispose people to straightforward responses, one of which might be "if you try to make me work, I will pretend to be sick?" Conversely, does the covert expression of power so commonly used within families, paternalistic societies, and some religions encourage disguised responses? If so, the common persuasion "we are only asking you to work (or conform to certain rules) for your own good" may well be answered with "I truly want to work and be good, but unfortunately I am very ill."

Although the effects of cultural beliefs on the prevalence of hypochondria are hard to pin down, it is somewhat easier to see how different beliefs affect the superficial trappings of hypochondria. A rich combination of folklore and medical history determines which parts of the body are considered most vulnerable and which diseases and dysfunctions are most feared. Religion or, more broadly speaking, the relationship an individual has with figures of great power also affects his or her willingness to adopt or reject a posture of helplessness.

OCCUPATIONAL
HYPOCHONDRIA

Becoming a "hypochondriac" may be an
occupational hazard for those who are in
process of becoming medical experts.
  —Paul Atkinson
    "Becoming a Hypochondriac"

All creative writers are hypochondriacs, since
those of them who do not worry about the
state of their bodies are certain to worry
about the state of their minds.
  —Harold Nicholson
    "The Health of Authors"

■

CERTAIN ACTIVITIES, such as doctoring, performing, and
arguing with God, expose their devotees to disturbing
ideas not the least of which is the unsettling reminder that "all
flesh is grass." As was the case with military men, part of the
predisposition toward hypochondria experienced by doctors, musicians, painters, and the like comes from social circumstance and
part from pressures inherent in the occupation itself. The latter
can be as obvious as a doctor's intimate association with death
and disease or as subtle as the relationship between action and
self-disclosure.

Starting with medical students, it is a commonplace to say that many of them briefly become hypochondriacal, if not during their first-year anatomy laboratories when they anxiously confront their first patient, a cadaver, then a year or so later in response to the vivid teaching technique of making hospital rounds. In their third year medical students are abruptly surrounded by illness. There are apprehensive patients, embarrassing examinations, and painful open lesions to deal with daily. The students cannot help but be amazed by the number and kinds of things that can go wrong with the human body. Quite naturally many develop a sense of personal vulnerability, and as Paul Atkinson described in his account of making rounds with medical students, "as we heard more and more case histories, and as patients recounted the insidious onset and development of grave illness, so we came to take our own continuing good health less and less for granted."[1]

Most of the students in Atkinson's acquaintance soon began to diagnose the symptoms of daily stress in themselves, their professors, and their fellow students as signs of fatal illness. Many took their own first cases of imagined ankylosing spondylitis and brain tumor to a doctor and were hurt by his casual dismissal of both their problem and their diagnosis. With experience, however, the same students learned to tolerate their symptoms for longer periods before consulting a doctor. In theory at least, their growing realization that healthy bodies produce vast arrays of temporary and inexplicable symptoms that are amplified during periods of anxiety allowed them to survive attacks of ear-ringing and indigestion. The commonness of unimportant symptoms would be further underscored when they entered private practice and began treating the less acutely ill. If current medical autobiographies can be trusted, the hypochondria so common in medical school is left behind. It reappears, if at all, only as anecdote.

Studies of the mental health of doctors do not entirely agree. (See Ford for a review.)[2] Physicians, investigators note, are under considerable occupational pressure and suffer more psychiatric illness than the general population. Although their psychiatric problems largely fall into two categories, depressions and addictions, hypochondriacal fears are also prevalent.

Studies suggest that physicians adopt one of two rather extreme stances vis-à-vis disease. The majority come to consider themselves invulnerable. A minority fear the most dangerous or unusual diseases that their patients present to them and often seek to control this painfully sophisticated form of hypochondria with self-prescribed drugs. "I would be an absolute cripple if I had even the normal amount of suggestibility," said a Cape Cod physician, Dr. Virginia Biddle, when asked if she feared contracting her patients' diseases.[3] "No, no, no. I go in the opposite direction. I have to believe it can't happen to me."

Many of her colleagues say essentially the same thing. E. Langdon Burwell, for example, began having trouble speaking and even seeing when he was a young doctor doing his military service in the Azores.[4] One morning his legs gave way beneath him as he tried to get out of bed and he fell flat on the floor. "Even then I did not make a diagnosis," he recalls with mild surprise, "and by that time I was seeing double." Fortunately a pediatrician recognized the onset of a dangerous form of polio and began treatment immediately.

And does a doctor learn from so dramatic an illustration that he is the last person to suspect his own illness and therefore should have periodic checkups with another doctor? Rarely, according to Burwell, who even now has a physical examination once every ten years, which is when his life insurance policy absolutely requires one. The recent death of one of Burwell's colleagues from advanced prostate cancer did not send many local doctors rushing to the doctor.

Turning to doctors who exhibit the opposite reaction and are chronically afraid of illness, many model their diseases on the infirmities of their most desperate patients. "I suffered extremely in the Symptomatic Fever, by violent Headaches, great Sicknesses and Sinking," wrote Dr. George Cheyne describing his own case in the early 1700s. "And lately having had two full-bodied Patients, who had died of Mortifications from that Distemper, I was much frightened at mine."[5]

Like his former patients, full-bodied Cheyne, who weighed over four hundred pounds and "exhibited in his immense hulk most of the diseases in which he specialized,"[6] had thick, dark-colored blood. He bled himself—as he had bled his patients—and "found one continued *impenetrable Mass of Glew*."[7] He was reduced to the last degree of misery.

As his brethren still do today, Cheyne tried to drive off his vague and ever-changing symptoms first with overwork and then with drugs. Finally he reached "a perpetual Anxiety and Inquietude, [with] no Sleep or Appetite . . . a constant Colick, and an ill Taste and Savour in my Mouth and Stomach . . . , a melancholy Fright and Pannick, where my Reason was of no use to me: So that I could scarce bear the Sight of my Patients or Acquaintances . . . , and yet could not bear being a Moment alone, every Instant expecting the Loss of my Faculties or Life. . . . In fine, I had recourse to Opiates."[8] Cheyne knew these were "slow Poison." Nevertheless, he was in such torment that he took them and in the ever-increasing doses he knew were necessary for relief.

> All this time, I attended . . . the Business of my Profession . . . , but in such a wretched, dying Condition as was evident to all that saw me. I had many and different Contradictory Advices from my Friends and Acquaintances.[9]

In the main, the advice given Cheyne was to go to London and consult the best doctors he could find. For months he delayed, finding himself in the same awkward position that doctors anxious about their health do today. On the one hand, if a doctor is as sick as he believes himself to be, he is reluctant to go to a doctor and have his worst fears confirmed. On the other hand, if no illness is found, or much less than he tells his doctor to expect, he may feel reassured but also ashamed, for he will be revealed within the medical community as a hypochondriac. He may hesitate further, knowing that because he will not be asked to pay for his care, his visits cut into the time his doctor would normally spend with paying patients.

Cheyne finally went to London and, having "promised to be passive," did for a time follow the prescriptions of six doctors, although not without modifying their suggestions. He put himself on a vegetarian diet—a regime thought by John Bull Englishman to be fit only for effeminate Italians—and in spite of his doctor's advice to return gradually to the customary meats, puddings, and gravies, Cheyne stuck to his seeds and milk. He recovered slowly and after several years proclaimed himself in perfect health with "as much Activity and Cheerfulness, with the full, free and perfect Use of my Faculties . . . , and of going about the Business of my Profession . . . , as I was ever capable of in my best Days."[10] "I am myself come to that Time of Life when Hopes and Fears ought to be contracted into a very narrow Compass," he wrote later. "I have done my best, and pursu'd in my own Case the same Rules I have given to Others, and have at present, I thank God, inward Peace, Health and Freedom of Spirits."[11]

Styles of self-revelation have changed since Cheyne appended "The Author's Case" to his famous book on the spleen, vapors, lowness of spirits, and hypochondriacal and hysterical distempers, and it is rare now for a doctor to make himself the subject of a treatise on hypochondria. That far less charming literary form, the sociological study, with its touching lust for quantification, has replaced Cheyne's confessions, but modern articles still indicate that some doctors are prone to hypochondria.

In *The Emotional Health of Physicians*, J. C. Duffy and E. M. Litin describe ten specialists who, diagnosed as suffering from "depressive reactions," all interpreted their problems as physical illness.[12] It could be argued that none was a hypochondriac and that all were depressed instead, but the case histories of the pathologist who thought he had cardiac symptoms, the surgeon who spent months worrying about a cut on his finger that other doctors said was healed, and so on certainly suggest that these doctors were expressing their troubles in terms of physical disabilities.[13] "The physician fears a psychiatric diagnosis," the authors concluded, "and with some justification."[14]

This seems true of a group of forty-seven doctors in another study whose methods of coping with emotional distress were compared to those of a carefully matched group of laypersons.

> At times of adult life crises, hypochondriasis and turning against the self . . . were seen twice as often among the physician sample as among controls. . . . During interviews nonphysicians frequently repressed critically painful events in their lives. In contrast, physicians told us in detail about their medical symptoms.[15]

And yet, the authors of this study go on to note, few of these anxious physicians had consulted other doctors. "It was as if . . . the physician said 'There is a lot wrong with me, but I will not inconvenience anyone else.'"[16]

If this is typical behavior for a hypochondriacal physician— and the modern doctors cited believe it is—then the vast majority might be trying to treat themselves and will never come to the attention of other doctors or therapists. If reduced to the last degree of misery and unable to function, many might seek treatment for and be classified as drug abusers or alcoholics.

"Tenth month, 1753. Morose on trifles," wrote Dr. Rutty, an Irish physician who experienced every addiction and obsession in spite of himself.[17]

> Second month, 1754. Weak and fretful.
> Third month. The pipe enslaves.
> Twelfth month. An hypochondriack . . . , wind and indigestion.
> Fifth month. O my doggedness.
> Ninth month. An overdose of whiskey.

Sixth month, 1756. Feasted a little piggishly.
Second month, 1757. Snappish on fasting. 27th—Avant, Satan! the Lord is strengthening and promoting my progress.

A second place to look for a greater-than-normal concentration of hypochondria is in the performing arts. Dancers, singers, actors, and musicians—all rely far more than most on the full functioning of their bodies. Their concerns for the health of leg muscles, vocal chords, or hands can become so intense that they seem hypochondriacal, but it is difficult to tell if their preoccupations are realistic in view of the risks that physical disabilities pose to their social, emotional, and financial well-being.

The attention that the famous tenor Enrico Caruso gave to his vocal chords seems an example of realistic if not ordinary concern. Caruso rose every morning at 8:00 A.M. and began a long and complicated routine. Wrapped in an enormous white robe, he swept into his steamy bathroom and for half an hour lay in a scented tub while an inhalator added moisture to the already hazy atmosphere. He never sang in the bathroom. Next he moved to his dressing room and, after setting a mirror against a window, opened his mouth as wide as he could and examined his vocal chords with a dentist's mirror. If they looked at all irritated, he would paint them with a special solution procured from his personal laryngologist. After this daily examination Caruso proceeded into his living room and while his barber shaved him, his accompanist played whatever score the tenor was working on. Caruso followed the music silently. By late morning—bathed, examined, shaved, and dressed—he was finally ready to sing.

At times, however, the attention that performing artists and serious athletes lavish on parts of their bodies exceed the bounds of common sense, and their preoccupations weave back and forth across the boundaries of hypochondria. Frequently an approaching performance produces bizarre rituals and examinations as the musicians or hurdlers suffer the anxious anticipation that precedes many forms of acting. Like doctors, performers are initiating a string of irreversible actions and reactions. Their performance cannot be taken back. A play, a ballet, a concert—all are gestures of self-disclosure that will inevitably be followed by responses, which in turn will act upon the performer. "To do and to suffer are like opposite sides of the same coin," wrote Hannah Arendt.[18]

Nonperforming artists—painters, sculptors, writers, and composers—also work within the realm of "authentic perplexities." Although their statements may be retouched or rewritten many times, these too are acts of self-disclosure. When released into the public domain, the works initiate response (one of the worst is silence), and these reactions cannot help but heighten an author's self-awareness.

"[Mental] disease prevails most among those whose minds are most excited by hazardous speculations and by works of imagination and taste," wrote Amariah Brigham, medical superintendent of the State Lunatic Asylum in Utica, New York. "The registers of the Bicêtre [an asylum] in France, show that the insane of the educated classes consist chiefly of priests, painters, sculptors, poets, and musicians."[19]

The first comprehensive study of occupational hazards was made a century before Brigham's time by Bernardino Ramazzini. In 1700 he published *De Morbis Artificum,* or *Diseases of Workers,* which included both physical problems, such as hernias among trumpet players, and mental ones. ("Those who hold appointments at the court of princes . . . head the list of hypochondriacs.") Ramazzini was aware that the occupation of painter, scholar, judge, or sculptor posed a double or even triple threat to tranquility. "To begin with, nearly all learned men . . . suffer the drawbacks of a sedentary life. . . . As a general rule [they] suffer from weak stomachs."[20] The perspicacious Ramazzini noted that in addition to this imbalance between mental and physical activity, the excitement of ideas, combined with the need to please, led to hypochondria and other forms of distress.

Ramazzini could have used the life of the Florentine painter Jacopo Pontormo to illustrate the hazards of painting.

Pontormo was born in 1494 and orphaned as a small child. At the age of eleven he was apprenticed and over the next seven or eight years painted in the workshops of such great painters as Leonardo da Vinci and Piero di Cosimo. Pontormo's first important work was a fresco of the figures of Faith and Charity executed in honor of Pope Leo X.

> That work . . . was of such a kind, and so beautiful, what with the novelty of the manner, the sweetness in the heads of those two women, and the loveliness of the graceful and lifelike children with the Charity . . . , that one is not able to praise them enough.[21]

As Pontormo's reputation rose and the demand for his work increased, the painter became increasingly solitary and eccentric. At the slightest outbreak of the plague in Florence he fled to the country even if this meant interrupting his work for months at a time.

> He was so afraid of death that he could not bear to hear it mentioned, and he fled from the sight of corpses. He never went to festivals or to any place where people gathered, so as not to be caught in the crowd; and he was solitary beyond belief.[22]

During the last years of his life, when he was working on frescoes for the chapel of San Lorenzo, he kept a diary in which he recorded day by day, or even hour by hour, his concerns for work and health.

> March, 1555: Wednesday I did the rest of the *putto* and had to stoop uncomfortably all day, so that on Thursday I had a pain in my kidneys; and on Friday, apart from the pain, I was ill-disposed and did not feel well and had no supper that night; and on the morning that was the 29th day I did the hand and

half the arm of that large figure and the knee and that part of the leg on which rests his hand. That was on the said Friday, and the said evening I did not sup. And had no food until Saturday night when I ate 10 oz. of bread and two eggs and a salad of borage flowers. Sunday the 31st I had lunch in the house of Daniello, fish and capon; and in the evening I had no meal and on Monday morning I was distracted by pains in my body. I got up and then, owing to wind and cold, I returned to bed and stayed there until 6 o'cl. and all day long I felt unwell, yet in the evening I supped a little on boiled meat with beets and butter; and I remained thus not knowing what was the matter with me. I think my returning to bed must have harmed me, yet now, at 4 o'cl. in the morning I seem to feel much better.[23]

Pontormo, who died a year later at the age of sixy-five, lived during a period when the artist-as-craftsman and artist-as-workshop-member was being replaced by the image of the artist as an inspired individual. Thus singled out as the lone worker who took personal responsibility for the success or failure of his projects, the artist joined the ranks of other individual "actors" and was prone to their characteristic pressures and distress. In addition, the old ideas of the allegiance between genius and insanity were being revived during the Renaissance and became so widely accepted that the public actually expected painters and writers to have certain peculiarities. As time went on, circumstance deprived other artists of the protection of anonymity and they too felt singled out—torn between the excitement of their ideas and the desire, or financial need, to please.

By the nineteenth century the picture of the high-strung intellectual given to chronic indigestion and deep anxieties over health applied to scholars and men of letters as well as to painters and poets. Not only did Lord Byron "roll in agony through long assaults of acute dyspepsia" but Percy Bysshe Shelley catch imagined elephantiasis from seeing a lady with swollen legs, and Alfred Lord Tennyson become convinced that he would be bald, blind, and dead by fifty, but scientists and scholars began to recite the same tedious litany of morbid symptoms. Of the dozens upon dozens of famous lives that could serve as examples, Charles Darwin's is one of the clearest illustrations of the anxious hazards that await a person working in the realm of ideas. Even before the publication of *The Origin of Species*, Darwin suffered—in the culturally accepted manner of his day—from his anticipation of the violent response he knew his work must elicit.

Charles Darwin was raised in Shrewsbury, England, by a strict father, described by one relative as "a very considerable tyrant," and a mother who died when Charles was only eight. Even more than most upper-middle-class Victorians, Charles learned to respect the authority of God, Queen, and father and to direct any rebellious thoughts down his own throat. Like many of his contemporaries, he never learned to handle the conflicts and confusions of disobedience.

Following the wishes of his father, who was a doctor, Charles enrolled in medical school at the University of Edinburgh but did not enjoy it. After witnessing "two bad operations, one on a child . . . [which] fairly haunted me for many a long year,"[24] he changed without great enthusiasm to a program of geology and natural history. As a student he already suffered from the gastrointestinal complaints that would plague him all his life and also complained of problems with his hand and lip. It was not until he took the adventurous step of embarking on an around-the-world voyage on the *Beagle* (against his father's better judgment), however, that his serious complaints began. He wrote many years later:

> These two months at Plymouth [waiting for the ship to sail] were the most miserable which I have ever spent. I was out of spirits at the thought of leaving all my family and friends for so long a time, and the weather seemed to me so inexpressibly gloomy. I was also troubled with palpitations and pain about the heart, and like many a young ignorant man, especially one with a smattering of medical knowledge, was convinced that I had

heart disease. I did not consult any doctor, as I fully expected to hear the verdict that I was not fit for the voyage, and I was resolved to go at all hazards.[25]

Once safely embarked on the *Beagle*, Charles did not complain much about his health, though he did suffer terribly from seasickness. Upon his return his health remained good until he married. Then, about the time that his patient wife (and cousin), Emma, became pregnant, Charles's health deteriorated and was rarely restored to what most persons would consider normal for the rest of his seventy-three years. Although he used his father as his doctor until the latter died, he did not get the sympathy he craved from the elder Darwin. "I told him of my dreadful numbness in my finger ends," he wrote Emma, "and all the sympathy I could get was 'Yes-yes-exactly-tut-tut, neuralgic, exactly, yes, yes!!'"[26] But from Emma it was different. "Without you when I feel sick I feel most desolate. . . . I do so long to be . . . under your protection for then I feel safe."[27]

After three years of marriage and a second pregnancy, which "knocked me up almost as much as it did Emma," the Darwins moved to the country, where Charles's delicate health would not be taxed by social obligations. As was mentioned before in connection with the privileges of illness, Emma's "whole day was planned to suit him, to be ready for reading aloud to him, to go his walks with him, and to be constantly at hand to alleviate his daily discomforts."[28] Gradually she came to plan his rest cures and vacations, monitor the number of his guests, and even determine the length of his conversations with visiting scientists.

But it was not a simple desire for privilege and pampering or even an aversion to social gatherings that had Charles retching over his washbasin night after night or lying awake feeling "so much afraid though my reason was laughing & told me there was nothing." As he worked on the quantities of data gathered on the *Beagle*, he began sketching a broad hypothesis that would make sense of information that, if viewed traditionally, seemed difficult to fit together. To his first confidant, the botanist Joseph Hooker, he admitted that he was engaged "in a very presumptuous work, and I know no one individual who would not say a very foolish one. . . . At last gleams of light have come, and I am almost convinced (quite contrary to the opinion I started with) that species are not (it is like confessing a murder) immutable. . . . I think I have found out (here's presumption!) the simple way by which species become exquisitely adapted to various ends. You will now groan, and think to yourself, 'on what a man have I been wasting my time and writing to.' I should, five years ago, have thought so [too]."[29]

With as much sorrow as conviction, Charles Darwin inched his way toward a position that put him painfully at odds with people whose professional feelings he feared to offend and whose personal affection he trembled to lose. Darwin, who so hated arguments that it made him sick to think about them, realized that his theory of natural selection would be vehemently rejected by many. And Darwin, who so wanted to please his wife by being a Christian of unwavering faith, knew he was basing his life's work on a natural process so "clumsy, wasteful, blundering, low and cruel" that it could not possibly be an expression of God's will.

Darwin published *On the Origin of Species by Means of Natural Selection* in 1859 and with it broke the link between moral and natural sciences. Nature no longer had a moral lesson to teach. As expected, *The Origin* was violently attacked by the Church, but not in Darwin's presence. He was already doing penance. He was sick.

> I am glad I was not at Oxford, for I should have been overwhelmed, with my stomach in its present state. . . . I would as soon have died as tried to answer the Bishop [Samuel Wilberforce] in such an assembly.[30]

As Darwin grew older he gradually gained insight into the part his illnesses had played in his personal economy. He had learned from taking water cures that it was possible for him to "walk & eat like a hearty Christian" for the regime of long walks, simple food, and scrubs and showers "dulls one's brain splendidly. I have not thought about a single species of any kind since leaving home."[31] Yet in another letter to his friend Joseph Hooker he admits that although his "head will stand no thought" without making him sick, "I would sooner be the wretched contemptible invalid, which I am, than live the life of an idle squire."[32] "My abstract [*The Origin of Species*] is the cause, I believe, of the main part of the ills to which my flesh is heir to."[33]

In addition to realizing that his controversial theory of natural selection brought on a great deal of his physical distress, Darwin also began to see that the illnesses themselves had functioned as regulators. They had protected him from "the distractions of society and amusement" and, more important, from the very real possibility of mental collapse. "I know well that my head would have failed years ago had not my stomach saved me from a minute's over-work."[34]

During the last decade of his life Darwin worked almost exclusively on plants, which he loved. Although his health was gradually undermined by heart disease, his vomiting and anxious insomnia largely ceased. His reputation as a scientist was secure, his personal relationships less demanding, his daily routine set beyond disruption. There were fewer threats and conflicts in his country life and far less anxiety to channel into his own stomach. Even the words he had underlined in his manuscript to remind himself that when a species has vanished the same form never reappears gave him less sorrow. With that knowledge, wrote Philip Appleman more than a century later, "we know we are mortal as mammoths, / we know the last lines of our poem."[35]

Darwin was by no means alone in preferring illness to open conflict or in paying excessive attention to his health. For many of his contemporaries in literary as well as scientific circles, the quest for health in such a time of rapid change seemed a search for a physical, emotional, and moral unity that could replace the traditional faiths that were being so badly shaken. As is the case today, an exaggerated concern for health was an acceptable avenue of retreat from a disheartening world both for some hypochondriacs who denied the problems of the larger world altogether and for persons such as Darwin, T. H. Huxley, Lytton Strachey, Robert Burns, Alfred Lord Tennyson, and so many others whose painfully honest dealings with their part of the world seemed to drive them toward a partial retreat.

In Darwin's case, as with the others mentioned, there has long been talk of "creative maladies," of the impetus that anxiety can lend to a career, and of the part that suffering plays in the getting of wisdom. But although hypochondria has been used as a synonym for excruciating sensitivity and is associated with the lives of such artists, writers, and composers as Molière, Voltaire, Jonathan Swift, Samuel Johnson, James Boswell, Immanuel Kant, Beethoven, the de Goncourt brothers, André Gide, and Sara Teasdale, these persons could hardly think or write during their severest bouts of hypochondria. All struggled *against* their disorder with the tremendous activities that made them famous.

Hypochondria might be something of an occupational hazard for doctors, performers, and intellectual rebels, and it might sometimes serve as a defense against or regulator of conflicts that could overwhelm, but it certainly does not seem to be a prerequisite of creativity.

"Disease is not the soil from which the best products of our culture spring."[36]

GETTING BETTER

We pay our past little honor by pretending
we can shed it easily.

              —Robert May
              Sex and Fantasy

■

I
T IS USELESS TO imagine that hypochondria is a pattern that
yields easily to change. Although at one time or another our
entire stock of mechanical, pharmacological, and psychotherapeu-
tic tools has been utilized in its treatment, no reliable cures have
emerged. As has been the case for centuries, dozens of treatments coexist for this common malady, some promising a veneer
of tranquility, others a chemical fix, and still others the distant
prospect of what Samuel Johnson called the stability of truth.

Although it is common to compare treating a hypochondriac to shaping a piece of flint with a toothpick, the fifteen or
so studies in which hypochondriacs have actually been followed
after therapy (reviewed in Kellner)[1] present no clear picture of
prognosis. Certain trends can be discerned, however.

■   The shorter the duration of the hypochondria before therapy
       is begun, the better the outcome.

- If a personality disorder, such as might be seen in an extremely dependent or socially isolated individual, accompanies the hypochondria, the outcome is less likely to be favorable.
- If a hypochondriac is miserably anxious or depressed, there may be a better chance of his changing than if he is emotionless.
- The hypochondriac who suffers a rapid succession of transient but recurring symptoms usually does better than an individual whose symptoms are unremitting.[2]
- Suicide among hypochondriacs is rare unless they are also seriously depressed, in which case the hypochondria increases the risk.

In addition, there are various subgroups of hypochondriacs who seem to respond to treatment differently. For example, a "developmental" hypochondriac whose troubles have begun in early adulthood and whose hypochondria is an ingrained part of his strategy for living will probably be more difficult to treat than a "reactive" hypochondriac who becomes hoarse after his brother dies of laryngeal cancer and is sure that he too is dying of the same disease.

Dividing hypochondriacs another way, those who embrace chronic invalidism and suffer no significant displeasure from being sickly—Etty Darwin, for example—are more difficult to get into treatment, much less treat, than those who are emotionally and physically distressed by their constant succession of symptoms.

Combining trends and types, it seems that basically four things can happen to hypochondriacs. They can get worse, as did Sara Teasdale and Jacopo Pontormo, the former committing suicide and the latter dying of natural causes after years of emotional paralysis. Alternatively, they can labor against recurring bouts of hypochondria that remain at about the same level of severity but become more manageable. Such a chronic course was suffered by Boswell, vexed "to find a return of that distemper," and Darwin, afraid of being considered a "wretched contemptible invalid." Or they can remain the same, either by embarking on a career as an invalid as did Smollett's Matt Bramble, Molière's Argan, and Etty Darwin, or by embracing a lifelong series of alternate obsessions such as health and fitness fads or mind cures.[3] Finally, hypochondriacs can get better, as triumphantly illustrated by the corpulent George Cheyne, who attained, "thank God, inward Peace, Health and Freedom of Spirits."[4]

There are no reliable estimates of improvement, but after reviewing the modern literature, Kellner cautiously concludes that psychotherapies seem to accelerate the improvement that might occur from routine medical care, and tranquilizers and antidepressants reduce symptoms. Roughly half the hypochondriacs who seek treatment seem to substantially improve.[5]

We now come to treatment. As we have seen, the hallmark of a hypochondriac is that he wishes to deal with his emotional or psychosocial problems as if they were purely physical problems over which he has no control and for which he can take no blame. This being the case, he registers his problems as physical symptoms and seeks treatment either from a medical doctor or, more actively, from some self-styled regime of diet and exercise that would seem to address the physical problem. Only if these treatments repeatedly fail *and* if he is miserable will a hypochondriac consider psychotherapy.

Before considering either physical or emotional treatments, we must look at the terms "cure" and "improvement." Using a narrow definition, a cure for hypochondria might be expected to straighten out wrong-headed beliefs, eliminate the symptoms of bogus disease, and dissipate anxiety or depression. But these happy changes do not usually occur. Just as persons who consider themselves physically healthy sustain a wide variety of disabilities such as nearsightedness, high blood pressure, and migraines, so the mentally healthy person is not so much symptom-free as he is unhampered by the symptoms he exhibits.[6] Thus for a hypochondriac, "cured" does not necessarily mean that he will never worry about having a heart attack again; rather, it means that he will handle such an occurrence very differently.

"Improvement" is just as broad and slippery a concept as

"cure," and this makes it difficult to compare the outcomes of different treatments. One of the more common ways of judging improvement is for both physician or therapist and client independently to rate the progress made and for the client to continue to evaluate his condition at six-month or twelve-month intervals. Nevertheless, even when the method of evaluation is roughly the same among studies, terms such as "much improved" can mean a number of things.

Returning to treatments, we have two categories to consider—first, the treatments hypochondriacs initially favor, such as medical doctors, specialists, and personal regimes, and, second, various psychotherapies. Extracting the "active ingredients" from the self-styled treatments used by the hypochondriacs described in this book, we find that seeking support from a trusted physician is a most common recourse. The literature of hypochondria has its famous couples, patient and doctor, and it would be interesting to discover if the healthier hypochondriacs are those who put their trust in a single doctor (or kick the doctor habit entirely) compared to those who seek out and discard a succession of physicians. A variation of this desire for support from a doctor is the hypochondriac's urge to shore up his fragile body by taking the waters or retreating to rest homes and special institutes. Taking a more active hand in their own management, hypochondriacs might put themselves on special diets, cut out alcohol, or try to walk or run off their anxieties. Also on the first line of defense for someone like Boswell or Johnson is reading Burton's *Anatomy of Melancholy* or in some other way actively mastering the offending distemper. Both Cheyne and de Mandeville became physicians, then wrote about hypochondria (including their own cases), and helped others control their fears. Even Molière's Argan becomes a doctor at the end of the play; and, more recently, Kate, who followed Boswell through Holland, has finished medical school and is specializing in psychosomatic medicine. Still another ingredient of the most common self-styled cures is diversion—working hard on a career and being actively involved with other people. "Be not solitary; be not idle."[7]

There is no clear distinction between these self-styled and largely physical treatments and psychotherapy primarily because a supportive medical doctor provides some of each. Kellner recommends that any physician who suspects a patient of being hypochondriacal first try to handle the case by slowing down, encouraging the patient to talk about emotional and social problems as well as physical ones, and listening. Once the necesssary physical examinations and tests are performed, Kellner suggests that the physician give a simple, accurate explanation of the problem, which usually includes explaining how anxiety augments the perception of pain. Given such an explanation, many patients feel reassured both by knowing what is going on and what they can expect in the future.

Next the physician helps the patient unlearn the delicate art of creating symptoms. The patient has probably been so attentive to one part of his body and has brooded so anxiously over the possible meanings of each creep of the skin and thump of the heart that he has constructed a half-dozen equally appalling constellations of decay any one of which could radically shorten his time on earth. Kellner's ideal physician takes these maladaptive processes into account and tells the patient how to interrupt these ruminations and, if necessary, how to accept setbacks philosophically. (Another expert on hypochondria, F. E. Kenyon,[8] further suggests instruction in relaxation, "a proper holiday," autosuggestion, keeping occupied, cutting out medications, staying away from quacks, and being as open as possible with the doctor.) If, despite all these suggestions, the patient's apprehensions are not allayed in several weeks, then it is time to suggest psychotherapy.

But what kind? One of the talking therapies or talk-plus-drugs that seek to change the hypochondriac in the belief that the cause of the problem lies mainly within the individual? Or one of the far less common family or community therapies that seek to change the environment in the belief that the source of distress lies primarily in the relationships that the hypochondriac has with others?[9]

Because most people believe that hypochondria comes from within, therapies of self-adjustment are common. In fact, in the United States today there are at least fifty different kinds from which to choose. The differences among such methods as analysis, behavior modification, and psychodrama seem tremendous, but the similarities are impressive too. All attempt to explain the sufferers to themselves—that is, to give them an acceptable explanation for why they are feeling and acting the way they are. Further, all attempt to introduce them to alternative ways of dealing with their problems.

A further similarity is that most of these therapies reflect the dominant values of our culture and thus present themselves as scientific rather than religious or purely intuitive, and as democratic and permissive rather than authoritarian. In contrast, German therapies, for example, are more authoritarian, not because these methods have been shown to work better than democratic ones but because they fit better within German society.

A wonderfully vigorous German doctor, Karl Leonhard, believes that a hypochondriac should be forced to do exactly what he fears most. When a patient appears who is terrified of heart failure, Leonhard leaps from behind his desk and leads the sufferer through a breathtaking series of deep knee bends right in his office. The person afraid of ulcer or stomach cancer is ordered to eat regular food—wursts, sauerkraut, beer, and pastries. Those fearing insanity get a reading list of melancholic philosophers. In addition, Leonhard orders all his patients to spend several hours a day exercising vigorously and to stop talking about their symptoms. With the support of weekly therapy sessions that usually last only a month or two, Leonhard maintains that "this method of therapy will cure almost all hypochondriac cases."[10] If therapists used this autocratic method of dealing with hypochondriacs in the United States, however, both their patients and colleagues would probably complain of their heavy-handedness.

If a hypochondriac embarks upon a course of self-adjustment, he or she is likely to get one of three broad types: psychodynamic therapy, behavior modification, or (less often) group therapy. The first concentrates on giving the patient personal insight into the nature of the basic conflict that underlies the hypochondria.

Many psychodynamic therapies are variations of Freudian methods and of the ego psychology that grew from them. In simplest terms, these schools of thought proceed as if each person has an ego that seeks to defend itself against the onslaughts of the person's own instinctual drives or impulses. These basic and unreasoning urges push the person toward the getting of pleasure and toward the release of tension by means of aggression. When these urges pass into consciousness on the way to fulfillment, however, the ego insists that they respect the demands of reality and, further, that they obey the rules of social custom and morality. If the ego can bend the instinctual drives into socially acceptable forms without denying them entirely, the common struggles of the emotionally healthy ensue.

But if the balance of power between the force of desire and the ego's control is upset by any one of a number of deficiencies in childhood, then the ego may feel it cannot handle the overpowering urges. According to Freudian analysts, the ego counterattacks and tries to put the disruptive desire for pleasure or aggression permanently out of commission by using one or more carefully selected defenses. For example, an urge may be repressed and pushed right out of one's consciousness; it may be reversed so that aggression surfaces an oversolicitous concern and sexual desire as prudery; it may be projected onto others as if they were the driven ones; or it may be turned against oneself. This last mechanism of defense is common among hypochondriacs, especially those who punish themselves both to avoid a harsher punishment at the hands of a powerful person and as a retribution for the deep feelings of aggression they harbor toward these powerful persons.

Psychotherapies that explain hypochondria in terms of egos and urges generally try to reverse the defensive process and allow the instinctual urges and volcanic emotions associated with them back into consciousness so that the rest of the person (his ego and consciousness) can come to terms with the troublesome urges in a more realistic and less disruptive way. To do this, therapists ally themselves with the urges as they fleetingly surface in memories, present conflicts, and dreams.

Reconstruction of the first attack of hypochondria is especially valuable as it is likely to present a relatively clear picture of the instinctual urge or the conflict it engenders being driven below the surface of consciousness with a defensive tactic. Later attacks of hypochondria are likely to be distorted and embellished with the hypochondriac's reactions to the attacks themselves and their social consequences. When the therapist tries to exhume the emotionally charged urges that seem so unbearably threatening to the patient that he has been willing to be sick and afraid just to deny their existence, the hypochondriac strenuously resists. He denies, he charms, he fabricates, he intellectualizes. But if therapist and patient persist, excuses finally collapse; personal myths of goodwill, self-sufficiency, and much else crumble; and the battle to survive illness gradually shifts to a different ground. The new battlefield is often one on which the hypochondriac's desire for independence runs headlong into his old inability to stand up to (and thus possibly break from) a powerful parentlike person. Psychodynamic therapy tries to give such persons enough self-confidence and insight into their own behavior and the behavior of those around them to enable them to act in accordance with this new understanding. It is not enough for them to think independent thoughts or to use the therapist's explanations as an excuse for continued dependence and hypochondria.

Some therapists feel that although psychodynamic therapy provides insight into underlying problems, it is not particularly effective in giving patients the skills they need to put their new insight into practice in the outside world.

A very different process goes on, at least in theory, during behavior modification, or behavior therapy, as it is often called. For behaviorists, who deny the existence of the free inner self and believe, with B. F. Skinner, that "the environment determines the individual," there are no neuroses, only simple learned habits.[11] Individuals acquire these habits as they respond to the situations they encounter during their lifetime. Because they have no choice in becoming what they become, it makes no sense to blame them for developing the bad habit of hypochondria, for example, or for hanging onto it once the habit is acquired. The goal of behavior therapy is to get patients to unlearn their habit by which is meant get rid of their symptoms. "There is no neurosis underlining the symptom but merely the symptom itself—get rid of the symptom and you have eliminated the neurosis."[12]

In the case of hypochondria, which behaviorists prefer to call "a somatic response to stress," the patient is first taught one of several relaxation techniques so that anxiety is reduced and the unlearning process can begin. Next therapist and patient study the situations that trigger an attack and the responses that follow. Once the cues that initiate the hypochondriacal behavior are identified, the patient begins practicing a different response to those cues. This is called counterconditioning. If the habit does not readily respond, a system of rewards for the new response and punishment might be added to prod the sufferer toward better health. For a chronic hypochondriac the cues eliciting anxiety or illness behavior are piled around him like jackstraws. Unexpected agreement as well as arguments, the threat of success as well as failure, a major acquisition as well as loss—any change whatsoever can trigger a hypochondriacal response.

Nevertheless, behavior therapists concentrate on the more common cues and try to teach the hypochondriac to respond to them in a new way. This usually involves assertiveness training or practice in getting mad, for hypochondriacs often direct their anger toward themselves rather than delivering it directly and unambiguously to others. Such patients are encouraged to substitute the clear expression of their own feelings for their former recourse to illness, even if this means frightening confrontations with powerful persons.

If a hypochondriac suffers primarily from the fear of disease, and his anxiety attacks are triggered more by seeing a program on cancer or walking into a doctor's office than by social conflicts, then desensitization may be preferable to counterconditioning. Using this procedure, the patient first constructs a hierarchy or weighted list of anxieties. Once the patient has rated the objects or events he fears according to their degree of disturbance, he and the therapist usually find that his fears cluster around three or four foci. For example, there might be fears of illness associated with doctors, injections, the sight of open wounds, or medical odors; fears of personal vulnerability associated with criticism, teasing, or rejection; and fear of aggression linked to fighting, loud noises, bullying, knives, anger, and so forth.

Next, the patient is led through a relaxation procedure and then, in the safe setting of the clinic, is repeatedly exposed to one of his minor fears. He is asked to imagine being teased or walking into a hospital over and over again until it elicits no anxiety at all. The desensitization procedure is repeated for each of his fears.

Behavior modification, with its frequent use of relaxation techniques and assertiveness training, seems fully conscious of the need to prepare the hypochondriac for reentry into the outside world. There is some doubt, however, as to whether the elimination of symptoms without insight into the underlying problems is the equivalent of mental health. When counterconditioning was used on anorexia nervosa patients who were starving themselves to death, for example, the system of rewards and rather disagreeable punishments led to rapid gains in weight but also increased the patients' feelings of helplessness.[13] Now they were being manipulated by a therapist as well as by their parents. Several girls adopted measures of countermanipulation. They took to gorging themselves before weighing time and vomiting as soon as the therapist was out of sight. Treated with behavior therapy, these girls gained some weight, but they still felt out of control and still faced life as anorexics. George Ladee, among others, found that the same kind of thing happened when hypochondriacs were given a pure form of behavior therapy.[14] Their anxiety was reduced but their pattern of preoccupations remained.

A few therapists have used hypnotism in conjunction with behavior therapy both to give their patients insight into their deeper problems and to involve them more actively in the therapeutic process. For example, one woman, who was so preoccupied with her supposedly failing health that she gave up all housekeeping and lay on a sofa ten hours a day, was told under hypnosis that her real problems stemmed from loneliness and rejection, not ill health. She was told,

> When you wake up, you will think of yourself as a person with 'problems in living'. . . . You haven't had time to think about these important problems because of your other concerns. Now you will have time to do so, because your mind will be very curious to discover such problems in living in your own life, and you will be very eager to discuss them and solve them. . . . You *will* be able to solve them with hard work. Your other problems will seem less important than these problems in living.[15]

Within a month this woman gave up fourteen of her seventeen symptoms, resumed keeping house, and lay on the sofa only an hour each day. Interviewed a year later, she still had only three symptoms—none major—and was napping about two and a half hours a day. The combination of hypnosis and talking therapy had apparently enabled this woman to give up her substitute problems and address her real concerns more quickly than is usual among hypochondriacs.

There is still lively disagreement between behaviorists and other psychotherapists as to whose model of emotional development is closer to the truth and whose therapy is more effective. Authors of one of the more careful comparisons noted that a warm, friendly behaviorist inadvertently gives his or her patients more than a set of directions for unlearning a habit. Listening in on the sessions, observers were sometimes hard put to distinguish psychodynamic therapists from behavior therapists.[16]

The third and least likely of the talking therapies that a hypochondriac is likely to encounter and one that begins the transition to what might be called social therapies is group therapy. In this case the disorder is thought of as involving an underlying difficulty in interpersonal relations. Introduced in this country at the turn of the century, group methods were first used to treat the medically ill and then tried on "nervous troubles" in the 1930s.[17] By the 1950s the interpersonal relationships of the group members rather than their illnesses had becme the focus of treatment, and each member's overreactions and distortions were regarded as characteristic of the problems each suffered with family members or other important persons. Early sessions of a group of "high somatizers" are commonly dominated by a discussion of symptoms and medications, and group members are often relentless in their attempts to get the group leader to prescribe medication or in some way make them instantly well, as a good doctor should be able to do. However, discussions usually turn to anger, disappointment, and previously unacknowledged feelings of failure. Even when this shift does not occur, it has been reported that hypochondriacs dramatically reduce their visits to the medical clinic,[18] and when somatic complaints are exchanged for problems in living, the results are even better. (See Schoenberg and Senescu for a brief review.)[19]

Before leaving therapies of self-reform and moving to the wider arena of social reform, we should take a brief look at drug therapy.
By far the most common prescription drugs given to hypochondriacs are minor tranquilizers. If a hypochondriac is seeing a medical doctor, he will almost surely be given one of the benzodiazepines to manage his distress, and if he embarks on psychotherapy, he may continue to receive tranquilizers on the

theory that a relaxed patient makes quicker progress. By themselves, however, these drugs neither cure nor control hypochondria. The example provided by D. V. Sheehan's fifty-seven patients, who before participating in a trial of antidepressants had taken more than half a million doses of tranquilizers and were still beset by their original problems, does not stretch the imagination.[20]

A far more promising group of drugs is the antidepressants. In the 1950s these and several other classes of drug that alter the functioning of the brain's neurotransmitters—chemicals that regulate the passage of nerve impulses from one nerve cell to another—were introduced from Europe. At first they were used on schizophrenics, manic-depressives, and other psychotics, but by the 1960s some were being used in conjunction with talking therapy in the treatment of affective disorders. Because hypochondriacs and anxious persons sometimes benefited from antidepressants, investigators initially concluded that such patients must have been suffering from a masked or disguised depression. As more was learned, however, it was seen that there were different kinds of biochemical imbalances and that a single drug could alleviate more than one problem. Although specific imbalances cannot yet be matched to particular psychiatric syndromes, some neurologists tentatively assume that a functional deficit of certain neurotransmitters is associated with depression and that a functional excess (which could result from low levels of *inhibitory* neurotransmitters) is somehow involved in mania and anxiety states.

Using this oversimplified and clearly transitional model of mental distress, hypochondria, anxiety neuroses, panic disorders, illness phobias, and a host of related problems are all believed to be associated with abnormally low levels of inhibitory neurotransmitters, which in turn are affected by inheritance, metabolism, stress, and other factors. The millions of Americans affected thus find it difficult to dampen or inhibit the nerve impulses that ricochet through their central nervous systems. Beset by a chronic overabundance of sensations, some associate their gurgles, jangles, and palpitations with disease. From this point it is a short step to hypochondria. According to neurologists, who embrace a biochemical explanation of hypochondria, the goal of treatment is not to understand the symbolic meaning of "illness" or even to ask sufferers how they are using their fears to cope with their environment. Instead, the aim is to correct the subtle imbalance within their central nervous systems with the appropriate drug.

This kind of drug therapy was given to fifty-seven persons, all of whom were severely and chronically disabled by anxiety.[21] In a double-blind experiment, one-third of the patients received a placebo and the others were given one of two types of antidepressant. At first, members of all three groups suffered dramatic side effects, and the investigators dourly noted that "the propensity of these patients to experience all varieties of side effects . . . is reinforced by their hypochondriacal fears and makes their management very difficult in the first four weeks."[22]

At the end of twelve weeks, however, 83 percent of the patients on antidepressants showed a remarkable degree of improvement, whereas only half the group on placebos noticed any improvement at all. Although no follow-up study could be done on the placebo group because they were immediately put on antidepressants, the investigators predicted that, if left untreated, members of the placebo group would soon have lost their modest improvement because their panic attacks never stopped recurring. Consequently, their hypochondriacal or phobic life-styles were continuously reactivated. The patients on drugs had no further anxiety attacks after six weeks of treatment and were able to drop their fears and restrictions with a minimum of retraining (behavior therapy).

Several years later the authors of this investigation were less sanguine concerning the long-term effectiveness of antidepressants. "If a patient has had a satisfactory period of stability," reported the director of the Psychosomatic Medicine Clinic at Massachusetts General Hospital, "the drug may be discontinued after six months to a year. Relapses are common."[23]

Now to therapies of social reform—programs that have shifted their focus from the distressed individual to the family or community in which he or she lives. The belief is that *"there is an intimate relationship between the social organization of the community and the individual psychological organizatin of its residents."*[24] This orientation does not negate the importance of either physiology or personality but insists that social factors are so important that they can make the difference between health and disease.

"Mental health can only be achieved in an environment which provides opportunities for self-expression, social usefulness, and the attainment of human satisfactions."[25] Social psychiatrists further maintain 'that the resolution of socially generated mental disorders often lies beyond the powers of either the physician or the psychotherapist.

In family therapy, however, the therapist tries to effect social reforms on a small scale. Frequently a family comes into therapy with an "identified patient," a member who seems to be having all the trouble. The therapist's goal is to show the family that the real problem does not belong to an individual and that that member's symptoms are not saying "I am sick" as much as they are proclaiming "this is no way for a group of people to live." The therapist believes he will find that the whole family is somewhat disordered or that its members are taking turns being disordered, with the result that a restrictive and maladaptive system of family communication has developed.

Structural family therapy has been particularly useful in ameliorating the restrictive conditions that stimulate and maintain psychosomatic illness in children. It has been noted that when the family gathers for an interview there is rarely a lot of noise and bickering but, rather, an excess of apparent goodwill. Each member of the family seems remarkably aware of how the actions of each will affect the others—they live in one anothers' pockets, as the expression goes—and the mother or older daughter will often speak for or interpret what someone else in the family has said. Such families have often developed complicated methods for avoiding overt conflict: one member getting sick instead of angry, another helpfully managing instead of directly manipulating, a third following directions to avoid trouble, and so on. Each responds to the indirect coercion of the other with countermanipulative techniques of his or her own. No problems are confronted, or even stated, and no answers are found to unformulated questions.

In this situation individual therapy is sometimes less effective than family therapy, for if the legitimately upset and disordered "patient" is prompted to find the source of discontent solely within himself he may well pull back from family conflicts that are among the most important to resolve. Even with the assertiveness training or insight that individual therapy can supply, the patient will have an extremely hard time convincing family members who are intent upon avoiding conflict, blame, and change that they should abandon their pretense of cooperation and confront their disagreements.

Of course family therapists face the same awesome resistance, and they have had to devise subtle methods to trick, cajole, and persuade. Not least among these is "paradoxical intervention" in which the therapist appears neither to want nor to expect the family to change its uncomfortable way of doing business. When confronted with the hypochondriacal complaints in a child, for example, the therapist urges the family to take the symptoms at face value and brushes off any suggestion that they represent an emotional problem. Such a therapist may tell the child in a matter-of-fact way that it is a good idea to keep the asthma or stomachaches. Getting rid of them would deny the whole family too many benefits, such as the child's own favored position among brothers and sisters, an acceptable excuse for the mother to stay home and not get a job, and a made-to-order focus for the whole family's discontents.

The family is confounded. They were sure the therapist would challenge their literal interpretation of the problem, and although they would not admit it—hardly knew it, in fact—they were prepared to resist. They were not going to be controlled by a therapist. But if the therapist insists on *no change*, the family can spite him only by changing.

Some studies have found that family therapies help roughly two-thirds of the persons who use them. If the father participates, the rate of improvement is higher. If he does not, it is lower.[26]

Although a mental health act was signed in 1946 establishing the National Institutes of Mental Health and making federal funds available for the investigation of social problems, no major programs in community psychiatry were launched until the 1960s. At that time community mental health centers were established across the country both to treat the mentally ill—especially persons who could not afford private therapies—and to upgrade communities in hopes of lowering the incidence of alcoholism, delinquency, suicide, and other expressions of distress.

Exactly what changes a mental health center should try to effect were by no means clear, but gradually what might be called a social-psychiatric model of mental health and disease evolved that helped community workers recognize groups of persons who were at risk of developing mental disorder. The model was based in large part on a five-year study of community mental health undertaken in Nova Scotia.[27] According to Alexander Leighton, senior author of this study, mental health is dependent upon the pursuit of ten basic satisfactions, which he listed as physical security, sexual satisfaction, the expression of hostility, giving love, getting love, recognition, the expression of creativity, a sense of social position, membership in a group, and a sense of what could loosely be called righteousness. These constitute each person's "essential strivings." Block a person from striving for any of these—that is, convince him that any of these goals are unattainable or mutually exclusive—and "disagreeable feelings" will ensue. Such feelings set off a struggle to set things right, and this leads either to a solution and renewed striving or to a stalemate in which the individual obtains partial relief from his disagreeable feelings by restricting the full scope of his life.

Thus the sociologist describes mental disorder as a process by which we lock away one or more essential parts of our lives in an effort to survive without unendurable emotional pain.[28] Once an individual has hobbled himself in exchange for a measure of peace, he might become more or less disordered, Leighton asserts, depending on the strengths and weaknesses of his body, his emotional development, and his community.

Social psychiatrists use this or a related model of mental disorder to look for groups of persons within a community who are blocked from pursuing some of their essential strivings and who are therefore at risk of mental breakdown. When such groups are found, a community mental health center can treat individuals or try to institute community reforms that will unblock their striving and, it is hoped, prevent future distress.

The treatment half of the remedy involves traditional therapies of self-adjustment which seek to change the behavior of distressed individuals in ways that make it more socially acceptable. Politicians thus speak of mental health centers as a form of "fire insurance," a smart expenditure for a community to make in exchange for reduced incidence of arson, assault, and vandalism. The poor, for whom the center was established, are wary of this philosophy, and the residents who work at the center warn that "we must not allow the establishment to use us to pacify the community . . . to 'cool out' the poor, especially [the] blacks."[29]

Prevention by means of reform is the more radical part of the remedy, involving, as it invariably does, criticism of some aspect of the community. A fine example comes from Somerville, Massachusetts, a nonacademic suburb of Boston.[30] There Victor Cardoza, a politician inspired by Leighton's project in Nova Scotia, worked with the Somerville Mental Health Center to see if the Center could initiate social changes that would affect mental health. Guided by an academic group working on preventive psychiatry, Cardoza first identified three high-risk groups: kids on drugs, the unemployed, and elderly persons who were bedridden. Judging that the community would be most responsive to the needs of senior citizens, Cardoza then tried to determine what the isolated themselves thought they needed. From their suggestions he might institute social reforms to reduce the depression and suicide that were alarmingly common.

Against considerable opposition mounted by established services for the elderly, Cardoza finally managed to set up a central information and coordination service for senior citizens. The new service, totally independent of the mental health center, offered two visiting programs, one for persons in nursing homes and another for the elderly who lived by themselves. Before leaving Somerville, Cardoza helped the mental health center begin this "catalytic" process all over again for a second high-risk group.

It will never be possible to measure precisely the effects of Somerville's social reforms on mental health and certainly not on a single group of persons such as hypochondriacs. Common sense suggests, however, that the no-longer-so-isolated elderly who now receive regular visits from their contemporaries, the clergy, and high school students are less likely unconsciously to cultivate disease as an excuse for calling the doctor or for creating a family emergency. They may no longer need hypochondria as an excuse to relieve their loneliness.

Thus far help for the hypochondriac has been described in general terms, which does not say much about how the process of getting better actually proceeds in a real person's life. If we pick up from chapter 4 the story of Anita, who as a child was punished by her mother for getting sick until illness and badness seemed all but synonymous, we can follow the progress of a woman who gradually put together her own eclectic regime as she struggled to outgrow her acutely uncomfortable hypochondria.

Anita had suffered from a series of undiagnosable illnesses from childhood and was particularly upset when two of her playmates died suddenly. Gradually her fear of illness fastened on heart failure, a choice that was underscored when a relative who had attributed his chest pains to asthma died suddenly of a heart attack. During her college years Anita was rarely bothered by thoughts of illness, but when she married and had two children in rapid succession her hypochondria returned in force.

One of Anita's most vivid and painful memories from this period is of lying in bed next to her sleeping husband and feeling her chest begin to tighten. It became painful to breathe and then, was she imagining it, or was the pain spreading upward toward the left side of her jaw and downward into her arm? She rolled over on her side. The pain got worse. She shifted quietly onto her back again.

"So this is what it feels like to have a heart attack," she said to herself. Questions, half-formulated and curiously immobile, clamped themselves around her fears. The pain would increase gradually or suddenly. She would live or she would die. But two things were certain. Her chest hurt horribly and she must not disturb her husband.

Having miraculously survived the night, Anita was much too upset for the next several days to see the absurdity of her situation. She finally told her husband of her attack but deemphasized its fearfulness, agreeing outwardly that it might well have been indigestion. At the same time she fretted over whether or not to "bother" her doctor. If she told him how terrifyingly bad the attack had been, she was sure he would insist on extensive tests, even hospitalization, but if she described it as she had for her husband, then the doctor would probably tell her it was heartburn. She wished fervently that she did not have to carry the burden of these secret illnesses any longer. The attacks were so utterly uncontrollable when they came, and yet people's response to them seemed easy to manipulate. Although she could not yet put it into words, she felt the confusion and inconsistency of dealing with her heart attacks on two entirely different levels. Privately they were real in every sense of the word, yet publicly she treated them almost as if they were products of her imagination. She apologized for the inconvenience they caused others as if she were creating the attacks on purpose. The unintentional deceitfulness of Anita's heart attacks was uncomfortably close to the surface. She knew and she didn't know at the same time. During the next five years, from the age of thirty to thirty-five, Anita got much better. She not only recognized that her pains and fears were substitutions for deeper fears of confrontation and rejection but managed to rechannel a major portion of her anxiety into family relationships, where it belonged. Her transition from a fearfully anxious hypochondriac to a confident yet appropriately watchful hypochondriac in remission seemed largely undirected, yet with hindsight Anita could see that she had inadvertently embraced much of the advice handed on to hypochondriacs since ancient times.

Anita had taken up running, for example, ostensibly to keep her weight down but actually, she realized later, as a powerful insurance policy against heart disease.

> As long as I run, I am convinced that I won't have a heart attack. Even today, if I haven't run for five or six weeks, I am very reluctant to shovel heavy snow or carry anything heavy. I know this isn't rational. But it's the way I think.

About a year after she began to run (a treatment used by some therapists to speed up talking therapies),[31] Anita revived her interest in music, first by returning to her piano lessons and then by getting a part-time job in a music store. At the same time, she, her husband, and her brother-in-law bought a big wooden boat and began to restore it. She was neither solitary nor idle.

The social aspects of Anita's life were also improving. She made new friends through her interests in running, sailing, and music and especially among musicians began to feel part of an intimate group for the first time since college. Gradually she gained enough self-confidence to admit to herself that she had indeed been in bad shape for the past several years. Not surprisingly, it was at this point tht she elected to try therapy. By this time she was no longer seeking help with heart attacks but asking for guidance with family problems. Her weekly sessions lasted six months.

As Anita left her hypochondria behind, she did not have the sense of choosing to solve her problems in a new way. Instead, the nature of the problems themselves seemed to change. The "heart attacks" occurred less frequently, and the uncomfortable but not invasive problems concerning her husband's dissatisfaction with his career and her parents' recurrent attempts to stir up family crises over money were confronted more directly. Only much later did Anita realize that as her self-confidence had risen in response to feeling better, she had begun facing her real problems and letting the substitutions go.

> I don't think I will ever get over being a hypochondriac—not completely. If I am stressed beyond a certain point I still get chest pains and I guess I'll always be afraid those chest pains mean a heart attack. But at least now I know what's going on. When I get a pain I ask myself, "What's bothering you?" Or, "are you about to get your period?" If the answers are "nothing" and "no," then I talk it over with my husband and sometimes call the doctor. I don't want to be such an anti-hypochondriac that I pretend all pain is caused by anxiety. I think by now I can tell the difference. It's an amazing discovery.

Three years after this vignette was written, Anita had a dramatic recurrence of her psychogenic heart pain. Forty-six years old, her children leaving home, her husband finally changing careers, and she herself picking up the slack by working fifty hours a week, Anita got so wound up that she couldn't either get to sleep or stay asleep. Exhausted, she began taking sleeping pills, which eased the stress but also made her feel heavy and tired. Soon old thoughts of cancer and heart disease began to flicker through her mind, but Anita blamed the symptoms on her pills. Eventually, however, she became so anxious about heart disease that she didn't dare give up the sleeping pills for fear that her symptoms would persist, which, to her, would prove they were serious. Trapped between work, which she felt she had to continue, and what seemed like the growing probability of a heart attack, Anita awoke early one morning in excruciating pain. Within minutes half her body went numb. "You predicted it," she told herself and felt relieved that the suspense (and work) were over.

Once she was admitted to the hospital, it was quickly discovered that Anita did not have heart disease. A few days later she reviewed her entire history of apprehensions with her doctor and, at the latter's suggestion, cut out the pills, took a leave of absence from work, and embarked on a brief course of marital therapy. Although the attack had been terrifying, weeks of secret shame and guilt did not follow as they had before. Anita knew the score. "When the mind has been hurt by hypochondria . . ." Boswell had written, ". . . one learns how to manage distress," Anita added.

Anita's is a fairly typical case of waxing and waning hypochondria except in one respect. Her major symptom—a psychogenic heart attack—has remained the same. This is somewhat unusual, for many hypochondriacs who are getting better report that over the course of several years their symptoms change in at least one of three ways. The first type of shift is a displacement of symptoms from the center of their bodies. No matter what the complaint, it seems to represent a less threatening problem if it moves from the center of the person—chest, belly, or bowels— toward the extremities or exterior. For example, Kate, who in chapter 1 was nearly paralyzed by her conviction of throat and stomach cancer and who for years feared cancer of the intestines and pancreas, gradually shifted her concern to joint problems and arthritis. Skin eruptions and itching are other common concerns that occur as deep problems surface. So are tight muscles, especially if the muscular aches rise through the shoulders and neck into the head as if trying to get out.[32]

A second type of shift involves physiological changes. If a hypochondriac exchanges heart palpitations and a dry mouth for muscle tightness, for example, some psychotherapists believe he is unconsciously selecting symptoms that are more under his control. Such a person apparently feels his problems are becoming more manageable.

The third kind of shift concerns the quality of the disability that the hypochondriac fears. Damage is the most threatening; disturbance or change less so. A sports medicine doctor reported that a man who had feared heart attacks, (i.e., damage) began running and within a year or so was seldom bothered by his former concern. Although his attention still returned to his heart when he was under pressure, his worries now focused on the possibility of increasing his heart rate by drinking too much coffee. In other words, his concern had shifted from damage to disturbance.

Pulling all this information together, what is a hypochondriac to do when his or her life becomes intolerable and it is time to change? Extending the Socratic maxim to cover the social aspects of a person's life, it seems clear that body, soul, and society must be cured together. A hypochondriac needs to reach for every kind of available help in these three areas. The improvements in physical health that come from eating and exercising in moderation have helped hypochondriacs at least since Hippocrates advised some of his patients to roll in warm sand and keep to a diet of boiled grains, new cheese, and figs.

As with exercise, diet must be tailored to the individual. Many hypochondriacs have noisy, responsive bodies that make it clear what foods are not easily digested. "Every Body ought to consult his Stomach, and whatever agrees with that perfectly well, is wholesome for him,"[33] wrote Bernard de Mandeville almost three hundred years ago. His advice is still good, although to the dismay of some it places the responsibility of choosing, modifying, and continually adjusting a diet on the individual and not on some expert.

Even today we are not sure why Socrates and so many thoughtful persons were right to maintain that curing the body strongly affects the health of the soul and vice versa. Galen said a good regime balanced the humors. Others said it purified the blood. Now exercise is believed to stimulate the brain and to release opiatelike chemicals that give the fit person a natural high and, in the laboratory, put sparkle in a rat's eye. Directly or indirectly, exercise and diet may influence the biochemical balance in the central nervous system and thus help a person avoid excessive anxiety or depression. The explanations keep changing, but the fact remains that good physical health is conducive to good mental health.

As hypochondriacs tend to their physical health, even using antidepressants if they suffer severely from panic attacks, they can help themselves immensely by reevaluating their work, study, and amusements. At best, these should be challenging and exciting enough to distract them from thoughts of disease. At the least, the activities should be exhausting enough to do the same. When no activity is capable of providing this temporary release, hypochondriacs have turned to helping the truly unfortunate— the poorest of the poor, the loneliest of the elderly, the suicidal. That works.

> Through the history of the race, deeper in time than historians usually tell, one thing most of all has offered relief from dilemmas: keeping busy.[34]

Good friends provide comfort as well as distraction, and this is especially true if, like Boswell's Johnson, the friend has had experience with hypochondria. As Burton knew, the best kinds of friends for anyone to have are those intimate enough to discuss openly the threat of change, the embarrassment of rejection, and the sadness of loss. Empathetic physicians and therapists of almost any persuasion increasingly function as an adjunct to or, sad to say, a substitute for friends and family. As with diet, drug, or exercise, the fit between helper and sufferer is important. If hypochondriacs are to be supported as they apprehensively experiment with a more direct language of distress, they and their therapists or friends must hold views of the world that are somewhat compatible and all must agree on what constitutes progress.

Finally, hypochondriacs' community—especially their household and workplace—must be critically surveyed. Does their environment allow them to strive for physical security, recognition, love, and the other essentials with a good chance of success? Does it let them express affection, anger, and sexual desire without threat of violent disapproval and rejection? If the answer to any of these is no and if the restrictions come from outside, not from fantasies based on the hypochondriacs' own inabilities or fears, then family therapy and socioeconomic help are needed in addition to self-reform. Better health, better work, better friends and family, better environment—progress in any one of these areas halts the downward spiral and gradually facilitates advances on other fronts.

Getting better takes a long time, and the difficult tasks of unearthing true feelings and expressing them in honest actions never proceed smoothly. It is well to remember in the hours before dawn and on rainy Sunday afternoons that all therapies seek only to imitate and enhance the natural healing process that proceeds every minute of every day. The drive to get better goes on whether we will it or not, sabotage it or not, even believe in it or not. Like our bodies, our minds are meant to survive.

APPENDIX

THE WHITELEY INDEX is one of about a dozen questionnaires developed to identify hypochondriacs. This particular test tries to distinguish among subgroups of hypochondriacs, namely those who are preoccupied with symptoms, those who fear developing a serious disease, and those who are convinced they are already ill.

Answer yes or no.

A. Do you often worry about the possibility that you have a serious illness?

B. Are you bothered by many aches and pains?

C. Are you frequently aware of various things happening in your body?

D. Do you worry a lot about your health?

E. Do you often have the symptoms of very serious illnesses?

F. If a disease is brought to your attention through radio, television, newspapers, or someone you know, do you worry about getting it yourself?

G. If you are ill and someone tells you that you are looking better, are you annoyed?

H. Do you find that you are bothered by many different symptoms?

I. Is it easy for you to forget yourself and think about all sorts of other things?

J. Is it hard for you to believe the doctor when he tells you there is nothing to worry about?

K. Do you get the feeling that people are not taking your illness seriously enough?

L. Do you think that you worry about your health more than most people?

M. Do you think there is something seriously wrong with your body?

N. Are you afraid of illness?

Questions such as A, D, E, and J are answered in the affirmative by almost all hypochondriacs who are willing to acknowledge their apprehensions. Individuals also answering yes to B, C, and H are said to have a greater-than-usual preoccupation with their bodies. Something is always wrong somewhere, and their complaining has probably become habitual.

Persons answering yes to F, L, and N and no to I are categorized as disease phobic. These people are afraid of getting certain diseases. Under stress they may be terrified that they are getting sick, but when life is going well their apprehensions may be expressed only as a concern for eating right, not taxing themselves, and not coming into contact with germs or pollutants.

Yes answers to G, K, and M suggest a conviction of disease and a somewhat suspicious attitude toward others. This may be a more settled form of hypochondria.

The Whiteley Index is taken from I. Pilowsky, "Dimensions of Hypochondriasis," *British Journal of Psychiatry* 113 (1967): 89–93.

NOTES

INTRODUCTION

1. A. J. Barsky and G. L. Klerman, "Overview: Hypochondriasis, Bodily Complaints and Somatic Styles," *American Journal of Psychiatry* 140 (1983):273–283. Ewald W. Busse, "Hypochondriasis in the Elderly: A Reaction to Social Stress," *Journal of the American Geriatric Society* 24 (1976):145–149. F. E. Kenyon, "Hypochondriacal States," *British Journal of Psychiatry* 129 (1976):1–4. I. Pilowsky, "Primary and Secondary Hypochondriasis," *Acta Psychiatrica Scandinavia* 46 (1970):273–285.
2. E. Fitzgerald, letter of November 1848, quoted in Christopher Ricks, *Tennyson* (New York, 1972), p. 206.
3. Alfred Lord Tennyson, "In Memoriam A.H.H.," in *Tennyson, Poems and Plays* (London, 1975), p. 230.
4. Miguel de Unamuno, *The Tragic Sense of Life* (New York, 1954), p. 36.
5. Herbert E. Klarman, "The Financing of Health Care," in *Doing Better and Feeling Worse: Health in the United States*, ed. John H. Knowles (New York, 1977).
6. Plutarch, quoted in Gregory Zilboorg and George Henry, *A History of Medical Psychiatry* (New York, 1941), p. 67.
7. Robert Burton, *The Anatomy of Melancholy (A Selection)* (East Lansing, Mich., 1965), p. 379.

1. BEING A HYPOCHONDRIAC

1. James Boswell, letter to John Johnston, 15 August 1763, quoted in Frederick A. Pottle, ed., *Boswell in Holland 1763–1764* (New York, 1952), p. 6.

2. James Boswell, letter to William Johnson Temple, 16 August 1763, quoted in Pottle, *Boswell in Holland*, p. 8.
3. Ibid., p. 10.
4. Frederick A. Pottle, *James Boswell, the Earlier Years, 1740–1769* (New York, 1966), p. 12.
5. Frederick A. Pottle, ed., *Boswell's London Journal, 1762–1763* (New York, 1950), p. 178.
6. Ibid., p. 319.
7. Pottle, *Boswell, the Earlier Years*, p. 126.
8. Ibid., p. 130.
9. Pottle, *Boswell in Holland*, p. 160.
10. Margery Bailey, ed., *The Hypochondriak, Being the Seventy Essays by the Celebrated Biographer, James Boswell* (Palo Alto, Ca., 1928), 1:203.
11. Ibid., p. 215.
12. Ibid., p. 327.
13. Pottle, *Boswell in Holland*, p. 196.
14. Ibid., p. 387.
15. Charles Ryskamp and Frederick A. Pottle, eds., *Boswell: The Ominous Years, 1774–1776* (New York, 1963), p. 233.
16. Bailey, *The Hypochondriak*, 1:23.
17. Bailey, *The Hypochondriak*, 2:43.
18. William James, quoted in Jean Strouse, *Alice James, A Biography* (New York, 1982), p. 139.

2. "A DISEASE SO GRIEVOUS, SO COMMON"

1. Robert James, *Medical Dictionary*, quoted in G. S. Rousseau, introduction to facsimile copy of John Hill, *Hypochondriasis. A Practical Treatise on the Nature and Cure of That Disorder: Commonly Called the Hyp and Hypo* (London, 1766), p. v.
2. *The Aphorisms of Hippocrates*, trans. J. W. Underwood (London, 1831).
3. G. Sheldon, *History of Deerfield, Massachusetts* (Massachusetts, 1895), 1:448.
4. Giovanni Pietro, quoted in Rudolph Wittkower and Margot Wittkower, *Born under Saturn: The Character and Conduct of Artists* (New York, 1963), p. 79.
5. Robert Burton, *The Anatomy of Melancholy* (New York, 1927), p. 21.

6. Ibid., p. 152.
7. Ibid., p. 137.
8. Ibid., p. 212.
9. Thomas Sydenham, quoted in Ilza Veith, "Psychiatric Nosology," *American Journal of Psychiatry* 114 (1957):387. The belief that men and women could be either hysterical or hypochondriacal and that "there is no essential difference between these two afflictions" (Stahl, quoted in Michel Foucault, *Madness and Civilization: A History of Insanity in the Age of Reason* [New York, 1973], p. 145) required that the traditional connection between the uterus and hysteria be broken or that men be given some similarly troublesome organ to account for their hysteria. Physicians moved in both directions, and one even maintained that hysterical women with irregular menses had a direct counterpart in men who vomited blood and had hemorrhoids (ibid.).
10. Andrew Duncan, quoted in Guenter B. Risse, "Managing 'Neuroses' in a General Hospital: Edinburgh 1750–1800" (unpublished manuscript), p. 9. See also idem, *Hospital Life in Enlightenment Scotland: Care and Teaching at the Royal Infirmary of Edinburgh* (New York, 1986).
11. Risse, "Managing 'Neuroses,' " p. 6.
12. Benjamin Rush, *An Inquiry into the Natural History of Medicine among the Indians of North America and a Comparative View of Their Diseases and Remedies with Those of Civilized Nations* (1774), quoted in Ilza Veith, *Hysteria, the History of a Disease* (Chicago, 1965), p. 174.
13. Bailey, *The Hypochondriack*, 1:136.
14. Jean-Pierre Falret, *De l'Hypochondrie et du suicide* (Paris, 1822), p. vi.
15. Ibid., p. 372.
16. Sigmund Freud, quoted in Phillip Greenberg, "Hypochondriasis," *Medical Journal of Australia* 47 (1960):675.
17. In spite of analysts' disinterest in hypochondria, some cases remained within the purview of psychiatry usually because they were seen as part of a severe depression or schizophrenic episode. Examples might include the Scottish poet Robert Burns, who was so afraid he would suffocate during the night that he kept a tub of cold water at his bedside which he frequently leapt into; or one of the Princes of Bourbon, who stood in his rose garden and insisted upon being watered for fear of dessication.
18. Kenyon, "Hypochondriacal States."

19. Alfred Lord Tennyson, letter to his Aunt Russell, 1847, quoted in Ricks, *Tennyson*, p. 65.
20. Charles Darwin, letter to Joseph Hooker, 1864, quoted in Ralph Colp, Jr., *To Be an Invalid: The Illness of Charles Darwin* (Chicago, 1977), p. 77.
21. A. L. Comrey, "A Factor Analysis of Items on the MMPI Hypochondriasis Scale," *Educational and Psychological Measurement* 17 (1957):568–577. J. P. O'Connor and E. C. Stefic, "Some Patterns of Hypochondriasis," *Educational and Psychological Measurement* 19 (1959):363–370.
22. I. Pilowsky, "Dimensions of Hypochondriasis," *British Journal of Psychiatry* 113 (1967):89–93.
23. G. N. Bianchi, "Patterns of Hypochondriasis: A Principal Components Analysis," *British Journal of Psychiatry* 122 (1973):541–548.
24. D. V. Sheehan, J. Ballenger, and G. Jacobsen, "Treatment of Endogenous Anxiety with Phobic, Hysterical and Hypochondriacal Symptoms," *Archives of General Psychiatry* 37 (1980):51–59.
25. American Psychiatric Association, *Diagnostic and Statistical Manual of Mental Disorders*, 3d ed. (Washington, D.C., 1980).
26. Ibid., p. 251.
27. Although hypochondriasis is distinguished in the *DSM-III* from something called somatization disorder or Briquet's syndrome, the distinction is hazy, and in common parlance both are called hypochondria. The main difference is thought to be that persons with somatization disorder have multiple psychogenic "illnesses" and are career patients. Hypochondriacs may do the same but focus on fear of disease rather than on symptoms per se.
28. C. V. Ford, *The Somatizing Disorders: Illness as a Way of Life* (New York, 1983).
29. "Hypochondriasis—USA," editorial in the *American Journal of Psychotherapy* 16 (1962):187.
30. Dr. Margaret Gildea, personal communication.
31. R. Meister, *Hypochondria: Toward a Better Understanding* (New York, 1980), p. 30.
32. D. R. Lipsitt, "Medical and Psychological Characteristics of 'Crocks,' " *Psychiatry in Medicine* 1 (1970):15.
33. I. Pilowsky, "The Response to Treatment in Hypochondriacal Disorders," *Australian and New Zealand Journal of Psychiatry* 2 (1968):88.
34. A. J. Barsky and G. L. Klerman, "Hypochondriasis," *Harvard Medical School Mental Health Letter* 2 (1985):4.

35. Milton Mazer, *People and Predicaments* (Cambridge, Mass., 1976), pp. 112–115.
36. *The Harris Survey Yearbook of Public Opinion* (New York, 1970), pp. 197–204.
37. J. A. Ryle, "The Twenty-First Maudsley Lecture: Nosophobia," *Journal of Mental Science* 94 (1948):1.
38. S. Agras, D. Sylvester, and D. Oliveau, "The Epidemiology of Common Fears and Phobias," *Comprehensive Psychiatry* 10 (1969):151–156.
39. S. Weir Mitchell, quoted in Ilza Veith, *Hysteria, History of a Disease* (Chicago, 1965), p. 217.
40. J. C. McKinley and S. R. Hathaway, quoted in F. E. Kenyon, "Hypochondriasis: A Survey of Some Historical, Clinical and Social Aspects," *British Journal of Medical Psychology* 38 (1965):121.
41. A. Barsky, G. Wyshak, and G. Klerman, "Hypochondriasis: An Evaluation of the *DSM-III* Criteria in Medical Outpatients," *Archives of General Psychiatry* 43 (1986):493–500.

3. THE SOCIAL SIGNIFICANCE OF BEING ILL

1. Howard Brody and David S. Sobel, "A Systems View of Health and Disease," in *Ways of Health: Holistic Approaches to Ancient and Contemporary Medicine*, ed. David S. Sobel (New York, 1979), p. 93.
2. World Health Organization's definition of health, quoted in Meister, *Hypochondria: Toward a Better Understanding*, p. 9.
3. B. Baumann, "Diversities in the Conceptions of Health and Physical Fitness," *Journal of Health and Human Behavior* 2 (1961):39–46.
4. Andrew C. Twaddle, "Illness and Deviance," *Social Science and Medicine* 8 (1973–1974):756.
5. In *The Profession of Medicine*, Eliot Freidson maintains that our medical system is an agency of social control on a par with our legal system or with organized religion but with one significant difference. In matters of health and disease we submit to the judgment of a professional, usually a doctor, who decides who is sick and what should be done, whereas, after centuries of struggle, ordinary people have insisted on the right to be judged by their peers in courts of law and to interpret the Scriptures themselves. Eliot Freidson, quoted in John Ehrenreich, *The Cultural Crisis of Modern Medicine* (New York, 1978).

6. Charles Rosenberg, *No Other Gods: On Science and American Social Thought* (Baltimore, 1961).
7. Susan Sontag, *Illness as Metaphor* (New York, 1979).
8. Charles Caldwell, quoted in Charles Rosenberg, *The Cholera Years: The United States in 1832, 1849, and 1866* (Chicago, 1962), p. 96.
9. Rosenberg, *The Cholera Years*.
10. Colp, *To Be an Invalid*, p. 92.
11. William Allingham's diary, in ibid., p. 87.
12. Milton Mazer, personal communication.
13. Anthropologists identify three phases in the transition from one role to another. First there is separation from the former classification with its attachments and responsibilities, next a transition through a disagreeable state in which one is an outcast and a misfit, and finally full admittance into a new role. Many hypochondriacs seem to get stuck in the transitional stage. Being neither well nor sick (and rejecting the possibility of being emotionally disturbed), they are in limbo. There are no guidelines in a society for treating persons who cannot or will not fit into a recognized role. How do we regard a three-week-old fetus? A person in an irreversible coma? Or a person who is sick and well at the same time?
14. M. Field, *Doctor and Patient in Soviet Russia* (Cambridge, Mass., 1957).
15. E. F. Schumacher, *Small Is Beautiful: Economics as if People Mattered* (New York, 1975), p. 38.
16. Thomas Szasz, *The Myth of Mental Illness* (New York, 1961), p. 248.

4. PATHWAYS TOWARD CHILDHOOD HYPOCHONDRIA

1. Mary Preston, "Physical Complaints without Organic Basis," *Journal of Pediatrics* 17 (1940):279–304.
2. American Psychiatric Association, *Diagnostic and Statistical Manual*, p. 230.
3. Douglas Hubble, "The Life of the Shawl," *The Lancet* 2 (1953):1351–1354.
4. Gwen Raverat, *Period Piece* (London, 1952), chap. 7.
5. Ibid.
6. E. L. Richards, "Following the Hypochondriacal Child for a Decade," *Journal of Pediatrics* 18 (1941):531.

7. Robert Kellner, *Somatization and Hypochondriasis* (New York, 1986).
8. Felix Brown, "The Bodily Complaint: A Study of Hypochondriasis," *Journal of Mental Science* 82 (1936):308.
9. Ibid.
10. For example, Kellner, *Somatization and Hypochondriasis*, p. 67.
11. David Mechanic, "The Influence of Mothers on Their Children's Health Attitudes," *Pediatrics* 33 (1964):450.
12. Ibid., p. 451.
13. David Mechanic, "The Development of Psychological Distress among Young Adults," *Archives of General Psychiatry* 36 (1979):1233–1239.
14. Kellner, *Somatization and Hypochondriasis*, p. 71.
15. K. Dunnel and A. Cartwright, *Medicine Takers, Prescribers and Hoarders* (Boston, 1972), table 38.
16. Mechanic, "The Influence of Mothers," p. 453.
17. Michael Balint, *The Doctor, His Patient, and the Illness* (New York, 1972), p. 259.
18. Ibid., p. 261.
19. Anna Freud, "The Role of Bodily Illness in the Mental Life of Children," *The Psychoanalytic Study of the Child* 7 (1952):69–81.
20. John Bowlby, *Attachment and Loss*. Volume 3: *Loss* (New York, 1980), p. 398.
21. Anna Freud, *Writings of Anna Freud* (New York, 1969), 5:235.
22. Leo Kanner, *Child Psychiatry*, 4th ed. (Springfield, Ill., 1972), p. 590.
23. Freud, "Role of Bodily Illness," p. 79.
24. Freud *Writings* 5:114.
25. Charlotte Brontë, quoted in Winfred Gérin, *Charlotte Brontë, the Evolution of Genius* (Oxford, 1967), p. 114.
26. Charlotte Brontë, *The Professor* (New York, 1965), p. 202. This, her first novel, was written in 1846 but not published until 1857.
27. Paul Atkinson, "Becoming a Hypochondriac," in *Medical Encounters: The Experience of Illness and Treatment*, ed. Alan Davis and Gordon Horobin (New York, 1977).
28. In the nineteenth and early twentieth centuries it was so common for young men to fall into a panic over the possibility of developing syphilis from "abusing themselves" that doctors coined a special term for the problem: "malignant syphilis-from-masturbation type of hypochondria." The prevalence of this illogical fear was blamed on quack literature, and doctors raged that the "harmful effects on the adolescent are incalculable." Brown, "The Bodily Complaint," p. 312.

29. Sir William Petty, M.D., letter to Robert Boyle, 15 April 1653, quoted in Richard Hunter and Ida Macalpine, *Three Hundred Years of Psychiatry 1535–1860* (London, 1963), p. 246.
30. Atkinson, "Becoming a Hypochondriac," in Davis and Horobin, *Medical Encounters*, p. 19.
31. S. M. Woods, J. Natterson, and J. Silverman, "Medical Students Disease: Hypochondriasis in Medical Education," *Journal of Medical Education* 41 (1966):785–790.
32. Ibid.
33. R. Kellner, R. G. Wiggins, and D. Pathak, "Hypochondriacal Fears and Beliefs in Medical and Law Students," *Archives in General Psychiatry* 43 (1986):487–489.
34. David Mechanic, "Social and Psychologic Factors Affecting the Presentation of Bodily Complaints," *New England Journal of Medicine* 286 (1972):1132–1139.
35. Cotton Mather, quoted in Otho T. Beall, Jr., and Richard Shryock, *Cotton Mather* (Baltimore, 1954), p. 8.
36. Charles Darwin, *The Autobiography of Charles Darwin 1809–1882* (London, 1958), p. 79.
37. Mechanic, "Factors Affecting Bodily Complaints," p. 1133.
38. William Drake, *Sara Teasdale, Woman and Poet* (New York, 1979), p. 7.
39. Ibid., p. 8.
40. Jay Haley, *Strategies of Psychotherapy* (New York, 1963), p. 132.
41. Bernard de Mandeville, *A Treatise of the Hypochondriak and Hysterick Passions* (London, 1711), p. 238.

5. HYPOCHONDRIA IN THE FAMILY

1. Haley, *Strategies of Psychotherapy*, p. 148.
2. Norman Kreitman, P. Sainsbury, K. Pearce, and W. R. Costain, "Hypochondria and Depression in Outpatients at a General Hospital," *British Journal of Psychiatry* 3 (1965):615.
3. G. A. Ladee, *Hypochondriacal Syndromes* (New York, 1966), p. 97.
4. A bizarre illustration of hypochondria's usefulness in staving off psychosis can be found in the case of a forty-three-year-old schizophrenic whose attention was purposely focused on physical complaints "to provide a new outlet for the expression of his illness which would be socially acceptable." Having ascertained that the man, a frequent resident of mental hospitals, was unresponsive to ordinary treatments, the hospital staff embarked upon a three-month campaign to

convince him that he suffered from chronic back pain and that an old injury had been the cause of his troubles all along. Gradually the man developed a classic low-back pain that waxed and waned with his anxieties. It was reported that the new complaints successfully replaced the schizoid behavior and that the man, though never gaining any insight into his problems, was much happier with the hypochondriacal concerns. He left the mental institution and only rarely needed to be hospitalized. R. C. Cowden and J. E. Brown, "The Use of a Physical Symptom as a Defense against Psychosis," *Journal of Abnormal and Social Psychology* 53 (1956):133–135. In similar fashion a paranoid schizophrenic was encouraged to express his apprehensions in terms of heart problems. Adrian Verwoerdt, *Clinical Geropsychiatry* (Baltimore, 1976), p. 117.

5. Raverat, *Period Piece*, p. 121.
6. Ibid., p. 122.
7. Ibid., pp. 123–125.
8. Ibid.
9. Ibid.
10. Jonathan Swift, *Journal to Stella*, quoted in George Sampson, *The Concise Cambridge History of English Literature*, 2d ed. (Cambridge, 1961).
11. Jules and Edmond de Goncourt, *Journal*, entry for 6 October 1869.
12. Jules and Edmond de Goncourt, quoted in Robert Baldick, *The Goncourts* (New York, 1960), p. 9.
13. de Goncourts, *Journal*, entry for 18 December 1860.
14. Ibid., 10 June 1870.
15. Ibid., 20 June 1870.
16. de Goncourts, quoted in Baldick, *The Goncourts*, p. 14.
17. Marriages in which *both* partners are ambivalently dependent, reluctantly responsible, compulsively authoritarian, hypochondriacal, or something of that sort are what psychologists term "neurotic marriages." Some data suggest that such unions occur substantially more often than they should if chance alone distributed neurotic traits among marriages. Norman Kreitman, Joyce Collins, Barbara Nelson, and Jane Troop, "Neuroses and Marital Interaction," *British Journal of Psychiatry* 117 (1970):33–46, 47–58. Some psychologists believe selection is at work—neurotic men select neurotic wives and vice versa—whereas others feel that "pathogenic interaction" during years of marriage gradually changes the more normal partner until he or she comes to resemble the spouse.
18. Haley, *Strategies of Psychotherapy*, p. 148.

19. Sara Teasdale, quoted in Drake, *Sara Teasdale*, p. 91.
20. Ibid., p. 45.
21. Ibid., p. 136.
22. Ibid., p. 71.
23. Stephen Wolkind, "Psychological Facotors and the Minor Symptoms of Pregnancy," *Journal of Psychosomatic Research* 18 (1974):161–165.
24. David V. Sheehan, "Diagnosis and Treatment of Anxiety Disorders" (Paper presented at The Ninth Annual Clinical Psychopharmacology Symposium, Pine Manor College, Chesnut Hill, Mass., 3 November 1982).
25. Sara Teasdale, quoted in Drake, *Sara Teasdale*, p. 171.
26. Sara Teasdale, "The Broken Field" in *The Collected Poems of Sara Teasdale* (New York, 1937), p. 167.
27. Drake, *Sara Teasdale*, p. 294.
28. Tobias Smollett, *The Expedition of Humphrey Clinker*, letter from Matt Bramble to Dick Lewis, 20 April (London, 1966).
29. Ibid., letter of 28 April.
30. Szasz, *The Myth of Mental Illness*, p. 264.
31. Ford, *The Somatizing Disorders*.
32. Gerard Chrzanowski, "Neurasthenia and Hypochondriasis," in *American Handbook of Psychiatry*, ed. Silvano Arieti (New York, 1959).
33. Ibid., p. 261.
34. M. Blinder and M. Kirschenbaum, "The Technique of Married Couple Group Therapy," *Archives of General Psychiatry* 17 (1967):44–52.
35. Leo Kanner, quoted in Lawrence Grolnick, "A Family Perspective of Psychosomatic Factors in Illness: A Review of the Literature," *Family Process* 11 (1972).
36. Ibid., p. 461.
37. Melita Sperling, "The Role of the Mother in Psychosomatic Disorders in Children," *Psychosomatic Medicine* 11 (1949):377–385.
38. Ibid.
39. Haley, *Strategies of Psychotherapy*, p. 148.
40. Edward Albee, *A Delicate Balance* (New York, 1966), p. 144.

6. HYPOCHONDRIACS AND THEIR DOCTORS

1. C. W. Wahl, ed., *New Dimensions in Psychosomatic Medicine* (Boston, 1964), p. 202.

2. R. Hutchison, quoted in R. D. Gillespie, "Hypochondria: Its Definition, Nosology, and Psychopathology," *Guys Hospital Report* 8 (1928):414.
3. Ibid.
4. Wahl, *Pyschosomatic Medicine*, p. 203.
5. Reverend Heinrich Melchior Muhlenberg, quoted in J. W. Leavitt and R. L. Numbers, eds., *Health and Sickness in America: Readings in the History of Medicine and Public Health* (Madison, Wis., 1978), p. 45.
6. de Mandeville, *The Hypochondriack and Hysterick Passions*, p. 31.
7. Smollett, *The Expedition of Humphrey Clinker*, letter from Matt Bramble to Dick Lewis, 20 April.
8. Letter to the editor, *Lancet* 2 (1970):830.
9. Overheard in the Fishmonger's Café, Woods Hole, Massachusetts.
10. John Moore, quoted in Hunter and Macalpine, *Three Hundred Years of Psychiatry 1535–1860*, p. 496.
11. Ford, *The Somatizing Disorders*, p. 210.
12. E. Langdon Burwell, M.D., personal communication. To be on the other end of this problem is distressing as well. Patients who have been erroneously labeled hypochondriacs, a group that is estimated to include from 25 to 63 percent of their number (G. C. Davison and J. M. Neale, *Abnormal Psychology*, 3d ed. [New York, 1982], p. 181), justifiably complain of the treatment they received before the physical cause of their problem was discovered. "It was suggested that I was obsessed, bored and depressed and that I was bothering busy doctors," wrote a woman later diagnosed as having Lyme arthritis. "[Doctors] later suggested that the entire family had a psychogenic problem" (letter to the editor, *New England Journal of Medicine* 305 [1981]:895). A truly ironic example of this mislabeling occurred when a Swiss psychoanalyst contracted an amoebic infection that resisted diagnosis for ten years. During that entire time the analyst was torn between analyzing what others had told her was a psychological problem and insisting that the disease was physical.
13. David Mechanic, *Medical Sociology: A Selective View* (New York, 1968), p. 169.
14. Ibid.
15. Balint, *Doctor, Patient, Illness*.
16. "It is one of the sadnesses of medical evaluation," wrote Nobel Laureate P. B. Medawar, "that in spite of the earnest advocacy of people in the know, ordinary medical students tend to be bored by and are even a little contemptuous of the study of social medicine and public

health. In British medical schools public health is traditionally taught alongside forensic medicine in a course compendiously known to medical students as 'rape and drains.' " P. B. Medawar, review in *The New York Review of Books* 27 (1980):10.

17. Balint, *Doctor, Patient, Illness*, p. 216.
18. Burton, *The Anatomy of Melancholy*, p. 158.
19. Strouse, *Alice James*, p. 252.
20. Ibid., pp. 251–252.
21. J. E. Groves, "Taking Care of the Hateful Patient," *New England Journal of Medicine* 298 (1978):883–887.
22. B. K. Singh, J. Nunn, J. Martin, and J. Yates, " Abnormal Treatment Behaviour," *British Journal of Medical Psychology* 54 (1981):67–73.
23. Thomas Szasz and M. H. Hollender, "A Contribution to the Philosophy of Medicine: The Basic Models of the Doctor-Patient Relationship," *Archives of Internal Medicine* 97 (1956):585–592.
24. Ford, *The Somatizing Disorders*, p. 227.
25. Haley, *Strategies of Psychotherapy*.
26. Balint, *Doctor, Patient, Illness*, p. 277.
27. Ibid.
28. Strouse, *Alice James*, p. 332.
29. Ibid., p. 333.
30. W. C. Alvarez, *Minds That Came Back* (New York, 1961).
31. B. G. Harrison, "Profound Hypochondria," *Ms* 5 (1977):96.
32. Molière, "La Malade Imaginaire," Act I, *Oeuvres Complètes* (Paris, 1962), p. 628.
33. Haley, *Strategies of Psychotherapy*, p. 148.
34. Marianne LaFrance, personal communication.
35. Beverley Mead, "Management of Hypochondriacal Patients," *Journal of the American Medical Association* 192 (1965):33.
36. de Mandeville, *The Hypochondriak and Hysterick Passions*, third dialogue.
37. Balint, *Doctor, Patient, Illness*, p. 276.

7. HYPOCHONDRIA AMONG THE ELDERLY

1. Jaber F. Gubrium, "Self-Conceptions of Mental Health among the Aged," *Mental Hygiene* 55 (1971):399–403. See also Jeremy Tunstall, *Old and Alone, a Sociological Study of Old People* (London, 1966), p. 209; Simone de Beauvoir, *The Coming of Age* (New York, 1972), pp. 285 et seq.; and Peter Townsend, *The Family Life of Old People* (London, 1961).

2. S. E. Goldstein and F. Birnbom, "Hypochondriasis and the Elderly," *Journal of the American Geriatric Society* 24 (1976):150.
3. Eric Pfeiffer, quoted in James E. Birren and K. Warner Schaie, eds., *Handbook of the Psychology of Aging* (New York, 1977), p. 656.
4. Robert Hutchison, "Hypochondriasis: Individual, Vicarious and Communal," *British Medical Journal* 1 (1934):367.
5. Samuel Johnson, quoted in W. Jackson Bate, *Samuel Johnson* (New York, 1975), p. 9.
6. René Dubos, *Man Adapting* (New Haven, 1965), p. 395.
7. Tunstall, *Old and Alone*, p. 274.
8. K. Bergmann, "Sex Differences in the Neurotic Reaction of the Aged," *Journal of Biological Science, Supplement* 2 (1970):137.
9. Sophia Tolstoy, quoted in de Beauvoir, *The Coming of Age*, p. 311.
10. Samuel Johnson, *The Rambler*, No. 85. (New Haven, Conn., 1969).
11. Jonathan Swift, *Gulliver's Travels* (New York, 1972), pp. 210, 211.
12. Alex Comfort, *A Good Age* (New York, 1976), p. 10.
13. "Aging Goes On: The Questions Are How and Why," *New York Times*, 3 May 1981, E7.
14. In studying the vulnerability of middle- and working-class women to psychiatric disturbances, it was found that the number of "positive events" such as making a new friend, learning to crochet, or buying furniture declined with age. G. Brown, M. Bhrolchain, and T. Harris, "Social Class and Psychiatric Disturbance among Women in an Urban Population," *Sociology* 9 (1975):252.
15. de Beauvoir, *The Coming of Age*, p. 464.
16. André Gide, quoted in de Beauvoir, *The Coming of Age*, p. 453.
17. Ladee, *Hypochondriacal Syndromes*, p. 306.
18. Kellner, *Somatization and Hypochondriasis*, p. 153.
19. Ibid., p. 238.
20. Hutchison, "Hypochondriasis," p. 365.
21. Jerome K. Jerome, *Three Men in a Boat* (New York, n.d.), p. 2.
22. American Psychiatric Association, *Diagnostic and Statistical Manual*, p. 251.
23. Wayne E. Thompson and Gordon Streib, "Situational Determinants: Health and Economic Deprivation in Retirement," *Journal of Social Issues* 14 (1958):18–34.
24. Samuel Johnson, quoted in Bate, *Samuel Johnson*, p. 273.
25. Frieda Fromm-Reichman, "Loneliness," *Psychiatry* 22 (1959):3,15.
26. Ninon de Lenclos, quoted in de Beauvoir, *The Coming of Age*, p. 435.
27. de Beauvoir, *The Coming of Age*, p. 366.

28. Samuel Johnson, quoted in Bate, *Samuel Johnson*, p. 579.
29. François Mauriac, quoted in de Beauvoir, *The Coming of Age*, p. 362.
30. Leo Tolstoy, in ibid., p. 370.
31. L. W. Early and O. von Mering, "Growing Old the Outpatient Way," *American Journal of Psychiatry* 125 (1969):963–967.
32. Richard Hughes and Robert Brewin, *The Tranquilizing of America* (New York, 1979), p. 164.
33. Louis Kuplan in de Beauvoir, *The Coming of Age*, p. 481.
34. May Sarton, *As We Are Now* (New York, 1973), p. 81.
35. François René de Chateaubriand and Paul Claudel, quoted in de Beauvoir, *The Coming of Age*, p. 303.
36. Bergmann, "Neurotic Reaction of Aged," pp. 137–145.
37. A. W. McMahon and P. J. Rhudick, "Reminiscing: Adaptational Significance in the Aged," *Archives of General Psychiatry* 10 (1964):292–297.
38. Verwoerdt, *Clinical Geropsychiatry*, p. 115.
39. Bate, *Samuel Johnson*, p. 235.
40. Samuel Johnson, quoted in Bate, *Samuel Johnson*, p. 371.
41. Samuel Johnson, in ibid., p. 510.
42. James Boswell, *The Life of Samuel Johnson* (Roslyn, N.Y., 1952), p. 36.
43. Sigmund Freud, quoted in de Beauvoir, *The Coming of Age*, p. 451.
44. T. L. Brink, D. Capri, V. De Neeve, C. Janakes, and C. Oliveira, "Hypochondriasis and Paranoia: Similar Delusional Systems in an Institutionalized Geriatric Population," *Journal of Nervous and Mental Disease* 167 (1979):226.
45. Kellner, *Somatization and Hypochondriasis*, p. 263.
46. Ibid.
47. Goldstein and Birnbom, "Hypochondriasis and the Elderly," p. 151.
48. Ibid., p. 154.
49. Busse, "Hypochondria in the Elderly," p. 145.
50. Szasz, *The Myth of Mental Illness*, p. 292.
51. Florida Scott-Maxwell, *The Measure of My Days* (New York, 1979), p. 32.
52. Samuel Johnson, quoted in Bate, *Samuel Johnson*, p. 510.
53. Ibid., p. 598.
54. Ibid., p. 599.
55. Ibid., p. 597.

8. HYPOCHONDRIA AND OUR CULTURAL VALUES

1. H. Jack Geiger, book review of Paul Starr, *The Social Transformation of American Medicine* in *New York Times Book Review*, 9 January 1983, p. 1.
2. Harry Schwartz, "Looking at the Ways We Die," *Wall Street Journal*, 9 December 1980.
3. For example, Robert N. Bellah, Richard Masden, William M. Sullivan, Ann Swidler, and Steven M. Tipton, *Habits of the Heart: Individualism and Commitment in American Life* (New York, 1986), chaps. 2 and 3.
4. Joseph Pernica, "The Second Generation of Market Segmentation Studies: An Audit of Buying Motivations," in *Life Style and Psychographics*, ed. William D. Wells (American Marketing Association, 1974). At one end of the consumer spectrum are the "extrapotency" people whose stronger-than-ordinary needs prompt them to buy extra-strength everything and lots of it. The second and largest group is concerned with living the good life *now* and is motivated to buy whatever helps maintain a high level of social functioning. Members of this group are especially prone to buy in order to express themselves and impress their friends. They are said to be responsive to fads. The third group consists of apprehensive consumers—fussy hypochondriacs where drugs are concerned or helpless car buyers in search of endless warranties. When a product doesn't meet their impossible demands, they try another and another. Pragmatists form a small fourth group. They buy what works and are said to respond to a product's intrinsic value rather than its image-enhancing qualities. They keep what they buy longer. Most people belong to several groups depending on what they are buying.
5. Heinz Kohut and Ernest Wolf, "The Disorders of the Self and Their Treatment: An Outline," *International Journal of Psychoanalysis* 59 (1978):413–425.
6. Edward E. Jones and Steven Berglas, "Control of Attributions about the Self through Self-Handicapping Strategies: The Appeal of Alcohol and the Role of Underachievement," *Personality and Social Psychology Bulletin* 4 (1978):200–206.
7. Timothy W. Smith, C. R. Snyder, and Suzanne C. Perkins, "The Self-Serving Function of Hypochondriacal Complaints: Physical Symptoms as Self-Handicapping Strategies." *Journal of Personality and Social Psychology* 44 (1983):787–797.

8. Atkinson, "Becoming a Hypochondriac," in Davis and Horobin, *Medical Encounters*, p. 28.

9. Dunnell and Cartwright, *Medicine Takers, Prescribers and Hoarders*, p. 118.

10. Pointing out that "it needs no social scientist to observe that society in the United States is in a demoralized state, with citizens lacking a common purpose and evincing massive distrust of their fellows, leaders and institutions," professor of psychiatry Jerome Frank asserts that in stable periods demoralized persons look for help from traditional institutions such as the family and organized religion. In times of rapid change, however, before such institutions have had time to adjust to new conditions, the many persons who feel powerless to help themselves turn to some form of therapy. "The mushrooming of psychotherapies, which typically occurs in periods of social transition, can be seen as society's effort at filling the gap until new institutions and value systems appropriate to the conditions of modern life emerge." Jerome Frank in B. H. Kaplan, R. N. Wilson, and A. H. Leighton, eds., *Further Explorations in Social Psychiatry* (New York, 1976), p. 123.

11. Jean-Paul Sartre, quoted in Bruce Haley, *The Healthy Body and Victorian Culture* (Cambridge, Mass., 1978), p. 257.

12. A. H. Leighton, *My Name is Legion, the Stirling County Study of Psychiatric Disorder and Sociocultural Environment.* (New York, 1959), vol. 1. August B. Hollingshead and Fredrick C. Redlich, *Social Class and Mental Illness: A Community Study* (New York, 1958).

13. Marc Fried, quoted in John Kosa and Irving K. Zola, eds., *Poverty and Health: A Sociological Analysis* (Cambridge, Mass., 1975), p. 154.

14. M. Harvey Brenner, "Losing Jobs, Losing Lives," *Johns Hopkins Magazine* (October, 1981).

15. Brown et al., "Social Class and Psychiatric Disturbance."

16. Gillespie, "Hypochondria."

17. Szasz, *The Myth of Mental Illness*, p. 248.

18. Hollingshead and Redlich, *Social Class and Mental Illness*, p. 340.

19. Marc Fried, quoted in Kosa and Zola, *Poverty and Health*, p. 157.

20. Irving K. Zola, "Culture and Symptoms: An Analysis of Patients' Presenting Complaints," *American Sociological Review* 31 (1966):615–630.

21. Virginia Biddle, M.D., personal communication. See also R. Diaz-Guerrero, "Neurosis and the Mexican Family Structure," *American Journal of Psychiatry* 112 (1955):411–417.

22. S. Cole and R. LeJeune, "Illness and the Legitimation of Failure," *American Sociological Review* 37 (1972):348.
23. Ibid.
24. Quotations are from F. E. Kenyon, *Hypochondria* (London, 1978), pp. 5, 6; Ladee, *Hypochondriacal Syndromes*, p. 363; and E. Langdon Burwell, personal communication.
25. H. Fabrega, Jr., Richard J. Moore, and John R. Strawn, "Low Income Medical Problem Patients: Some Medical and Behavioral Features," *Journal of Health and Social Behavior* 10 (1969):334-343.
26. Inge K. Broverman, Donald M. Broverman, Frank E. Clarkson, Paul S. Rosenkrantz, and Susan R. Vogel, "Sex-Role Stereotypes and Clinical Judgments of Mental Health," *Journal of Consulting and Clinical Psychology* 34 (1970):6.
27. Robert May, *Sex and Fantasy. Patterns of Male and Female Development* (New York, 1980), chap. 4.
28. H. Gerald Hare, M.D., personal communication. See also Kenyon, *Hypochondria*, Ladee, *Hypochondriacal Syndromes*, and Burwell, personal communication.
29. de Mandeville, *The Hypochondriak and Hysterick Passions*, p. 44.
30. Sontag, *Illness as Metaphor*, p. 7.
31. Balint, *Doctor, Patient, Illness*, pp. 60-63, 338-342.
32. Brown, "The Bodily Complaint."
33. Dunnell and Cartwright, *Medicine Takers*, chap. 1.
34. Jonathan Freedman, *Happy People* (New York, 1978).
35. Lewis Thomas, *The Medusa and the Snail* (New York, 1979), p. 46.

9. HYPOCHONDRIA IN OTHER CULTURES

1. P. M. Yap, "Mental Diseases Peculiar to Certain Cultures," *Journal of Mental Science* 97 (1951):318. Like the many other accounts of Koro, this one is based on the description by P. M. van Wulfften-Palthe in C. D. de Langen and A. Lichtenstein, *Textbook of Tropical Medicine* (Batavia, 1936).
2. A. M. Kleinman, "Depression, Somatization and the New Cross-Cultural Psychiatry," *Social Science and Medicine* 11 (1977):3-10.
3. José Ortega y Gassett, *Man and Crisis* (New York, 1962), p. 125.
4. Ibid., p. 163.
5. I. Pilowsky and N. D. Spence, "Ethnicity and Illness Behaviour," *Psychological Medicine* 7 (1977):447-452.

6. Kellner, *Somatization and Hypochondriasis.*
7. J. P. Hes, "Hypochondriasis in Oriental Jewish Immigrants," *International Journal of Social Psychiatry* 4 (1958):18–23.
8. Maurice Sendak, quoted in John Lahr, "The Playful Art of Maurice Sendak," *New York Times Magazine,* 12 October 1980, p. 56.
9. Andrew Twaddle, *Sickness Behavior and the Sick Role* (Boston, 1979), p. 96.
10. Zola, "Culture and Symptoms."
11. M. Zborowski, quoted in I. Pilowsky, "Dimensions of Abnormal Illness Behaviour," *Australian and New Zealand Journal of Psychiatry* 9 (1975):143.
12. R. R. Grinker and J. P. Spiegel, *Men under Stress* (New York, 1945).
13. L. G. Rowntree, K. H. McGill, and L. P. Hellman, "Mental and Personality Disorders in Selective Service Registrants," *Journal of the American Medical Association* 128 (1945):1084–1087.
14. Field, *Doctor and Patient in Soviet Russia,* p. 148. The Russians too ignored neuroses. "Presumably soldiers with complaints that we would term psychoneurotic were regarded either as malingerers subject to disciplinary action or medically ill and therefore treated by regular physicians" (ibid.).
15. Captain Harvey Greenberg, "Depressive Equivalents in the Pre-Retirement Years: 'The Old Soldier Syndrome,' " *Military Medicine* 130 (1965):252.
16. Ibid., p. 253.
17. Field, *Doctor and Patient in Soviet Russia,* pp. 148–168. See also David Mechanic, *Medical Sociology,* and Jerome Frank, *Persuasion and Healing. A Comparative Study of Psychotherapy* (Baltimore, Md., 1961).

10. OCCUPATIONAL HYPOCHONDRIA

1. Atkinson, "Becoming a Hypochondriac," in Davis and Horobin, *Medical Encounters,* p. 19.
2. Ford, *The Somatizing Disorders.*
3. Virginia Biddle, personal communication.
4. E. Langdon Burwell, personal communication.
5. George Cheyne, *The English Malady* (London, 1733), p. 344.
6. C. A. Moore, "The English Malady," in *Backgrounds of English Literature 1700–1760,* ed. C. A. Moore (Minneapolis, 1953), p. 222.

7. Cheyne, *The English Malady*, p. 345.
8. Ibid., p. 346.
9. Ibid., p. 348.
10. Ibid., p. 363.
11. Ibid., p. xv.
12. J. C. Duffy and E. M. Litin, *The Emotional Health of Physicians* (Springfield, Ill., 1967), p. 49.
13. Increasingly, studies of the mental health of physicians have included their wives, and investigations have found that many of these women use chronic pain and other apparently unfounded complaints both to get the attention of their husbands and to punish them for being absent or inattentive. M. O. Vincent, "Dr. and Mrs. _____, Their Mental Health," *Canadian Psychiatric Journal* 14 (1969):509–515. See also James L. Evans, "Psychiatric Illness in the Physician's Wife," *American Journal of Psychiatry* 122 (1965):159–163.
14. Duffy and Litin, *Health of Physicians*, p. viii.
15. G. E. Vaillant, N. C. Sobowale, and C. McArthur, "Some Psychological Vulnerabilities of Physicians," *New England Journal of Medicine* 287 (1972):374.
16. Ibid.
17. Dr. Rutty, quoted in James Boswell, *The Hypochondriack*, no. LXVI, "On Diaries" (March 1783). For this source see Bailey, *The Hypochondriak*, 1:266.
18. Hannah Arendt, *The Human Condition* (Chicago, 1958), p. 190.
19. Amariah Brigham, quoted in Hunter and Macalpine, *Three Hundred Years of Psychiatry 1535–1860*, p. 824. Priests and philosophers were often grouped with artists in treatises on mental distress, presumably because they succumbed to the same combination of strenuous thinking, sedentary habits, and excessive solitude.

Immanuel Kant is a good example of a hypochondriacal philosopher. He became so interested in his own malady, which he variously ascribed to his flat and narrow chest, an undisciplined mind, and the strains of society, that he devised several classifications of "emotional disease" and wrote articles on mental hygiene. One, "On the Power of the Mind to Master One's Pathological Feelings through Sheer Will Power," sprang from his personal experience of what he called "*hypochondria vaga*," in which "the patient fancies himself afflicted with all manner of diseases" and feels an absolute inability to combat or control them. Unlike the ordinary "self-tormentor [who] . . . in vain demands the aid of the physician," Kant brought the formidable powers of his mind to bear and tried to reason the anxiety out of his head. This regimen occasionally failed, at which point he would

close his eyes, think of Cicero, and breathe through his nose. No
remedy, he added, was entirely reliable. Immanuel Kant, quoted in
Sir John Sinclair, *The Code of Health and Longevity*, 2d ed. (London,
1807), p. 251.
20. Bernardino Ramazzini, *Diseases of Workers* (New York, 1964), p.
379.
21. Giorgio Vasari, *Lives of the Most Eminent Painters, Sculptors &
Architects* 7 (London, 1912–1914), p. 151.
22. Ibid., p. 182.
23. Wittkower and Wittkower, *Born under Saturn*, p. 70.
24. Charles Darwin, quoted in Hubble, "Charles Darwin and Psychotherapy," p. 129.
25. Darwin, *Autobiography*, p. 79.
26. Colp, *To Be an Invalid*, p. 37.
27. Ibid., p. 38.
28. Ibid., p. 92.
29. Ibid., p. 55.
30. Ibid., p. 69.
31. Ibid., p. 57.
32. Ibid., p. 60.
33. Ibid., p. 65.
34. Ibid., p. 70.
35. Philip Appleman, "The Skeleton of Dreams," *New York Times*,
29 November 1981, sect. 4, p. 20E.
36. Walther Riese, *The Conception of Disease, Its History, Its Versions,
and Its Nature* (New York, 1953), p. 31.

11. GETTING BETTER

1. Kellner, *Somatization and Hypochondriasis.*
2. Pilowsky, "The Response to Treatment in Hypochondriacal Disorders."
3. First gaining popularity at the turn of the century under such ban-
ners as the New Thought Movement and Christian Science, and pro-
liferating today at a remarkable rate, systems of mind cure seek to
reduce to insignificance conflicts that seem to exist between an individual and the outside world. In their stead problems of a more
manageable scope are substituted, namely those that might exist
within the mind. By repeating, "As you think, so you will be," or
"Day by day, in every way, I am getting better and better" (Joseph
Murphy and Emile Coué, quoted in Donald Meyer, *Positive Think-*

ers. *A Study of the American Quest for Health and Personal Power from Mary Baker Eddy to Norman Vincent Peale* [New York, 1965]), the anxious and the powerless can anchor his life in the untestable and therefore uncontestable belief that "I am fearless, powerful and wise in God's love" (Charles Fillmore, quoted in ibid., p. 92). But mind cures, like programs of positive thinking or even like hypochondria itself, are actionless forms of assertiveness or rebellion. They are comforting fantasies. "It was the genius of mind cure to discover how the weak might feel strong while remaining weak" (Meyer, *Positive Thinkers*, p. 121).

4. Cheyne, *The English Malady*, p. xv.

5. Kellner, *Somatization and Hypochondriasis*.

6. G. Gurin, J. Verhoff, and S. Feld, *Americans View Their Mental Health* (New York, 1960).

7. Burton, *The Anatomy of Melancholy*, p. 379.

8. Kenyon, *Hypochondria*, chap. 12.

9. This division, which obviously has a lot to do with the management of blame, is reflected in the ancient Greek belief that the god of medicine, Asclepius, had two daughters. Hygeia (or as we say, hygiene) helped people maintain their health by showing them how to live moderately, and Panakeia (panacea) helped people recover their health by finding the right drug or treatment to drive out an illness.

10. Karl Leonhard, "On the Treatment of Ideohypochondriac and Sensohypochondriac Neuroses," *International Journal of Social Psychiatry* 2 (1968):132.

11. B. F. Skinner, quoted in Floyd W. Matson, ed., *Being, Becoming and Behavior* (New York, 1967), p. 120.

12. H. J. Eysenck, ed., *Behavior Therapy and the Neuroses* (New York, 1960).

13. Hilde Bruch, *The Golden Cage, the Enigma of Anorexia Nervosa* (New York, 1979), pp. 97–98, 107–108.

14. Ladee, *Hypochondriacal Syndromes*.

15. T. Dieker and D. K. Counts, "Hypnotic Paradigm-Substitution Therapy in a Case of Hypochondria," *American Journal of Clinical Hypnosis* 23 (1980):122–127.

16. R. B. Sloane, F. R. Staples, A. H. Cristol, N. J. Yorkston, and K. Whipple, *Psychotherapy versus Behavior Therapy* (Cambridge, Mass., 1975).

17. Bernard Schoenberg and Robert Senescu, "Group Psychotherapy for Patients with Chronic Multiple Somatic Complaints," *Journal of Chronic Disease* 19 (1966):649.

18. M. A. Mally and W. D. Ogston, "Treatment of the 'Untreatables,' " *International Journal of Group Psychotherapy* 14 (1964):369–374.
19. Schoenberg and Senescu, "Group Psychotherapy," pp. 649–557.
20. David V. Sheehan, "Current Concepts in Psychiatry: Panic Attacks and Phobias," *New England Journal of Medicine* 307 (1982):158.
21. Sheehan et al., "Treatment of Endogenous Anxiety," p. 530.
22. Ibid.
23. Sheehan, "Current Concepts," p. 158.
24. H. B. Peck, S. R. Kaplan, and M. Roman, "Prevention, Treatment, and Social Action," *American Journal of Orthopsychiatry* 36 (1966):60.
25. T. A. C. Rennie and L. E. Woodward, *Mental Health in Modern Society* (New York, 1948), p. 385.
26. Alan S. Gurman and David P. Kniskern, eds., *Handbook of Family Therapy* (New York, 1981), pp. 747 et seq.
27. Leighton, *My Name Is Legion*, vol. 1.
28. The social-psychiatric, psychiatric, and biochemical models of mental disorder all postulate the onset of disagreeable feelings followed by a struggle to set things right, which may lead to success and further self-confidence or to defeat and the erosion of confidence. Each model traces the disagreeable feelings to a different source and largely treats the other sources as imponderables. Someday the knowledge of how our early childhood experiences, the social conditions of our lives, and the biochemical states of our brains *interact* will lie at the very center of our understanding of mental health and disease.
29. Roberta Boyette, "The Plight of the New Careerist," *American Journal of Orthopsychiatry* 42 (1972):600.
30. Victor Cardoza, William Ackerly, and Alexander Leighton, "Improving Mental Health through Community Action," in Kaplan et al., eds., (New York, 1976), *Further Explorations in Social Psychiatry*, pp. 212–227.
31. Arnold Orwin, "Treatment of a Situational Phobia—A Case for Running," *British Journal of Psychiatry* 125 (1974):95–98. O. C. Dodson and W. R. Mullens, "Some Effects of Jogging on Psychiatric Hospital Patients," *American Corrective Therapy Journal* 23 (1969):130–134.
32. Psychologists have attempted to learn more about the meaning of symptoms by artificially substituting one for another under hypnosis. Could nail-biting be substituted for uncontrollable eating? (No.) Could a disabling rigidity in a man's arms be replaced by a less restrictive symptom? In this particular case the patient, whose locked arms dated from a fierce fight he had had with his boss which he was not able to remember, was hypnotized and told he would wake

up without locked arms. He did, but his neck was uncontrollably twisted far to the left. Rehypnotized, he was asked the meaning of this and explained that it represented both strangling his boss and being hung in retribution. The patient was told he would awake without his locked arms and without a wry neck. He did, but began to gag and vomit. Again asked to explain, he said he was being choked. Encouraged that the symptoms were moving upward, which could mean that the moment of insight was at hand, the therapist brought the man out of his third trance. A headache replaced the gagging, but on the fourth try, the patient awoke somewhat dazed but with no visible symptoms. He rose from his chair, and with arms outstretched for the first time in years, he made straight for the therapist. As his hands approached the latter's throat, the therapist rehypnotized him and ended the experiment. The man was told he would have no recollection of the proceedings and that his arms would be locked at his sides as before. So he remains. Philip Seitz, "Experiments in the Substitution of Symptoms by Hypnosis," *Psychosomatic Medicine* 15 (1953):405–424.

33. de Mandeville, *The Hypochondriak and Hysterick Passions*, p. 325.
34. Meyer, *Positive Thinkers*, p. 58.

SELECTED BIBLIOGRAPHY

Agras, S., D. Sylvester, and D. Oliveau. "The Epidemiology of Common Fears and Phobias." *Comprehensive Psychiatry* 10 (1969): 151–156.

Alvarez, W. C. "A Gastro-Intestinal Hypochondriac and Some Lessons He Taught." *Gastroenterology* 2 (1944): 265–269.

———. *Minds That Came Back*. New York: Lippincott, 1961.

American Psychiatric Association. *Diagnostic and Statistical Manual of Mental Disorders*, 3d ed. Washington, D.C.: American Psychiatric Press, 1980.

Appleman, Philip. "The Skeleton of Dreams." *New York Times*, 29 November 1981, sect. 4, p. 20E.

Arendt, Hannah. *The Human Condition*. Chicago: University of Chicago Press, 1958.

Arieti, Silvano, ed. *American Handbook of Psychiatry*. New York: Basic Books, 1959.

Bailey, Margery, ed. *The Hypochondriak, Being the Seventy Essays by the Celebrated Biographer, James Boswell*, vol. 1. Palo Alto, Calif.: Stanford University Press, 1928.

Baldick, Robert. *The Goncourts*. New York: Hilary House Publishers, 1960.

Balint, Michael. *The Doctor, His Patient, and the Illness*. New York: International Universities Press, 1972.

Barsky, A. J., and G. L. Klerman. "Overview: Hypochondriasis, Bodily Complaints and Somatic Styles." *American Journal of Psychiatry* 140 (1983): 273–283.

———. "Hypochondriasis." *Harvard Medical School Mental Health Letter* 2 (1985): 4–6.

Barsky, A., G. Wyshak, and G. Klerman. "Hypochondriasis: An Evaluation of the *DSM-III* Criteria in Medical Outpatients." *Archives of General Psychiatry* 43 (1986): 493–500.

Bate, W. Jackson. *Samuel Johnson*. New York: Harcourt Brace Jovanovich, 1975.

Baumann, B. "Diversities in the Conceptions of Health and Physical Fitness." *Journal of Health and Human Behavior* 2 (1961): 39–46.
Beall, Otho T., Jr., and Richard Shryock. *Cotton Mather.* Baltimore, Md.: Johns Hopkins University Press, 1954.
Beauvoir, Simone de. *The Coming of Age.* New York: G. P. Putnam's Sons, 1972.
Bellah, Robert N., Richard Masden, William M. Sullivan, Ann Swidler, and Steven M. Tipton. *Habits of the Heart: Individualism and Commitment in American Life.* New York: Harper & Row, 1986.
Bergmann, K. "Sex Differences in the Neurotic Reaction of the Aged." *Journal of Biological Science, Supplement* 2 (1970): 137–000.
Bianchi, G. N. "Patterns of Hypochondriasis: A Principal Components Analysis." *British Journal of Psychiatry* 122 (1973): 541–548.
Birren, James E., and Warner K. Schaie, eds. *Handbook of the Psychology of Aging.* New York: Van Nostrand Reinhold, 1977.
Blinder, M., and M. Kirschenbaum. "The Technique of Married Couple Group Therapy." *Archives of General Psychiatry* 17 (1967): 44–52.
Boswell, James. *The Life of Samuel Johnson.* Roslyn, N.Y.: Black's Readers Service, 1952.
Bowlby, John. *Attachment and Loss.* Vol. 3: *Loss.* New York: Basic Books, 1980.
Boyette, Roberta. "The Plight of the New Careerist." *American Journal of Orthopsychiatry* 42 (1972): 596–602.
Brenner, M. Harvey. "Losing Jobs, Losing Lives." *Johns Hopkins Magazine* (October 1981).
Brink, T. L., D. Capri, V. De Neeve, C. Janakes, and C. Oliveira. "Hypochondriasis and Paranoia: Similar Delusional Systems in an Institutionalized Geriatric Population." *Journal of Nervous and Mental Disease* 167 (1979): 224–228.
Brody, Howard, and David S. Sobel. "A Systems View of Health and Disease." In *Ways of Health: Holistic Approaches to Ancient and Contemporary Medicine,* ed. David S. Sobel. New York: Harcourt Brace Jovanovich, 1979.
Brontë, Charlotte. *The Professor.* New York: Everyman Edition, 1965.
Broverman, Inge K., Donald M. Broverman, Frank E. Clarkson, Paul S. Rosenkrantz, and Susan R. Vogel. "Sex-Role Stereotypes and Clinical Judgments of Mental Health." *Journal of Consulting and Clinical Psychology* 34 (1970): 1–7.
Brown, Felix. "The Bodily Complaint: A Study of Hypochondriasis." *Journal of Mental Science* 82 (1936): 295–359.
Brown, G., M. Bhrolchain, and T. Harris. "Social Class and Psychiatric

Disturbance among Woman in an Urban Population." *Sociology* 9 (1975): 252–254.

Bruch, Hilde. *The Golden Cage, the Enigma of Anorexia Nervosa.* New York: Vintage, 1979.

Burton, Robert. *The Anatomy of Melancholy.* New York: Floyd Dell and Paul Jordan-Smith, 1927.

———. *The Anatomy of Melancholy (A Selection).* East Lansing: Michigan State University Press, 1965.

Busse, Ewald W. "Hypochondria in the Elderly: A Reaction to Social Stress." *Journal of the American Geriatric Society* 24 (1976): 145–149.

Cheyne, George. *The English Malady.* London: G. Strahan, 1733.

Chrzanowski, Gerard, "Neurasthenia and Hypochondriasis." In *American Handbook of Psychiatry,* ed. Silvano Arieti. New York: Basic Books, 1959.

Cole, S., and R. LeJeune. "Illness and the Legitimation of Failure." *American Sociological Review* 37 (1972): 347–356.

Colp, Ralph, Jr. *To Be an Invalid: The Illness of Charles Darwin.* Chicago: University of Chicago Press, 1977.

Comfort, Alex. *A Good Age.* New York: Crown Publishers, 1976.

Comrey, A. L. "A Factor Analysis of Items on the MMPI Hypochondriasis Scale." *Educational and Psychological Measurement* 17 (1957): 568–577.

Cowden, R. C., and J. E. Brown. "The Use of a Physical Symptom as a Defense against Psychosis." *Journal of Abnormal and Social Psychology* 53 (1956): 133–135.

Darwin, Charles. *The Autobiography of Charles Darwin, 1809–1882.* London: Collins, 1958.

Davis, Alan, and Gordon Horobin, eds. *Medical Encounters: The Experience of Illness and Treatment.* New York: St. Martin's Press, 1977.

Davison, G. C., and J. M. Neale. *Abnormal Psychology,* 3d ed. New York: John Wiley & Sons, 1982.

Diaz-Guerrero, R. "Neurosis and the Mexican Family Structure." *American Journal of Psychiatry* 112 (1955): 411–417.

Dieker, T., and D. K. Counts. "Hypnotic Paradigm-Substitution Therapy in a Case of Hypochondria." *American Journal of Clinical Hypnosis* 23 (1980): 122–127.

Dodson, O. C., and W. R. Mullens. "Some Effects of Jogging on Psychiatric Hospital Patients." *American Corrective Therapy Journal* 23 (1969): 130–134.

Drake, William. *Sara Teasdale, Woman and Poet.* New York: Harper
    & Row, 1979.
Dubos, René. *Man Adapting.* New Haven, Conn.: Yale University
    Press, 1965.
Duffy, J. C., and E. M. Litin. *The Emotional Health of Physicians.*
    Springfield, Ill.: Charles C. Thomas, 1967.
Dunnell, K., and A. Cartwright. *Medicine Takers, Prescribers and
    Hoarders.* Boston: Routledge & Kegan Paul, 1972.
Early, L. W., and O. von Mering. "Growing Old the Outpatient Way."
    American Journal of Psychiatry 125 (1969): 963–967.
Ehrenreich, John. *The Cultural Crisis of Modern Medicine.* New York:
    Monthly Review Press, 1978.
Evans, James L. "Psychiatric Illness in the Physician's Wife." *American
    Journal of Psychiatry* 122 (1965): 159–163.
Eysenck, H. J., ed. *Behavior Therapy and the Neuroses.* New York:
    Pergamon, 1960.
Fabrega, H., Jr., Richard J. Moore, and John R. Strawn. "Low Income
    Medical Problem Patients: Some Medical and Behavioral Features."
    Journal of Health and Social Behavior 10 (1969): 334–343.
Falret, Jean-Pierre. *De l'Hypochondrie et du suicide.* Paris, 1822.
Fenichel, Otto. *The Psychoanalytic Theory of Neurosis.* London: Rout-
    ledge & Kegan Paul, 1955.
Field, M. *Doctor and Patient in Soviet Russia.* Cambridge, Mass.: Har-
    vard University Press, 1957.
Ford, C. V. *The Somatizing Disorders: Illness as a Way of Life.* New
    York: Elsevier Biochemical, 1983.
Foucault, Michel. *Madness and Civilization: A History of Insanity in
    the Age of Reason.* New York: Vintage Books, 1973.
Frank, Jerome. *Persuasion and Healing. A Comparative Study of Psy-
    chotherapy.* Baltimore, Md.: Johns Hopkins University Press,
    1961.
Freedman, Jonathan. *Happy People.* New York: Harcourt Brace Jova-
    novich, 1978.
Freud, Anna. "The Role of Bodily Illness in the Mental Life of Children."
    The Psychoanalytic Study of the Child 7 (1952): 69–81.
————. *Writings of Anna Freud.* Vol. 5. *Research at the Hampstead
    Child-Therapy Clinic, and Other Papers, 1956–1965.* New York: In-
    ternational Universities Press, 1969.
Fromm-Reichman, Frieda. "Loneliness." *Psychiatry* 22 (1959): 1–15.
Geiger, H. Jack. Review of *The Social Transformation of American
    Medicine,* by Paul Starr. *New York Times Book Review,* 9 January
    1983.

Gillespie, R. D. "Hypochondria: Its Definition, Nosology, and Psychopathology." *Guys Hospital Report* 8 (1928): 408–460.

Goldstein, S. E., and F. Birnbom. "Hypochondriasis and the Elderly." *Journal of the American Geriatric Society* 24 (1976): 150–154.

Greenberg, Captain Harvey. "Depressive Equivalents in the Pre-Retirement Years: 'The Old Soldier Syndrome.' " *Military Medicine* 130 (1965): 251–255.

Greenberg, Phillip. "Hypochondriasis." *Medical Journal of Australia* 47 (1960): 673–677.

Grinker, R. R., and J. P. Spiegel. *Men under Stress*. New York: McGraw-Hill, 1945.

Grolnick, Lawrence. "A Family Perspective of Psychosomatic Factors in Illness: A Review of the Literature." *Family Process* 11 (1972): 457–486.

Groves, J. E. "Taking Care of the Hateful Patient." *New England Journal of Medicine* 298 (1978): 883–887.

Gubrium, Jaber F. "Self-Conceptions of Mental Health among the Aged." *Mental Hygiene* 55 (1971): 399–403.

Gurin, G., J. Verhoff, and S. Feld. *Americans View Their Mental Health*. New York: Basic Books, 1960.

Gurman, Alan S., and David P. Kniskern, eds. *Handbook of Family Therapy*. New York: Brunner/Mazel, 1981.

Haley, Bruce. *The Healthy Body and Victorian Culture*. Cambridge, Mass.: Harvard University Press, 1978.

Haley, Jay. *Strategies of Psychotherapy*. New York: Grune & Stratton, 1963.

Harrison, B. G. "Profound Hypochondria." *Ms* 5 (1977): 71 et seq.

Hes, J. P. "Hypochondriasis in Oriental Jewish Immigrants." *International Journal of Social Psychiatry* 4 (1958): 18–23.

Hippocrates. *The Aphorisms of Hippocrates*, trans. John Underwood. London, 1831.

Hollingshead, August B., and Fredrick C. Redlich. *Social Class and Mental Illness: A Community Study*. New York: John Wiley & Sons, 1958.

Hubble, Douglas. "Charles Darwin and Psychotherapy." *The Lancet* 1 (1943): 129–133.

———. "The Life of the Shawl." *The Lancet* 2 (1953): 1351–1354.

Hughes, Richard, and Robert Brewin. *The Tranquilizing of America*. New York: Harcourt Brace Jovanovich, 1979.

Hunter, Harriot, and John M. Lyon. "Clinic H: Haven for Hypochondriacs." *American Practice and Digest of Treatment* 5 (1951): 67–69.

Hunter, Richard, and Ida Macalpine. *Three Hundred Years of Psychiatry 1535–1860*. London: Oxford University Press, 1963.

Hutchison, Robert. "Hypochondriasis: Individual, Vicarious and Communal." *British Medical Journal* 1 (1934): 365–367.

"Hypochondriasis—USA." Editorial in the *American Journal of Psychotherapy* 16 (1962): 187–190.

Jerome, Jerome K. *Three Men in a Boat*. New York: Franklin Watts, Inc., n.d.

Johnson, Samuel. *The Rambler*, No. 85. New Haven, Conn.: Yale University Press, 1969.

Jones, Edward E., and Steven Berglas. "Control of Attributions about the Self through Self-Handicapping Strategies: The Appeal of Alcohol and the Role of Underachievement." *Personality and Social Psychology Bulletin* 4 (1978): 200–206.

Kanner, Leo. *Child Psychiatry*, 4th ed. Springfield, Ill.: Charles C. Thomas, 1972.

Kaplan, B. H., R. N. Wilson, and A. H. Leighton, eds. *Further Explorations in Social Psychiatry*. New York: Basic Books, 1976.

Kellner, Robert. *Somatization and Hypochondriasis*. New York: Praeger, 1986.

Kellner, R., R. G. Wiggins, and D. Pathak. "Hypochondriacal Fears and Beliefs in Medical and Law Students." *Archives in General Psychiatry* 43 (1986): 487–489.

Kenyon, F. E. "Hypochondriasis: A Survey of Some Historical, Clinical and Social Aspects." *British Journal of Medical Psychology* 38 (1965): 117–133.

———. "Hypochondriacal States." *British Journal of Psychiatry* 129 (1976): 1–4.

———. *Hypochondria*. London: Sheldon Press, 1978.

Klarman, Herbert E. "The Financing of Health Care." In *Doing Better and Feeling Worse: Health in the United States*, ed. John H. Knowles. New York: W. W. Norton, 1977.

Kleinman, A. M. "Depression, Somatization and the New Cross-Cultural Psychiatry." *Social Science and Medicine* 11 (1977): 3–10.

Kohut, Heinz, and Ernest Wolf. "The Disorders of the Self and Their Treatment: An Outline." *International Journal of Psychoanalysis* 59 (1978): 413–425.

Kosa, John, and Irving K. Zola, eds. *Poverty and Health: A Sociological Analysis*. Cambridge, Mass.: Harvard University Press, 1975.

Kreitman, Norman, P. Sainsbury, K. Pearce, and W. R. Constain. "Hypochondria and Depression in Outpatients at a General Hospital." *British Journal of Psychiatry* 3 (1965): 607–615.

Kreitman, Norman, Joyce Collins, Barbara Nelson, and Jane Troop. "Neuroses and Marital Interaction." *British Journal of Psychiatry* 117 (1970): 33–46, 47–58.

Ladee, G. A. *Hypochondriacal Syndromes.* New York: Elsevier Publishers, 1966.

Lahr, John. "The Playful Art of Maurice Sendak." *New York Times Magazine,* 12 October 1980.

Leavitt, J. W., and R. L. Numbers, eds. *Health and Sickness in America: Readings in the History of Medicine and Public Health.* Madison: University of Wisconsin Press, 1978.

Leighton, Alexander H. *My Name Is Legion. The Stirling County Study of Psychiatric Disorder and Sociocultural Environment 1.* New York: Basic Books, 1959.

Leonhard, Karl. "On the Treatment of Ideohypochondriac and Sensohypochondriac Neuroses." *International Journal of Social Psychiatry* 2 (1968): 123–133.

Lipsitt, D. R. "Medical and Psychological Characteristics of 'Crocks.' " *Psychiatry in Medicine* 1 (1970): 15–25.

Mally, M. A., and W. D. Ogston. "Treatment of the 'Untreatables.' " *International Journal of Group Psychotherapy* 14 (1964): 369–374.

Mandeville, Bernard de. *A Treatise of the Hypochondriak and Hysterick Passions.* London: Dryden Leach & W. Taylor, 1711.

———. *A Treatise of the Hypochondriak and Hysterick Passions.* Arno Press, 1976.

Matson, Floyd W., ed. *Being, Becoming and Behavior.* New York: George Braziller, 1967.

May, Robert. *Sex and Fantasy. Patterns of Male and Female Development.* New York: W. W. Norton, 1980.

Mazer, Milton. *People and Predicaments.* Cambridge, Mass.: Harvard University Press, 1976.

McMahon, A. W., and P. J. Rhudick. "Reminiscing: Adaptational Significance in the Aged." *Archives of General Psychiatry* 10 (1964): 292–297.

Mead, Beverley. "Management of Hypochondriacal Patients." *Journal of the American Medical Association* 192 (1965): 33–35.

Mechanic, David. "The Influence of Mothers on Their Children's Health Attitudes." *Pediatrics* 33 (1964): 444–453.

———. *Medical Sociology: A Selective View.* New York: Free Press, 1968.

———. "Social and Psychologic Factors Affecting the Presentation of Bodily Complaints." *New England Journal of Medicine* 286 (1972): 1132–1139.

_____. "The Development of Psychological Distress among Young Adults." *Archives of General Psychiatry* 36 (1979): 1233–1239.

Meister, R. *Hypochondria: Toward a Better Understanding.* New York: Taplinger Publishing Company, 1980.

Meyer, Donald. *Positive Thinkers. A Study of the American Quest for Health and Personal Power from Mary Baker Eddy to Norman Vincent Peale.* New York: Doubleday, 1965.

Molière. "La Malade Imaginaire," Act I. *Oeuvres Complètes.* Paris, 1962.

Moore, C. A., ed. *Backgrounds of English Literature 1700–1760.* Minneapolis: University of Minnesota Press, 1953.

Morgan, W. P. "Physical Fitness Correlates of Psychiatric Hospitalization." *Proceedings of the Second International Congress of Sports Psychology.* Washington, D.C., 1968.

O'Connor, J. P., and E. C. Stefic. "Some Patterns of Hypochondriasis." *Educational and Psychological Measurement* 19 (1959): 363–370.

Ortega y Gassett, José. *Man and Crisis.* New York: W. W. Norton, 1962.

Orwin, Arnold. "Treatment of a Situational Phobia—A Case for Running." *British Journal of Psychiatry* 125 (1974): 95–98.

Peck, H. B., S. R. Kaplan, and M. Roman. "Prevention, Treatment, and Social Action." *American Journal of Orthopsychiatry* 36 (1966): 57–69.

Pilowsky, I. "Dimensions of Hypochondriasis." *British Journal of Psychiatry* 113 (1967): 89–93.

_____. "The Response to Treatment in Hypochondriacal Disorders." *Australian and New Zealand Journal of Psychiatry* 2 (1968): 88–94.

_____. "Primary and Secondary Hypochondriasis." *Acta Psychiatrica Scandinavia* 46 (1970): 273–285.

_____. "Dimensions of Abnormal Illness Behaviour." *Australian and New Zealand Journal of Psychiatry* 9 (1975): 141–147.

Pilowsky, I., and N. D. Spence. "Ethnicity and Illness Behaviour." *Psychological Medicine* 7 (1977): 447–452.

Pottle, Frederick A., ed. *Boswell's London Journal, 1762–1763.* New York: McGraw-Hill, 1950.

_____. *Boswell in Holland 1763–1764.* New York: McGraw-Hill, 1952.

Pottle, Frederick A. *James Boswell, the Earlier Years, 1740–1769.* New York: McGraw-Hill, 1966.

Preston, Mary. "Physical Complaints without Organic Basis." *Journal of Pediatrics* 17 (1940): 279–304.

Ramazzini, Bernardino. *Diseases of Workers.* New York: Hafner Publishing, 1964.

Raverat, Gwen. *Period Piece*. London: Faber and Faber, 1952.
Rennie, T. A. C., and L. E. Woodward. *Mental Health in Modern Society*. New York: Commonwealth Fund, 1948.
Richards, E. L. "Following the Hypochondriacal Child for a Decade." *Journal of Pediatrics* 18 (1941): 528–537.
Ricks, Christopher. *Tennyson*. New York: Macmillan, 1972.
Riese, Walter. *The Conception of Disease, Its History, Its Versions, and Its Nature*. New York: Philosophical Library, 1953.
Risse, Guenter B. *Hospital Life in Enlightenment Scotland: Care and Teaching at the Royal Infirmary of Edinburgh*. New York: Cambridge University Press, 1986.
———. "Managing 'Neuroses' in a General Hospital: Edinburgh 1750–1800." Unpublished manuscript.
Rosenberg, Charles. *No Other Gods: On Science and American Social Thought*. Baltimore, Md.: Johns Hopkins University Press, 1961.
———. *The Cholera Years: The United States in 1832, 1849, and 1866*. Chicago: University of Chicago Press, 1962.
Rowntree, L. G., K. H. McGill, and L. P. Hellman. "Mental and Personality Disorders in Selective Service Registrants." *Journal of the American Medical Association* 128 (1945): 1084–1087.
Ryle, J. A. "The Twenty-First Maudsley Lecture: Nosophobia." *Journal of Mental Science* 94 (1948): 1–17.
Ryskamp, Charles, and Frederick A. Pottle, eds. *Boswell: The Ominous Years, 1774–1776*. New York: McGraw-Hill, 1963.
Sarton, May. *As We Are Now*. New York: W. W. Norton, 1973.
Schoenberg, Bernard, and Robert Senescu. "Group Psychotherapy for Patients with Chronic Multiple Somatic Complaints." *Journal of Chronic Disease* 19 (1966): 649–557.
Schumacher, E. F. *Small Is Beautiful: Economics as if People Mattered*. New York: Perennial Library, 1975.
Schwartz, Harry. "Looking at the Ways We Die." *Wall Street Journal*, 9 December 1980.
Scott-Maxwell, Florida. *The Measure of My Days*. New York: Penguin, 1979.
Seitz, Philip. "Experiments in the Substitution of Symptoms by Hypnosis." *Psychosomatic Medicine* 15 (1953): 405–424.
Sheehan, David V. "Current Concepts in Psychiatry: Panic Attacks and Phobias." *New England Journal of Medicine* 307 (1982): 156–158.
Sheehan, D. V., J. Ballenger, and G. Jacobsen. "Treatment of Endogenous Anxiety with Phobic, Hysterical and Hypochondriacal Symptoms." *Archives of General Psychiatry* 37 (1980): 51–59.

Sheldon, G. *History of Deerfield, Massachusetts*, vol. 1. Massachusetts, 1895.

Sinclair, Sir John. *The Code of Health and Longevity*, 2d ed. London: J. Murray, 1807.

Singh, B. K., J. Nunn, J. Martin, and J. Yates. "Abnormal Treatment Behaviour." *British Journal of Medical Psychology* 54 (1981): 67–73.

Sloane, R. B., F. R. Staples, A. H. Cristol, N. J. Yorkston, and K. Whipple. *Psychotherapy versus Behavior Therapy*. Cambridge, Mass.: Harvard University Press, 1975.

Smith, Timothy W., C. R. Snyder, and Suzanne C. Perkins. "The Self-Serving Function of Hypochondriacal Complaints: Physical Symptoms as Self-Handicapping Strategies." *Journal of Personality and Social Psychology* 44 (1983): 787–797.

Smollett, Tobias. *The Expedition of Humphrey Clinker*. London: Oxford University Press, 1966.

Sontag, Susan. *Illness as Metaphor*. New York: Vintage Books, 1979.

Sperling, Melita. "The Role of the Mother in Psychosomatic Disorders in Children." *Psychosomatic Medicine* 11 (1949): 377–385.

Strouse, Jean. *Alice James, A Biography*. New York: Bantam Books, 1982.

Szasz, Thomas. *The Myth of Mental Illness*. New York: Dell Publishing, 1961.

Szasz, Thomas, and M. H. Hollender. "A Contribution to the Philosophy of Medicine: The Basic Models of the Doctor-Patient Relationship." *Archives of Internal Medicine* 97 (1956): 585–592.

Thomas, Lewis. *The Medusa and the Snail: More Notes of a Biology Watcher*. New York: Viking Press, 1979.

Thompson, Wayne E., and Gordon Streib. "Situational Determinants: Health and Economic Deprivation in Retirement." *Journal of Social Issues* 14 (1958): 18–34.

Townsend, Peter. *The Family Life of Old People*. London: Routledge & Kegan Paul, 1961.

Tunstall, Jeremy. *Old and Alone, a Sociological Study of Old People*. London: Routledge & Kegan Paul, 1966.

Twaddle, Andrew C. "Illness and Deviance." *Social Science and Medicine* 8 (1973–1974): 752–762.

———. *Sickness Behavior and the Sick Role*. Boston: G. K. Hall and Co., 1979.

Unamuno, Miguel de. *The Tragic Sense of Life*. New York: Dover, 1954.

Vaillant, G. E., N. C. Sobowale, and C. McArthur. "Some Psychological

Vulnerabilities of Physicians." *New England Journal of Medicine* 287 (1972): 372–375.

Vasari, Giorgio. *Lives of the Most Eminent Painters, Sculptors & Architects* 7. London: P. L. Warner Publishers, 1912–1914.

Veith, Ilza. "Psychiatric Nosology." *American Journal of Psychiatry* 114 (1957): 385–391.

———. *Hysteria, History of a Disease.* Chicago: University of Chicago Press, 1965.

Verwoerdt, Adrian. *Clinical Geropsychiatry.* Baltimore, Md.: Johns Hopkins University Press, 1976.

Vincent, M. O. "Dr. and Mrs. ———, Their Mental Health." *Canadian Psychiatric Journal* 14 (1969): 509–515.

Wahl, C. W., ed. *New Dimensions in Psychosomatic Medicine.* Boston: Little, Brown, 1964.

Wells, William D., ed. *Life Style and Psychographics.* American Marketing Association, 1974.

Wittkower, Rudolph, and Margot Wittkower. *Born under Saturn: The Character and Conduct of Artists.* New York: Random House, 1963.

Wolkind, Stephen. "Psychological Factors and the Minor Symptoms of Pregnancy." *Journal of Psychosomatic Research* 18 (1974): 161–165.

Woods, S. M., J. Natterson, and J. Silverman. "Medical Students Disease: Hypochondriasis in Medical Education." *Journal of Medical Education* 41 (1966): 785–790.

Wulfften-Palthe, P. M. van. *Text-book of Tropical Medicine.* Batavia, 1936.

Yap, P. M. "Mental Diseases Peculiar to Certain Cultures." *Journal of Mental Science* 97 (1951): 313–327.

Zilboorg, Gregory, and George Henry. *A History of Medical Psychiatry.* New York: W. W. Norton, 1941.

Zola, Irving K. "Culture and Symptoms: An Analysis of Patients' Presenting Complaints." *American Sociological Review* 31 (1966): 615–630.

Alvarez, W. C., 108–109
Anita, 68–70, 203–207
Anxiety disorders, 33–34, 197–198
Appleman, Philip, 183
Arendt, Hannah, 177
"Argan," 109–110, 187
Atkinson, Paul, 62, 139, 171

Balint, Michael, 56, 100–101, 106–107, 111–112, 155
Barocci, Federico, 23
Barsky, A. J., 37
Bate, W. Jackson, *Samuel Johnson*, 127, 133
Beauvoir, Simone de, *The Coming of Age*, 120, 123
Berglas, S., 137–138
Bergmann, K., 116, 126–127
Bianchi, G. N., 33
Biddle, Virginia, 172
Boswell, James, 7, 10–17, 20, 24, 27, 49, 115, 186; his inviolable plan, 16; relapse, 16; "The Hypochondriack," 17
Bowlby, John, 58
Boyle, Robert, 62, 64
Brenner, M. Harvey, 143
Brigham, Amariah, 177
Brink, T. L., 131
Brontë, Charlotte, 61, 124
Brown, Felix, 54, 56, 155
Burlingham, Dorothy, 57
Burton, Robert, 9, 24, 101, 209; *The Anatomy of Melancholy*, 23–25, 101, 188

Burwell, E. Langdon, 98, 172
Busse, Ewald, 131–132

Cancer, 42–43; fear of, 1, 18, 45, 63, 154–156
Cardoza, Victor, 202–203
Caruso, Enrico, 176
Case, 9, 144–145
Charcot, Jean-Martin, 29
Cheyne, George, 27, 172–174, 187–188; *The English Malady*, 27
Chronic complainers, 30, 53, 57, 146
Chrzanowski, Gerard, 89
Comfort, Alex, 118

Darwin, Charles, 7, 31, 44, 46, 51, 63–64, 180–184, 186; hypochondria among his children, 52; *On the Origin of Species by Means of Natural Selection*, 182–183
Darwin, Emma, 46, 51–52, 181
Darwin, Etty, 52, 72, 74–76, 186–187
Death, fear of, 11, 15, 77, 135, 173, 178
Dependence, 4–5, 67, 78–81, 84, 90–91, 103–104, 110, 139–141, 145, 150–151, 162, 167
Despair, 11, 117, 128
Depression, 33, 35–36, 127–130, 161, 167, 174, 186, 197, 203
Diagnostic and Statistical Manual of Mental Disorders, 35, 36, 122, 149

Disease, fear of, 24, 30, 32, 38, 65, 86–87, 152–156, 159, 193–194
Disease phobia. *See* Disease, fear of
Drake, William, 66
Duffy, J. C., 174–175
Duncan, Andrew, 26–27

Edinburgh Royal Infirmary, 26

Falret, Jean-Pierre, 28
Filsinger, Ernst, 81
Ford, C. V., 36, 88, 98, 171
Freud, Anna, 57–59, 124–125
Freud, Sigmund, 29, 87, 129
Fried, Marc, 142
Fromm-Reichmann, Freida, 123

Galen of Pergammon, 22–23
Gide, André, 120
Goldstein, E. S., 131
Goncourt, Edmond and Jules de, 73, 76–78, 124; *Soeur Philomène*, 77
Greenberg, Captain Harvey, 167
Groves, James, 103

Haley, Jay, 67, 73, 79, 91, 105, 110
Hawkins, John, 25
Hippocrates, 21–22, 96
Hollingshead, August, 142–143, 146
Homosexuality, 42
Hooker, Joseph, 182–183
Humpty-Dumpty Syndrome, 88
Hutchison, R., 94
Hypochondria: and age, 54–55, 147; as an anatomical term, 22; and anatomy, 25, 29; behavioral causes of 34, 194–195, 234 n. 28; biochemical causes of, 5, 34, 197–198, 209, 234 n. 28; childhood causes of, 4–5, 53–61, 65–71; and creativity, 23, 76–77, 85, 179, 184; as a defense against psychosis, 73–74, 220–221 n. 4; definition of, 1, 3, 30,

35; and ethnicity, 55, 147–148, 160–165; and gender, 25, 29, 50, 54–56, 147–152, 215 n. 9; genetic causes of, 12, 27, 49, 53; history of, 2, 21–30, 49, 152–155; in military, 165–168; misdiagnosed, 223 n. 12; most common symptoms of, 31–32, 50, 146, 156–158; nosology of, 2, 22, 24, 28, 31, 35; and overeating, 19; and pregnancy, 83–84; prevalence of, 3, 36–39, 50; pure, 32, 35; sociological causes of, 5–6, 34, 234 n. 28; sociology of, 40–48, 134–159; tests for, 32–33, 38–39, 211–212
Hypochondrium, 21–22

Indirect communication, 47–48, 70, 80–81, 131, 145, 162

James, Alice, 102–105, 108
James, William, 19–20
Jerome, Jerome K., 121
Johnson, Samuel, 13–14, 24, 115–117, 122–124, 127–129, 132–133; advice on hypochondria, 13
Jones, E., 137–138

Kanner, Leo, 59, 89–90
Kant, Immanuel, 231–232 n. 19
Kate, 17–20, 35–36, 188; feelings of depersonalization, 18
Kellner, Robert, 131, 162, 185, 187, 189
Kenyon, F. E., 31–32, 189
Kleinman, A. M., 161
Klerman, G. L., 37
Kohut, Heinz, 136–137
Koro, 160–161
Kreitman, Norman, 73
Kuplan, Louis, 126

Ladee, G. A., 73–74, 120, 194–195
Leighton, Alexander, 201–202
Leonhard, Karl, 190
Lindsay, Vachel, 81

Litin, E. M., 174–175

Madness, fear of, 11, 13, 173
Malingering, 3, 166, 168–169
Mandeville, Bernard de, 71, 94–95, 112, 152–153, 188, 208
Mather, Cotton, 63
"Matt Bramble," 86–88, 95, 187
Mauriac, François, 125
May, Robert, 151
Mazer, Milton, 45
Meade, Beverly, 111
Mechanic, David, 63–64, 99
Medical mismanagement, 56–61
Medical students' disease, 61–65, 171, 180
Melancholia, 22, 24
Miss K, 155
Mitchell, S. Weir, 38
MMPI, 32, 38–39
Molière's "Imaginary Invalid," 109
Moore, John, 97
Mr. L, 155

National health services, 8, 37, 125
Neurotic marriages, 73, 221 n. 17
Nightmares, 9, 15, 18, 21, 23

Orphans, 60, 124–125
Ortega y Gassett, José, 162
Osler, Sir William, 3
Overprotective mothers, 54–56

Panic disorders. See anxiety disorders
Pilowsky, Ian, 32, 35
Plutarch, 9
Pontormo, Jacopo, 177–179, 186
Prohibition, 43
Psychosomatic illness, 3–4
Pusillanimata, 23

Ramazzini, Bernardino, Diseases of Workers, 177
"Rape and Drains," 223–224 n. 16

Reassurance, 106–108
Redlich, Frederick, 142–143, 146
Reece, Robert, 51
Reminiscence, 127
Relapse, 16, 61, 186, 198
Richards, Esther, 53–54, 56–57, 59
Rittenhouse, Jessie, 81
Rush, Benjamin, 27

Sartre, Jean-Paul, 141
Secondary gains, 5, 44, 56, 131
Self-blame, 19, 30, 68, 91, 128, 147–148, 187, 233 n. 9
Self-handicappers, 137–138
Sendak, Maurice, 163–164
Seneca, 101
Sheehan, D. V., 197
Shelley, Percy Bysshe, 179
Singh, B. K., 103–104, 110
Skinner, B. F., 193
Smith, T., 138
Smollett, Tobias, 86
Smythe, James, 26–27
Socrates, 208–209
Somatization disorder, 35, 122, 149, 216 n. 27
Sperling, Melita, 90–91
Suicide, 28, 41, 124, 143, 186, 202–203
Swift, Jonathan, Gulliver's Travels, 118–119
Sydenham, Thomas, 25
Sylvia, 52–53
Szasz, Thomas, 47–48, 87–88, 104, 145

Teasdale, Sara, 7, 65–67, 69, 72, 186
Temple, William Johnson, 12
Tennyson, Alfred Lord, 6, 31, 49, 179, 184
Therapy. See Treatments
Thomas, Lewis, 141, 159
Tolstoy, Leo, 117, 125
Treatments, 13, 16, 24, 26–27, 34–35, 83, 107–112, 131–132,

185, 187–210, 228 n. 10; behavioral, 192–196, 198; community psychiatry, 201–203; drug therapy, 196–198; family therapy, 199–201; group therapy, 196; hypnotism, 194, 234–235 n. 32; marital therapy, 79; mind cures, 232–233 n. 3; paradoxical interventions, 200; psychodynamic therapy, 191–192, 196
"Turkey" or social admissions, 51
Twaddle, Andrew, 164

Unamuno, Miguel de, 8

USSR, medical system in, 168–169

Venereal disease, fear of, 13, 26, 152–153, 156, 219 n. 28
Verwoerdt, Adrian, 127

Wahl, C. W., 93
Wheelock, John Hall, 85
Whiteley Index, 32–33, 211–212
Wolf, Ernest, 136–137
World Health Organization, 41
Worriers. See Disease, fear of

Zola, Irving, 164–165